DO-IT-YOURSELF CONVEYANCING

DO-IT-YOURSELF CONVEYANCING

J.C. POTTER LL.B(Hons)
and of The Middle Temple, Barrister

Foreword by
AUSTIN MITCHELL M.P.

PRISM PRESS

Published in Great Britain 1987 by

PRISM PRESS
2 South Street
Bridport
Dorset DT6 3NQ

ISBN 0 907061 95 8 Paperback
ISBN 0 907061 92 3 Hardback

Cartoons by David Rudd

Typeset by Maggie Spooner Typesetting, London
Printed by The Guernsey Press, Guernsey, Channel Islands.

Contents

Disclaimer

Whilst every effort has been made to ensure that the fees, etc, charged for the various services mentioned in this book were correct at the time of going to press, you should regard the figures quoted as a rough guide and check them out for yourself.

In some areas there is intense competition between solicitors and between solicitors and licensed conveyancers. In many ways this can only be good news for the house buyer and is endorsement of the advice to 'shop around'. However, price, whilst very important, should not be the only consideration when shopping around. Of even greater importance, I suggest, is the need to be sure that for the fee charged the client will get a good professional job. I regret to state that in my opinion where there is the intense competition referred to the standard of work in many instances is inferior and the client is the loser.

The fees quoted herein for the various services mentioned are based on the provision of a professional standard of work and I have ignored the cut throat fees referred to above.

Special Note

For the sake of simplicity, in preparing forms of Transfer and Conveyances etc. I have used the figure of £29,750 as the consideration (price paid). As stamp duty becomes payable at £30,001, by keeping the consideration below that figure the added complication of providing for it is avoided, and thus I hope makes the text easier to follow.

I realise, of course, that in many parts of the country property prices are way over £30,000.

Acknowledgements

I wish to express my thanks to Mr. Christopher (Chris) Maynard for his invaluable suggestions and practical assistance, to each of the 'Big Four' banks and to the many buildings societies for their ready co-operation and the provision of statistical material and other information, to The Frizzell Group who gave much information relating to insurances and to Leeds Permanent Building Society for permission to reproduce the chart on page 117. However, I am responsible for any figures quoted or views expressed.

The forms required in connection with applications to H.M. Land Registry are reproduced by kind permission of the Chief Land Registrar, and Forms 29A and 29D are reproduced by permission of the Law Society, the Association of County Councils, the Association of District Councils and the Association of Metropolitan Authorities by whose authority these forms are published.

Foreword

I did the conveyancing on my own house. The house and I both survived. Indeed we're still living together. Of course, I did it in those dim and distant days before Jim Potter wrote *Do-It-Yourself Conveyancing* and made the whole business simple and straightforward; if that doesn't give you the confidence to go ahead and do with ease what I did with trepidation, fear and a lot of self-generated confusion, then nothing will. If an MP can do conveyancing any idiot can. What's more, if he can do it without the advantage of this simple 'DIY manual' of conveyancing, with its flowcharts and practical explanations, then it should be perfectly easy for real people.

Thanks to Jim Potter we're now in a world where every man can be his own conveyancer. Which, as a democrat, is where I want us to be. The law still restricts conveyancing for profit to solicitors and our new breed of licenced conveyancers, yet anyone has the right to do the conveyancing on their own house whether for fun, to save money or out of simple masochism.

I set out to do mine for two reasons. Having successfully broken the solicitors' monopoly of conveyancing and gotten the government to agree to allowing licenced conveyancers to operate I was keen to put into practice what I'd been preaching for months. There was also a direct financial motive. My social climbing wife was determined to move out of Kilburn (or West Hampstead as some call it). Daringly we moved two streets away to Queen's Park and a house which she saw as taking us up in the world; somewhere fit to entertain the Hattersleys, even the Kinnocks, to become part of a glittering sophisticated metropolitan set, somewhere likely to enhance my prospects. That meant another fifteen thousand pounds up the price ladder, another decade on the mortgage mill. So it was essential to save on the conveyancing. It would have cost over five hundred pounds, even for allowing for the fact that solicitors' prices have come down with the arrival of competition.

'. . . somewhere likely to enhance my prospects. That meant another £15,000 up the price ladder, another decade on the mortgage mill. So it was essential to save on the conveyancing.'

I found the job relatively straightforward. Not easy. Yet far from difficult. Solicitors have succeeded in generating an atmosphere of awe and fear about conveyancing, as if it requires arcane legal skills, half-spectacles and a professional competance bred only in that privileged group. In fact, the only legal skill you need is the ability to write your own name. The real requirements are meticulousness, time, and organisational skills, though contacts in that mafia of legal/financial services which shapes our ends, rough hew them how we will, can also help.

If you have some, or all, of these, plus a cool nerve then do your own conveyancing. I have none. I got away with it even untutored as I then was by the excellent Jim Potter.

The first step is to find if the land is registered. Mine was. All Greater London is, another of those advantages of the soft southeast. Thanks to the agreement I got from the Solicitor General when I withdrew my House Buyers Bill most of the country will be before too long. He agreed to provide the staff and money to the Land Registry to extend compulsory registration to 85% of the country in five years (a target in fact reached in November 1985) and to all of it in ten, (now likely by 1990) provided computerisation of the Land Registry is as successful as it shows every sign of being. I wouldn't have done my own conveyancing if the land had not been registered. It can (though it usually doesn't) get more complicated, but Jim Potter has made even that easy.

The major requirement for successful conveyancing, and the thing I missed most, is a route planner. *Do-It-Yourself Conveyancing* provides several of these in a series of flowcharts. In addition it provides examples of all the relevant forms, filled in for your guidance. So with this book you're in business. Wait for the draft contract from the seller's solicitor. Send him 'Pre-Contract Enquiries'. Do your local search. For both you need some of the forms in the forms kit which is available to purchasers of this book. Have a survey done. Since the building society's survey (which you can now see) is primarily designed to re-assure them that the house will remain standing for the period of the mortgage, it's well worth while having your own. They cost. You can lose the money if you don't get the house. They can be depressing. Yet they're still worth it.

With all these reports in you sign the contract. I had no chain gang building up. Had there been one, a solicitor might have been better at getting them marching in step simply because he has prestige, pull and a built in institutional advantage. But don't give up oppressed by the fact that house buyers were born free but are everywhere in chains. You can badger and persuade too if its essential. Or take it calmly if it isn't. Just don't be in awe of anything.

Eventually we'll get conveyancing as simple as log book transfers for cars. Until then, the mystique surrounding it is put here to protect a host of entrenched interests. In my case the seller had intended to handle her side of things herself. She took one look at me and promptly employed a solicitor. The solicitor acting for the lady buying our house was coolly condescending, though in the event the only complication in a smooth sale came from him. An angry letter demanded to know why my house was divided into flats with a sitting tenant. After my usual reaction of total panic and running round the house three times to find the mystery guest I re-read the document. It was someone else's. Sent to me in error.

Act on time, pay careful attention to details, plan carefully as if for a military campaign and all will be well. Completion day brought the solicitors' revenge on me. Barclays Bank announced that they were appointing a solicitor to check my work. The excuse was that they needed good title, though if they did they should have paid the fee rather than charged the customer. The real reason was that they will only trust the professional old boy network with the money. I haggled. Yet I ended up paying about half of what I would have paid anyway.

Barclays' solicitor in Bradford knew nothing of the area, never saw the house, did very little and regarded me as if I'd crawled up through his floorboards. Yet by this stage I accepted this dirty trick in a spirit of resignation. The tension had got to me. With the vendor due to move out, us to move in, the removal van booked, the purchaser of our house banging on the door, I was too terrified of finding a descendant of the abbot of the monastery, which had probably owned this land up to the Reformation, at my doorstep with a shotgun or the Doomsday Book.

'With the vendor due to move out, us to move in, the removal van booked, the purchaser of our house banging on the door, I was too terrified of finding a descendant of the abbot of the monastery, which had probably owned the land up to the Reformation, at my doorstep with a shotgun or the Doomsday Book.'

I make my score Law Society 2 – Mitchell 4. So my own story isn't one of unalloyed success. The Hattersleys never came. The glitterati have remained well hidden; probably moved south of the river to be nearer Arthur Daley. The house took us so close to bankruptcy that we wouldn't have been able to afford to entertain anyone anyway. Yuppies saving to pay other large mortgages are the world's most boring neighbours. Middle class neighbourhoods greet Labour MPs like Rastafarian squatters. Queen's Park has all the warmth and affection of an open fridge, though I assume that's the South compared with the North.

Yet I enjoyed the conveyancing experience. No one has turned up and claimed our house. No one has attempted to assert 'sheepwalk' through the garden or 'jus primae noctae' elsewhere. Nor has the council tried to drive a motorway through the kitchen. Best of all I saved around £250 — even after the unearned solicitor's fee. As a Yorkshireman that makes everything worthwhile.

Like parachuting I had concluded that it was fun once, but not to be repeated. Until I met Jim Potter and read *Do-It-Yourself Conveyancing.* There is no better, more straightforward programmed learning guide for the layman, written by someone who knows conveyancing and land law backwards. He takes you step by step through the processes, simplifying and rationalising and providing the kind of route map which makes the job easy. Moreover the book works for both registered and unregistered land. It also helps in dealing with the institutions and organisations which are going to become increasingly important in the field of house buying as building societies, banks, estate agents and solicitors get into the real spirit of competition by setting out to provide a comprehensive service; the one-stop shopping which my Bill encouraged by breaking down the log jam of professional and institutional separation, solicitors doing one job, estate agents another, building societies a third.

Today those who want to have the job done for them are able to shop around for a much better, more competitive service. Yet I assume from the fact that you're reading this preface that you're not like that. You want to try it for yourself. Go ahead. With this guide it's easy. You'll learn the ropes. You'll develop a skill you'll almost certainly want to use again. You'll be able to give the job some things no solicitor and no institution can provide: personal attention, sustained interest, an insight into the real problems of neighbours and conditions on the spot. It's detailed niggling work. You'll be helped if you have an ordered mind and the propensities of a military campaign planner.

Even with none of those skills you can do it. If you do actually have any, or all, you're sure to be a success as your own conveyancer. You might even develop that side of your character to the full and become a solicitor. Then you'll be able to afford a bigger house!

AUSTIN MITCHELL
MP for Greater Grimsby

HOUSE OF COMMONS
LONDON SW1A OAA

Austin Mitchell M.P. is the member of parliament for Greater Grimsby. A well known author, broadcaster and TV personality, he sponsored the House Buyer's Members' Bill which brought about the ending of the solicitors near monopoly of conveyancing and the creation of a mini profession of 'licensed conveyancer' with its own qualifications and council.

Introduction: How to Use This Book

This book reflects conveyancing practice in England and Wales. If you live in Scotland or Northern Ireland, or intend to buy a home there, you will have to use something else, for the law and procedures are quite different in this case.

Every year many thousands of houses, bungalows, flats and other types of dwellings are bought and sold, and the legal steps that are taken to transfer legal ownership from one person to another are known under the umbrella term of 'conveyancing'.

The bulk of conveyancing is carried out by solicitors who, until recently, enjoyed a virtual monopoly in that field, and a smaller but growing number of licensed Conveyancers.

The monopoly of solicitors has largely been removed and Parliament has created a new breed of 'licensed Conveyancers'. These are persons who are licensed to undertake conveyancing, either on the basis of their experience of conveyancing procedures or by passing the relevant examinations.

Costs

Conveyancing firms' fees are usually appreciably lower than those of solicitors, so when contemplating buying or selling a property shop around and get more than one estimate of the costs from both solicitor and conveyancer. Not surprisingly, now that solicitors have lost their virtual monopoly and are facing competition from conveyancing firms, their fees are being reduced. However, in general a solicitor will charge more than a conveyancer.

The true cost of buying a property is not only the price that the vendor agreed to accept, but also includes solicitor's or licensed conveyancer's fees, stamp duty (if applicable), and land registry fees a valuation fee to the building society or bank, building society solicitor's fee and, most probably, a survey fee. An example of all these typical costs is on page 118.

The legal fees charged by solicitors on a typical sale of a house for £40,000 average around £410, and on a typical purchase of £45,000, the average fee is £450, both fees including VAT.

Thus, if the conveyancing is done entirely by solicitors, the cost would amount to about £860, which even in this era of funny money is quite a big outlay.

Yet there is no reason why the services of either solicitors or conveyancers need be employed. Anyone, but anyone, with the normal quota of intelligence and ordinary common sense can capably undertake the conveyancing procedures involved, and in the process not only make worthwhile savings, but do a more thorough job than either the solicitor or conveyancer.

Believe me, there is absolutely no reason why you should not buy and sell your own home yourself.

Step by Step Guide

The purpose of this book is to provide a step-by-step guide to the conveyancing of domestic property which will enable the average person, unburdened with legal qualifications but gifted with intelligence and common sense, to carry out his own transaction with confidence. It explains the procedures involved in the sale and/or purchase of a property and for the sake of simplicity, the word 'house' is used in the text as shorthand for a house that may be detached, semi-detached, or terraced, a bungalow, town house, maisonette, flat or whatever, and leasehold houses and flats. It does not cover the purchase of a new house from a developer or the grant of a new lease.

If you use this book as an 'operating manual', by following the procedures involved in logical sequence and reading the commentary you will realise that there is nothing involved that is not well within your capacity.

I have avoided legal mumbo jumbo wherever possible and in those cases where the use of a legal technical term is unavoidable I have also interpreted that term in ordinary language.

The book consists of four parts: the commentary which applies to both registered and unregistered land, a section dealing with the procedures involved in respect of registered land and another section with that relating to unregistered land, and a section containing completed forms and letters which latter you can copy or adapt.

I suggest that you start by studying the flow charts (on pages 16-17) to get a general idea of the procedure and then read the book through, referring to them from time to time.

Read the book with the intention of getting an overview; don't worry if the details escape you first time through. Then go back to the beginning and work through using the sample forms and letters.

Chapters 1 to 3 apply to any property you buy regardless of whether it is registered or unregistered. In every case the procedure is the same. But from page 55 the book divides into two sections, Chapter 4 dealing with the purchase procedure for registered land, and Chapter 5 with the procedure for property that is unregistered land.

Therefore, having leafed through the book to gain a general idea of what happens and when, you need only re-read up to page 55 and then select the section appropriate to your purchase, i.e. depending on whether the property is registered or unregistered.

Chapter 6 deals with the procedures for selling a property, and is divided between the procedures applicable for the sale of a registered property and those applicable for an unregistered property.

In Chapter 9 I have included sample forms and replies given in actual transactions (but have concealed identities), together with suggested letters that you may copy or adapt as necessary.

The book includes an extensive and comprehensive glossary which explains all the legal terms and phrases you are every likely to encounter in your dealings with solicitors, building societies and banks or anyone else concerned in your conveyancing transaction. Not all the terms used by lawyers are self explanatory, but have no fear. If you come across a term or phrase that is unfamiliar to you, you can confidently expect to find an explanation of what it means in the glossary.

A complete set of all the forms you will need to carry out your own conveyancing including even a small supply of the red seals for the Transfer or Conveyance is available — please see page 209 for order form.

A unique feature of *Do-It-Yourself Conveyancing* is the Backup Service. This has been carefully designed and set up to ensure that you are not isolated and 'on your own' by providing practical guidance and advice if you run across a problem which you yourself cannot resolve. If

How to Use this Book

Chapter 1 describes basic terms and concepts useful to everyone using this book.

If buying, or simultaneously buying and selling, chapters 2 and 3 cover the preliminaries up to exchanging contracts.

If the property being bought is registered go on to chapter 4. If unregistered go straight to chapter 5.

If you are merely planning to sell, everything you need to do is covered by chapter 6.

Chapter 7 has helpful hints about insurance and obtaining mortgages.

Lists of useful names and addresses, and tables of costs are to be found in Chapter 8.

Chapter 9 has draft samples of all the forms and letters you will be using.

Glossary of legal jargon and terminology.

Index

The Blank Forms Pack is to be used with your own conveyance and is available by using the order form on p. 209.

The Backup Service is there to be used if you become hopelessly stuck.

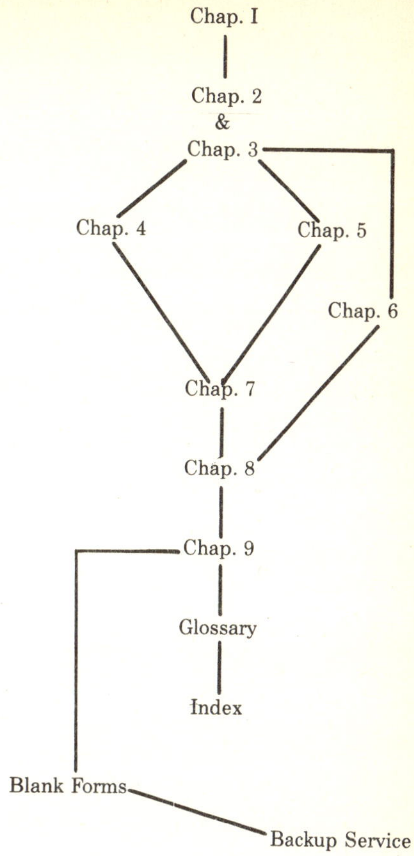

you carefully follow the procedures set out in the book, it is unlikely that you will encounter any problems, but the service is there if you need it. Think of it not as a 'panic button' but more as a reassuring 'support system' that will summon help and advice if and when you need it.

Working With the 'Other Side'

When you are carrying out your own conveyancing, whether it be a sale or a purchase, or more usually, a simultaneous sale and purchase, the person who has agreed to buy your house and the person from whom you are buying will each instruct a firm of solicitors or a licensed conveyancer to act for them.

In practice, it is unlikely that you will have many dealings with an actual solicitor. It is more likely that if solicitors have been instructed to act for your vendor or purchaser, your dealings will be with a clerk or secretary employed by the firm of solicitors.

If a licensed conveyancer has been instructed to act you are more likely to be dealing with the licensed conveyancer himself as conveyancing firms tend to be relatively small.

It is true that some solicitors can appear to be somewhat patronising when dealing with non-lawyers, but the majority just want to get on with the job with as little hassle as possible.

These facts alone should give you confidence, for in the usual conveyancing transaction, particularly of registered land, a knowledge of land law hardly intrudes.

The people who will be acting for the other side will be familiar with the forms and procedure, but you should not allow this to intimidate you. You, too, will gain in confidence as your familiarity with the forms and procedures increases.

Whichever your counterpart is, I suggest that the golden rule for a trouble-free transaction is to make a real effort right from the start to establish good relations with him (or her). This does not mean that you have to tug at your forelock, but courtesy costs nothing and helps to grease the wheels of a good relationship.

— You can start this off by a friendly phone call to the other side, introducing yourself. Few people can be boorish if they are greeted in a friendly way.

— Make a special point of promptly and efficiently replying to letters and phone calls. You should be meticulous about this and always ensure that the other side are never waiting for you.

— Leave a daytime phone number so that you can be readily contacted.

— Use the phone to sort out small snags and concerns, but try not to pester him with a barrage of phone calls unless there are real problems.

— Ideally, try to get the use of a typewriter if you don't already have one, or better still, the services of someone with nimble fingers on a typewriter. Not only does a neatly typed letter look more businesslike, but is usually easier to read! Keep copies of all incoming and outgoing letters and forms, and file them systematically so that you can readily find them.

— If yours is a simultaneous sale and purchase, keep the correspondence forms and documents in separate folders (I personally use foolscap envelope type folders. I rule columns on the back and keep a running record of the progress of the transaction).

— If you are to have a crisis-free transaction, you should try to develop, if you don't already possess it, obsessive attention to detail and by re-reading this book familiarise yourself with the procedures involved so that you can see at least the outline of a logical progression towards completion.

— Use the timetables on pages 55, 72, 93, and 112 as a progress check list and regularly review matters outstanding. Cross refer between the timetable and the filing system you set up.

Whilst solicitors acting for your purchaser and vendor can be expected to be helpful, they cannot release documents or money on trust as they can if they are dealing with a fellow solicitor. This is not a matter of the solicitor being difficult or obstructive, but of being obliged to follow the rules of his profession. Nor will solicitors agree to their client's deposit being held by you as stakeholder. I suggest that a third party, such as the estate agent if you used one, or a High Street bank, be asked to hold the deposit as stakeholder.

There are few High Street banks which might not be willing to hold a deposit of, generally a few thousand pounds for about one month, in the joint names of yourself and either the solicitor or your purchaser. Some solicitors may not agree to a bank holding the money, though I feel that a solicitor who objected to such an arrangement was being unreasonable.

However, if the alternative suggested by the solicitor is satisfactory to you, I do not consider that this is an issue of such significance as to risk losing your sale, and I would be inclined to go along with the solicitor's proposal for the holding of the deposit, ALWAYS PROVIDED that the deposit is held for you and your purchaser as stakeholder.

What If I Get Stuck?

At some stage in your transaction you may hit a snag that you cannot unravel or, worse, you feel completely lost. At this point you should go back in reverse order over what you have already done to make quite sure that you have followed the procedures precisely. Keep calm. Please believe me that the chance of you hitting a snag that cannot be put right is so small as to be almost inconceivable.

Take the example I relate on page 102. There a solicitor some 10 years ago had forgotten to apply for the merger of a lease into the freehold (fee simple) and his error had never been spotted. Instead of holding, as he thought, a freehold interest in the property he had offered for sale, the Vendor held both freehold and leasehold interests. Disaster? No. It was agreed that the contract would be altered and the purchaser would buy both freehold and leasehold interests and when applying for the change of ownership to be registered would ask the District Land Registry for the lease to be merged in the freehold. 'Problem' solved.

In particular, if you are dealing with registered land, or if yours is a sale of a house you bought or the purchase of a house from a vendor who himself bought the house, I repeat, I cannot readily think of any snag that you can meet that cannot be overcome.

If you are, say, selling as a personal representative, or the person you are buying from inherited the property, a snag could conceivably crop up; perhaps regarding the Grant of Probate or the Assent. But, in general terms, there is nothing that cannot be solved with patience and goodwill.

Take heart. Providing that you follow the procedures outlined in these pages precisely, that you do your searches in good time, get satisfactory answers to your preliminary enquiries and requisitions, and establish good rapport with the other side, if a snag does develop, a way around the problem can be found.

And do remember that if you really do get stuck or think you are, there is always the Backup Service to turn to — see page 6 and 207.

Simultaneous Sale and Purchase

Although selling and buying a house is dealt with in separate chapters so that the procedures can be fully understood, the vast majority of conveyancing transactions involve a purchase and a sale, usually simultaneously. That is to say, for most folk, whether or not they are getting a mortgage, the sale of their present house must help finance the purchase of their 'new' home.

When reading the chapters on sale and on purchase, therefore, you should keep in mind that in most cases these are not kept in separate watertight compartments; the procedures for your purchase proceed in tandem with those for your sale.

Timing of completion of a simultaneous sale and purchase is of crucial importance and you should read and re-read the procedure set out on pages 52-54.

A Short History of Who Owns What

You may find the following brief historical excursion helpful in understanding the background to land law in England and Wales.

It may be very difficult to accept that a man (or woman) cannot own land or the house on which it stands in the same way that he can own, say, a car.

It all goes back to 1066 — and all that. William the Conqueror considered the whole of England his by right of conquest, and parcelled it out to his followers and those of the English who submitted. It was not given absolutely but was held of the Crown under certain conditions.

These conditions varied, and included the provision of personal services, such as holding up the King's train (this was before British Rail), or providing a given number of fighting men and horses for forty days a year and so on.

At the time the Doomsday Book was compiled in 1086 there was thought to be around 1500 lords who held land directly of the King. They in turn granted occupation of parts of their vast lands to lesser lords in return for services, and so on down towards the base of the feudal pyramid.

This brings us to two words which appear frequently in the book, namely 'tenure' and 'estate'. Feudal services became standardised — service rendered personally to the King was known as 'grand sergeantry', the provision of armed fighting men as 'knight's service'. Each type of service was known as a tenure (from the French tenir — to hold, teneur — holder) since it showed the terms on which the land was held.

Now tenure might be held for different periods of time — for life (for so long as the grantee lived), in tail — entail — (for so long as the grantee or his heirs lived), or in fee simple (so long as the grantee and his successors lived whether descendants or not). Each of these interests in land was known as an estate.

If you are still with me, one other word requires a little explanation. 'Fee' is the right which a tenant (in the feudal sense of the word) has in land, rendering to his lord his due services. Thus we have the estate for life, the estate in fee tail, and the estate in fee simple. An estate in fee simple is the most extensive estate of inheritance a man can have. Simple in this context is used in contradistinction to a fee conditional, e.g. in tail.

900 Years Later

All that began 900 or so years ago and although considerable reforms were made in 1925, modern land law is still greatly influenced by its past history. It is still true today that a man cannot 'own' land absolutely. He can only have an 'estate' in it and the land can, in certain circumstances, revert to the Crown in accordance with the feudal principle 'No land without a lord' (Nulle terre sans seigneur).

Since the 1925 reforms the only estates in land are the 'fee simple absolute in possession' or freehold (which is as near to absolute ownership a man can get) and the 'term of years absolute' which is a leasehold estate.

However, both freehold and leasehold may be subject to a number of interests by third parties. Such interests include easements, covenants, mortgages, planning restrictions and so on.

Reverting to our analogy of a car purchase, when buying a car you

The simplified diagram below sets out the system by which land is owned in England and Wales.

1) All land is held ultimately by the Crown. A small part is occupied directly by the Crown. The rest is held by 'tenants', either directly or indirectly of the Crown.

2) Since 1925 only two estates in land have existed. Freehold land, or fee simple, implies absolute possession and is the closest you can get to outright ownership

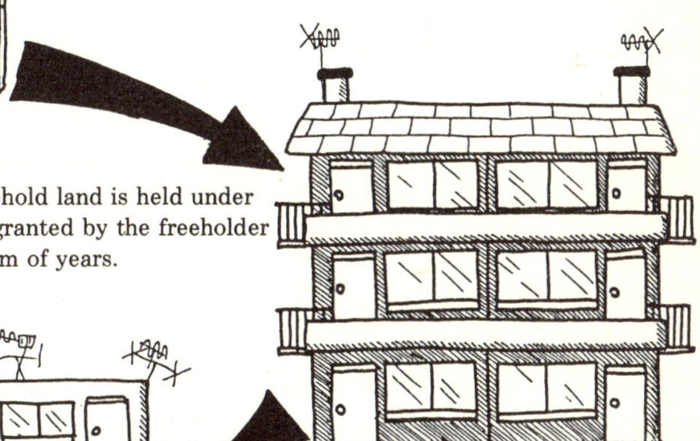

3) Leasehold land is held under a lease granted by the freeholder for a term of years.

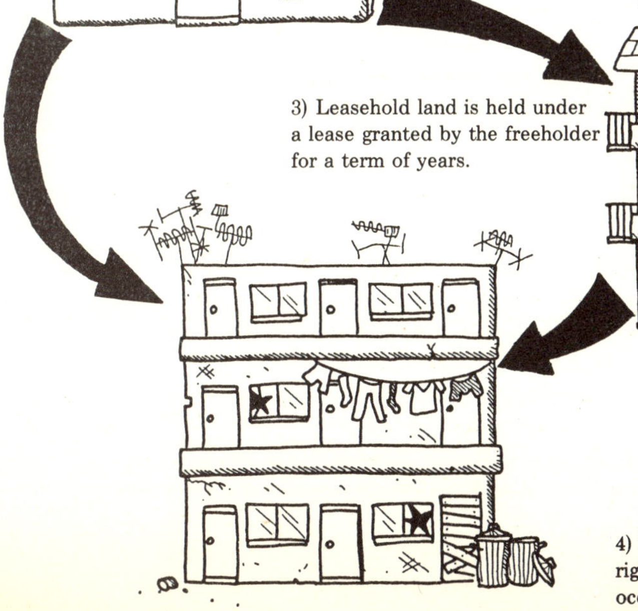

4) Rented property implies no rights of ownership but lawful occupancy is usually protected to some degree by Rent Acts.

hand over the purchase price or hire purchase agreement, and take possession. If you have paid the purchase price, or keep up the H.P. payments, the car is yours and you will own it. Not so with a house or flat. To transfer a freehold or leasehold estate from seller to buyer requires, with a few exceptions, that a deed be executed. A deed is a written document signed sealed and delivered by both parties and witnessed by a third.

Moreover, when buying a car from a reputable dealership one assumes that it is their property because they are in possession of it and, if the car is used, can produce the log book to support their implied claim to ownership.

But the same considerations cannot apply to a house or flat. The fact that the vendor appears to be living in it doesn't mean it is his. He may be a tenant, or a squatter, or a licencee (i.e. allowed to live there by the owner), or he might owe most of the value of the property to a building society. So 'title' (ownership) of the house or flat has to be investigated by a would-be purchaser.

Investigation of Title

'Investigation of Title' as the procedure is called has been much simplified by the Land Registration Act 1925. About 85% of all land in England and Wales is in areas of compulsory registration and within 10 years it is hoped that the whole of England and Wales will be one vast area of compulsory registration which will simplify things even more.

Until that glad day dawns, though, in areas within the 15% of England and Wales where registration is non-compulsory, a purchaser must investigate the title of his vendor by tracing the history of ownership through successive past owners right down to the current vendor.

As a deed is required each time an unregistered property changes hands, there can be quite a collection of deeds.

Cheer up, though. A vendor does not need to go back to the year dot. His title to the property he is selling is established if he can trace a chain of ownership to himself going back at least 15 years. In practice, this rarely involves more than three conveyances; on the other hand there may be only one conveyance to the vendor say 18 years ago.

Renting Property

Now, for completeness, a short discussion on the alternative to a freehold or leasehold interest in a house or flat — the renting of property.

Most rented dwellings are either owned by private landlords or by councils. In addition, there are Housing Associations and charities which provide dwellings for rent. The tenant pays a rent to the landlord in return for occupation. The terms of occupation typically provide for a weekly or monthly tenancy, but such a tenant may remain in occupation for a long time under the statutory protection provided by the Rent Acts, and if the tenant dies, his wife or children may be able to remain in the property and continue the tenancy.

The Rent Acts provide a measure of protection to a tenant against a eviction and harassment, and in controlling the rent that may be charged by a private landlord. The tenant is required to comply with the terms of the tenancy and to pay the rent. If the tenant fulfills his part of the tenancy agreement he has what is generally regarded to be a secure tenancy and a court will be very loath to grant re-possession to a landlord. There is of course no investigation by the tenant of a landlord's title, nor can the tenant by virtue of the tenancy ever gain a financial interest in the property he is renting. This latter point is the major difference between the occupation of a property one owns and the occupation of a rented property.

Buying and Selling Property

Before tackling conveyancing it is absolutely essential to have a clear idea of the ways property can be owned in England and Wales, and the various formal stages involved in buying and selling it.

Is the Property Freehold or Leasehold?

You may find it slightly confusing at first that when the word 'land' is used in the text we are referring not to acres of rolling English countryside but to the property you propose to buy or sell. In the context of this book, 'land' means a house, with any garage, workshop or other outbuildings, together with the garden and the land on which the buildings stand.

The terms on which the land is held, known as 'tenure', may be freehold or leasehold. By freehold we mean absolute ownership. This contrasts with leasehold by which is meant the possession of property for a fixed number of years under the terms of a lease.

Most houses are held on freehold tenure. Town houses, bungalows and maisonettes may be freehold or leasehold; flats are almost always leasehold.

A leasehold property is held under the terms of a lease by which a landlord grants a tenant rights of 'occupation and enjoyment of the property' for a fixed term of years. This, usually, is 99 years, but some exclusive properties are leased on 999 years leases.

Upon the grant of the lease the tenant (lessee) pays the landlord (lessor) a lump sum and agrees to pay an annual sum as ground rent. This ground rent is quite nominal.

Having paid the landlord for the grant of the lease, the tenant may 'assign' (sell) the lease to a purchaser; the procedures involved are little different from those involved if the property sold is freehold. Where there are differences these are referred to at the appropriate point in the text.

For the sake of simplicity, the word 'house' is used in the text as shorthand for a house that may be detached, semi-detached or terraced, a bungalow, town house, maisonette, flat or whatever.

It was also thought helpful, in some instances where a legal term is frequently used by conveyancers, to have both the legal term and its layman equivalent in brackets. Examples we will shortly be using include vendor (seller) and title (ownership). Other examples will be found at different stages in the book and I hope will be self-explanatory. But if you do encounter a term with which you are unfamiliar do please refer to the glossary.

Registered Land and Unregistered Land

There are two systems of proving title (ownership) of land running in parallel and this is really the first point to grasp.

Unregistered Land

One of the systems of proving title (ownership) to land is the venerable practice whereby the owner produces a series of deeds, tracing ownership to himself from some person or persons who previously owned the property, which go back at least fifteen years. A deed, in this context, is a document signed by the vendor (seller) — with a red disc or wafer after his signature — which conveys the ownership of an unregistered property from vendor to purchaser. This document is also referred to as a 'conveyance'. For our purpose we can say that until 1925 it was the only method of proving ownership. The most obvious defect of this traditional system is that title (ownership) must be investigated afresh every time the land is offered for sale. In brief, the system is wasteful and time consuming.

Registered Land

Under the Land Registration Act 1925, a new system was introduced whereby title (ownership) to land was to be registered and guaranteed by the State. This system of land registration is intended to replace the traditional system eventually, but until the whole of England and Wales is covered by areas of compulsory registration, the old and new systems will co-exist.

By 1986 it was estimated that about 85% of the land in England and Wales was in areas of compulsory registration, and new areas are being declared as quickly as the available facilities permit.

The Land Registry

The government department responsible for operating the land registration system is H.M. Land Registry under the control of the Chief Land Registrar. There are offices of the Land Registry in various part of the country known as District Land Registries. A list of addresses and telephone numbers is on pages 122-123.

Each District Land Registry maintains a register of all land in its areas of compulsory registration and issues a 'Land Certificate' to the registered owner of the property. This document is proof of title (ownership) and is guaranteed by the State. Some writers have described a Land Certificate as similar to a car log book, but it is much more than that. Whereas the person named in a car log book as the 'keeper' of the vehicle may or may not be the legal owner, the person listed on a Land Certificate as the proprietor of the land described is, in law, the legal owner and his title is guaranteed.

It will be seen that all an owner of property need do to prove his title, if the land is registered, is to produce the Land Certificate. All the costly, time consuming investigation of the history of ownership in the old traditional system is eliminated.

As already mentioned, additions are continually being made to the list of compulsory registration areas. It is thus not unusual to find that even though a house is within a compulsory registration area, title (ownership) to it may still be unregistered because it was last sold before the area was designated for compulsory registration. When a house is first sold after the area is so designated, title must be registered by the new owner.

The Two Stages of a Purchase or Sale

A transaction to sell or buy a house falls into two distinct stages. Stage one is up to exchange of contracts. For our purpose a contract is a written document of which there is an identical counterpart. Exchange of contracts takes place at the moment when the vendor (seller), having received the purchaser's (buyer's) signed copy of the contract, posts to the purchaser the copy countersigned by himself. At that moment the parties are contractually bound to go through with the deal. Incidentally, the buyer should satisfy himself in respect of insurance cover from the time of exchange of contracts. Of which more later.

The second stage is from exchange of contracts to completion. Completion is the moment when the Conveyance or Transfer is handed over in exchange for the purchase money and the purchaser becomes the legal owner of the house. Completion usually takes place about four weeks after exchange of contracts, but this can be and is often varied by mutual agreement.

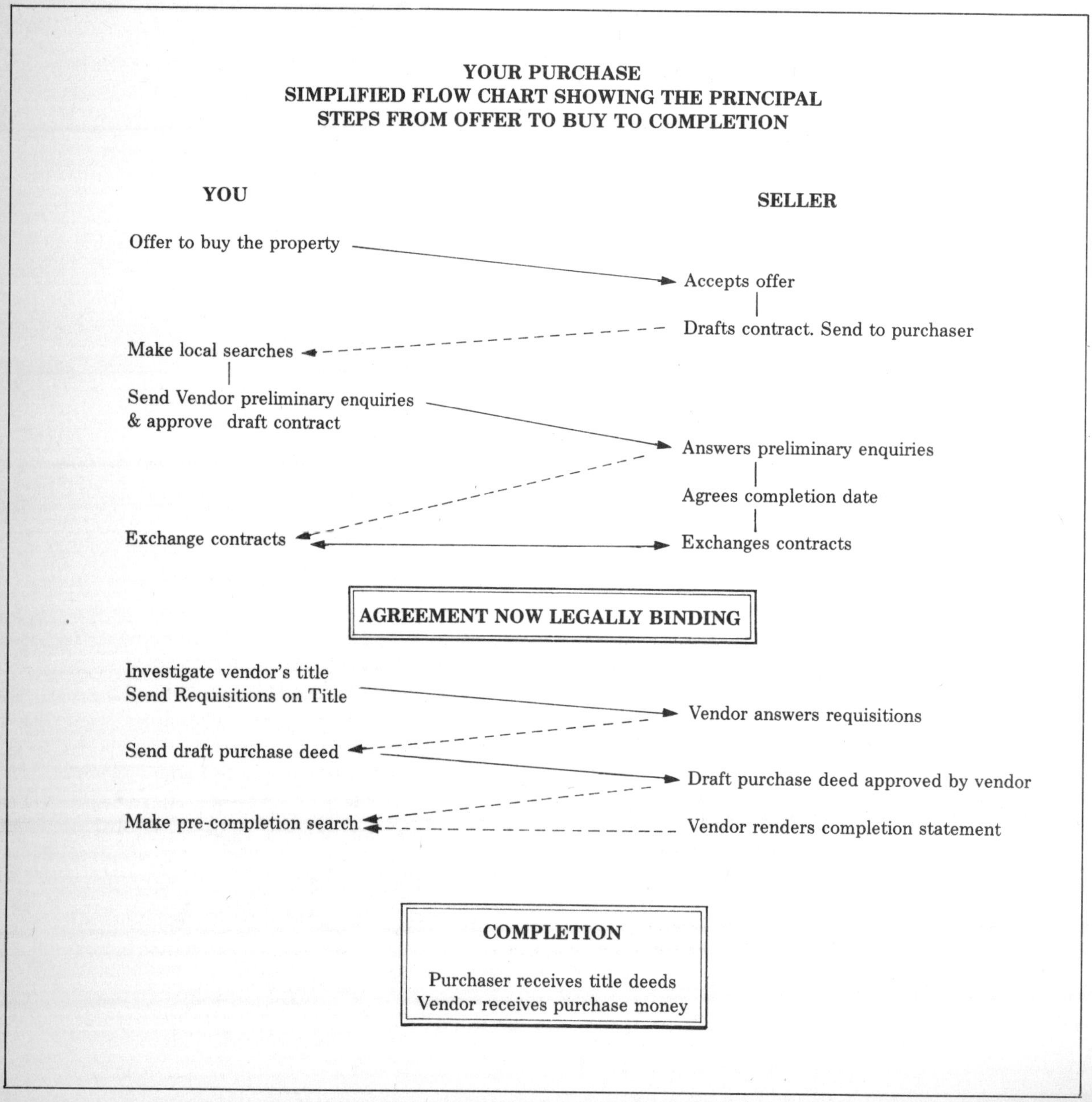

A Brief Recap

Let me repeat the first two points which are basic to your transaction, whether you are buying or selling or both.

Point 1 Land (including the land on which the house etc. stands) is either *registered land* or *unregistered land.*

Point 2 A transaction falls into two distinct stages:

Stage 1: Up to exchange of contracts. Prior to exchange either party may withdraw without giving a reason.

Stage 2: From exchange to completion. On exchange, purchaser and vendor are bound, i.e. neither may withdraw. Purchaser pays (usually) ten per cent of purchase price on exchange. At completion the purchaser pays the balance of the purchase price and in exchange receives the documents of title (ownership).

The steps involved in your purchase are illustrated by a flow chart on page 16 and for your sale by a flow chart below. Detailed step by step timetables for your purchase are on pages 55, 72 and 93 and for your sale on page 112.

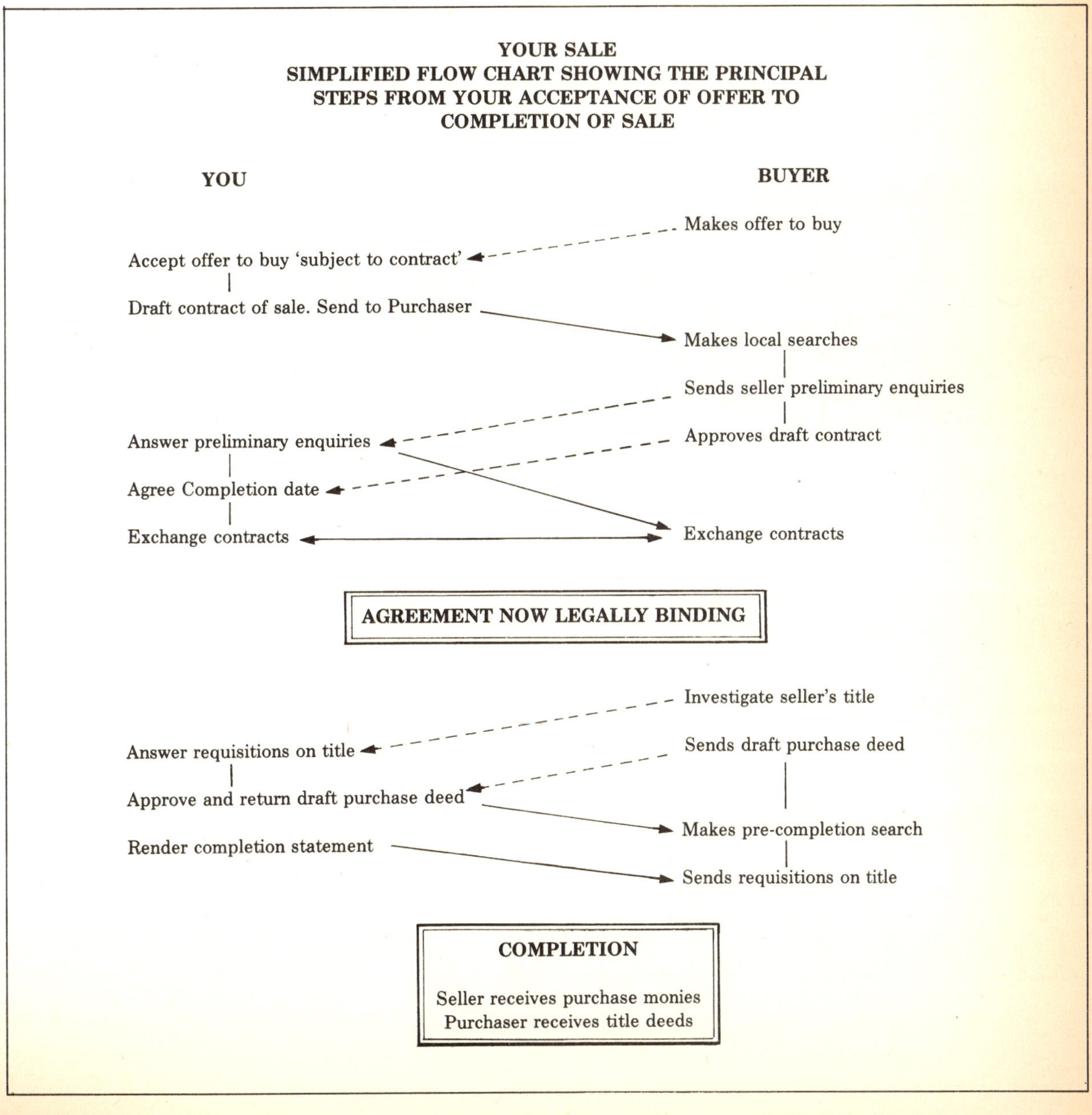

Making an Offer to Buy

Few people pay for a house or flat with cash. For most of us it's the biggest credit purchase we ever undertake, made possible only by mortgaging oneself to the hilt. Since the costs of mortgages can vary widely, there is every reason in the world to shop around to find the best buy.

Making An Offer — 'Subject to Contract'

You have agreed the price you are to pay to the vendor for his house, flat or whatever. This agreement will probably be a verbal one with the vendor, in which case telephone the estate agent acting for the vendor or call in and see him. Then write to the estate agent and the vendor, as suggested in the letter on page 127, making certain that you incorporate the phrase 'subject to contract'.

All correspondence concerning the transaction should also incorporate these magic words. Their effect is that the agreement is provisional and either party can withdraw without giving any reason.

If the vendor is selling through an estate agent, the latter will almost certainly send you a sales sheet similar to that on page 128. Having checked that the price and particulars are correct, you now have a handy contact sheet of the names and addresses you will be dealing with.

Conveyancing Forms

All the blank forms you require to do your own conveyancing are included in the forms pack available by completing the order form on page 209. Here is a check list of the forms you need and the quantities.

Completion of Form 96 Application for Official Search of the Index Map is essential if you are buying an unregistered property and it can be a very useful tool in other circumstances. If you are not certain whether the title to the land is registered an application on Form 96 should be made. An official certificate of the result of the search will then be sent to you within three days.

Purchasing Registered Land

1 Form 96:	Application for Official Search of the Index Map
2	Pre-Contract Enquiries (Ole series)
2 Con 29 A:	Enquiries of District Councils (England and Wales) *(or)*
2 Con 29D:	Enquiries of District Councils (London Boroughs and City of London)
1 LLC1:	Requisition for Search
2	Requisitions on Title (Ole series)
2 Form 19:	Transfer of Whole (for property being bought by sole purchaser) *(or)*
2 Form 19 (JP):	Transfer of Whole (for property being bought by joint purchasers)
1 Form K16:	Application for an Official Search (Bankruptcy only)

1 Form A4:	Application to Register Dealings
1 Form A44:	Application for Office Copies
1 Form Stamps L(A)451:	Particulars of Instruments Transferring or Leasing Land
1 Form Stamps 61:	To accompany Form Stamps L(A)451
4 Form A13:	List of Documents sent to H.M. Land Registry
1 Form 1A:	Application by Owners for First Registration Freehold Land
1 Form 2A:	Application by Owners for First Registration Leasehold Land
4 Seals:	For use on Form 19 or Form 19(JP)

Purchasing Unregistered Land

1 Form 96:	Application for Official Search of the Index Map
2	Pre-Contract Enquiries (Ole series)
2 Con 29A:	Enquiries of District Councils (England and Wales) *(or)*
2 Con 29D:	Enquiries of District Councils (London Boroughs and City of London)
2	Requisitions on Title (Ole series)
1 Form K15:	Application for an Official Search
1 Form K16:	Application for an Official Search (Bankruptcy only)
1 Conveyance Blank:	On which you copy the 'approved' conveyance
4 Seals:	For use on Conveyance

Both before and after exchange of contracts a purchaser asks questions of the seller. Until recently, these almost invariably were made by means of two forms produced by Oyez (The Solicitors Law Stationery Society Plc) called 'Enquiries before Contract' and 'Requisitions on Title' respectively. With the almost universal use of word processors in solicitors' offices, many solicitors now make up their own forms. I have drafted two such forms which are in the forms pack referred to on page 18.

Purchase in Joint Names

You will note that for the sake of simplicity, I have assumed that a husband and wife are buying as joint tenants, and a few words on this may be helpful.

When a married couple are buying jointly, it obviously is sensible to consider what they would like to happen to their share in the property in the event that one of them dies. Do they wish the share to form part of the estate of the deceased, or do they wish it to pass automatically on death to the survivor? Transfers of property between spouses are exempt from Inheritance Tax, and to an increasing extent married couples are choosing that their share in the matrimonial home shall pass to the survivor automatically (known as a joint tenancy) rather than form part of the estate of the deceased spouse (known as a tenancy in common).

The advantages of a joint tenancy are obvious; the property passes to the survivor automatically, there is no need to await the grant of probate or to refer to the will of the deceased; the survivor can deal with the property in every way, including the power of sale, and can give a valid receipt for money arising when the property is sold.

Of course, you may be purchasing in a sole name. Some married couples choose to buy in one name, usually of the husband, and the text also provides for this. Or else you may be an individual and would naturally purchase in a sole name.

Cold-Blooded Romance

When an unmarried couple buy a house jointly, it makes sense, even if it sounds somewhat unromantic, for them to agree what is to happen to the share of a partner who dies. Is the share of that partner to pass automatically to the survivor or is it to form part of the estate of the deceased?

What happens to the share of a deceased partner upon his death depends upon the manner by which the property is held. It may be held by the partners as 'joint tenants' or as 'tenants in common'.

For unmarried couples the distinction between a joint tenancy and a tenancy in common makes a big difference if one partner dies or, as is much more common, the relationship breaks down.

Joint Tenants

If they hold the property as joint tenants, each has an equal share in the whole, and the share of the deceased partner passes automatically to the survivor, who becomes the beneficial owner and can thus deal with the property in every way. As joint tenants they hold the property upon trust for themselves, and are therefore Trustees. See page 158 for a declaration of trust for joint tenants, and also see below.

Tenants in Common

If, the property is held as tenants in common, the deceased's share in the property forms part of the estate. If for example, the partners hold the property in equal shares, then 50% of the value of the property will pass into the deceased's estate. The property, can of course, be held in whatever proportions the parties agree. If, say, instead of 50/50 the shares were 60/40 and the partner with the 40% share died, 40% of the value of the property would pass into his estate.

Do note though, that whereas property transferred between spouses does not attract Inheritance Tax, the same concession does not apply to unmarried couples. Depending on individual circumstances, therefore, there may be a liability to tax upon the death of one of the co-habiting partners who hold property on a joint tenancy.

Consideration should also be given to what is to happen to their shares in the property if, as is increasingly common if they are a youngish couple, the partnership breaks down.

If, say, they each hold one half share in the property, each may dispose of his share independently of the other, and in the event of a breakdown in the relationship each is entitled to one half share of the proceeds of sale. Whilst each case must be decided on its facts it is my view, for what it is worth, that co-habiting couples should hold property as tenants in common. The completed form 19 (JP) on page 146, the Conveyance on page 158 and the Assignment on page 163 provide for the property to be held on a joint tenancy.

If you wish to hold as tenants in common delete 'can' in the declaration at (8) on Form 19 (JP) in respect of registered land. In respect of a tenancy in common of unregistered land refer to the Conveyance on page 192 which has been drafted to provide for a tenancy in common in equal shares.

If you would like more information on this topic, Pluto Press have published a very good book entitled 'The Cohabitation Handbook' which you may find helpful. Another helpful book is 'Living Together' by Dye and Berlins and published by Hamlyn Paperbacks. Both of these books should be available in your local library.

Financing Your Purchase

The availability of mortgage money has fluctuated violently over the past decade or so, and periods of mortgage 'famine' have alternated with times of mortgage 'plenty'.

The traditional sources of mortgage funds are the building societies, whose primary purpose is the provision of finance for house purchases. Many of these societies were established in the first half of the nineteenth century, and they have an unrivalled fund of experience in this field.

The building societies main competitors are the high street banks, but other lenders, notably The Mortgage Finance Corporation, have entered the market and are providing stiff competition as are some foreign banks. Large insurance companies such as Prudential have expressed their intention to become involved in domestic mortgage lending. To a much smaller extent mortgages may be forthcoming from trust funds and local authorities, but in most areas, mortgage money from the latter sources has dried up.

The other sources of mortgage loans referred to do so on much the same basis as do the building societies. That is to say, the lender will advance the mortgage loan and take a first mortgage over the property as security.

Building Society or Bank?

When the banks made their first hesitant steps into the mortgage market they offered large loans only, rather than the more modest loan usually sought by the owner-occupier, but later began to compete quite aggressively in most sectors of the market.

In doing so, the banks were very successful, and it is estimated that they secured around 25% of the mortgage market. This share has now steadied at a somewhat lower level.

I use the phrase 'most sectors' because the banks do not appear to be very interested in borrowers aged 55 years or over. Usually banks lay down a maximum term of 25 years and require the loan to be repaid by age 65 or upon retirement if this is earlier.

An intending borrower aged fifty or more would almost certainly find the building societies to be more flexible in this respect, their general

Mortgages can be obtained from a wide variety of sources.

Sources of Mortgages

1) Building Societies
2) High Street Banks
3) Foreign Banks (for mega-loans)
4) The Mortgage Corporation (and other specialist providers of mortgages)
5) Mortgage Brokers (carefully check arrangement fees)
6) Solicitors (on behalf of trust funds)
7) Local Authorities (a few still make mortgage loans)
8) And now even the Post Office Giro Bank

attitude being that they are concerned with the borrower's ability to repay the loan and not with his age. Indeed, I know of one building society which provided finance to tenants of a housing association to enable them to purchase their homes at a discount. A few of the tenants were in their sixties, another in her seventies, and one an octogenarian!

Mortgage Terms

Whilst mortgage lending sources all offer loans on a similar basis, the precise terms on which the loans are made differ. Certainly if funds are readily available, it is wise to compare what is on offer. The precise terms tend to change as the availability of mortgage funds fluctuates or the lending institutions strive to gain a competitive edge over their rivals, and the following comparison can only be made in general terms. It will, I hope, help to point you in the right direction and assist you in obtaining a mortgage on terms that suit your circumstances.

Building Society Terms

Building societies in general calculate the interest on the amount of the loan outstanding at the beginning of each year, whereas the banks calculate the interest on a daily basis. These different methods mean that when both banks and building societies quote identical mortgage rates, the true annual percentage rate of charge of the building societies would be slightly higher than the banks. However, the difference is relatively small, being of the order of about one quarter of one per cent.

Bank Terms

Banks fix the rate of interest to be paid by borrowers over periods of, usually, one year. This no doubt is for the administrative convenience of the banks and illustrates that they are not quite as flexible as are the building societies.

Whilst the banks insist that the property to be mortgaged is covered by a comprehensive index-linked policy of insurance for its full reinstatement value, only one bank requires that it places the insurance itself (and collects the commission); but all the banks are prepared to arrange appropriate cover.

On the other hand it is general policy for building societies to require that they themselves place the building insurance, although there is a limited choice of insurers and some societies will accept an insurance company nominated by the borrower. The Halifax Building Society is prepared to allow the borrower to place the buildings insurance himself with an approved insurance company, but charges an administration fee.

Some banks charge an 'arrangement' fee for providing a mortgage; usually this is £125 or more. Sometimes the intending borrower must also be a customer of the bank of at least six months standing.

All the banks either automatically send, or will make available to the borrower, a copy of the valuation report. In this respect the banks are ahead of those building societies which do not release the contents of the surveyor's valuation report.

A building society will usually readily agree to a further advance for home improvements and will incorporate the second loan into the first loan. As a few societies charge a slightly higher rate of interest for the second loan you should check this out beforehand.

On the other hand, some banks are not enthusiastic about further advances and would probably direct the borrower towards a short term personal loan on which the interest rate charged is much higher than the

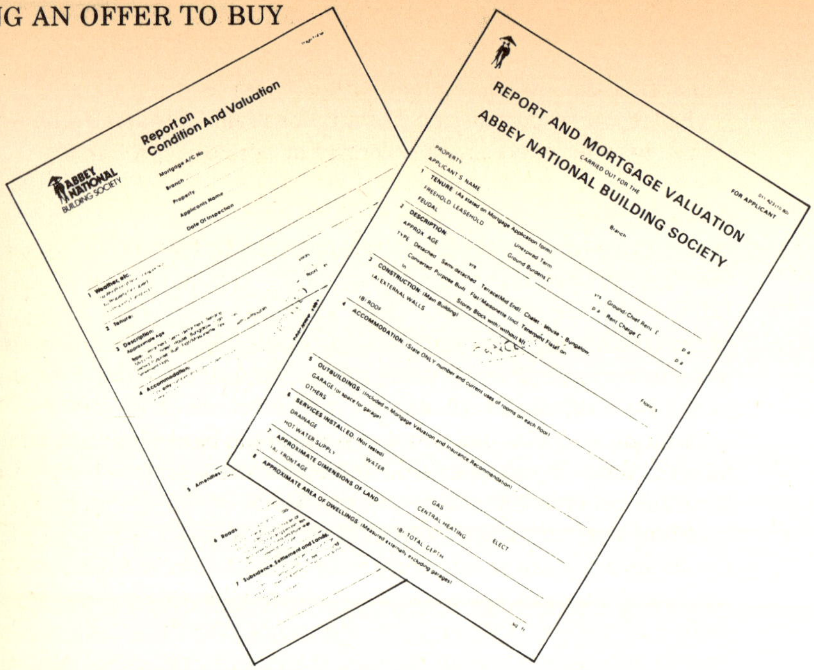

A 'report and mortgage valuation' runs to two and a half pages and is prepared by the building society's surveyor. It is used solely to value the property and a copy is provided to the borrower.

A 'report on condition and valuation' is more detailed. It runs to six pages and includes comments on the asking price and the future saleability of the property. It also contains a valuation for mortgage purposes.

A 'structural survey' is a detailed examination and report on the condition of a property. It does not normally include a valuation for mortgage purposes, although most building societies can arrange for this to be carried out at the same time.

standard mortgage interest rate, and is repayable over a much shorter period.

Amount Loaned

The amount that building societies and banks will advance on the security of the property to be mortgaged depends on the income of the applicant, and the purchase price or professional valuation of the property, whichever is the lower.

Both building societies and the banks generally use the following multipliers to ascertain the sum they will advance:

> 2½ times annual gross income or, if the applicants are both earning, 2½ times the larger annual gross income plus 1 times the smaller income.

Normally, both building societies and banks will advance up to 80% of the purchase price or valuation of the property, whichever is lower, but this percentage may be increased on payment of a single premium Indemnity Insurance. Usually the premium for this can be added to the loan. Do bear in mind that this policy does not confer any benefits on you such as obtain with an endowment or a life policy. Its only purpose is to increase the security for the loan.

There is a degree of flexibility exercised in respect of the multipliers, depending on the particular circumstances of the applicant and the availability of mortgage money. There can be no dispute that for large loans the banks are better equipped than building societies. Indeed, the banks first entered the home mortgage market via this route.

Large mortgages, though, account for a relatively small number of the total advances made on the security of domestic property.

Rising Prices

House prices are continuing to rise strongly. In 1986 as can be seen from the diagram the average rise was 14.5% nationally, whilst in Greater London the rise was 21.6%. These increases in house prices are largely mirrored in the increased average mortgage loan being made. The national average advance made by the building societies over the same period was about £24,000 and by the banks about £35,000.

One gains the impression that some of the banks tend to concentrate much of their effort towards the top end of the market, whereas building societies provide finance across the whole of the mortgage spectrum.

Some societies are also laudably active in inner city areas providing the finance for the repair and restoration of older housing stock.

The scenario thus described has recently been distorted by the entry on the mortgage scene of large institutions, including foreign banks and finance houses anxious to lend on the security of bricks and mortar.

In the main they are primarily interested in large loans — a £100,000 loan being regarded as quite normal. Their marketing is very aggressive but in the nature of things they cater for a fairly small segment of the house mortgage market.

I referred earlier to the degree of flexibility exercised in respect of the multipliers, which depends in large degree on the availability of mortgage finance. Some lenders have been operating very relaxed lending policies and granting mortgage loans based on increased multpliers and high percentages.

In practice this has meant that some lenders have been offering loans based on 3 times the main salary plus one times the subsidiary salary, others have offered 2¾ times the joint salaries. Some lenders are prepared to offer more. Often these higher than normal borrowing multpliers have been on offer coupled with one hundred percent of the property valuation.

It is not for me to pontificate on the social consequences of the growth in arrears and repossessions brought about, at least in part, by relaxed lending policies. I would only report the fact that it is estimated that 5 per cent of people with mortgage loans are seriously in arrears and that repossessions in 1985 jumped by 54 per cent over the previous year to an all time record of 16,770, and are still climbing.

The Building Societies Act 1986 could revolutionise the building society movement. The Act grants new freedoms to the societies. These include the right to engage in estate agency services, to offer property surveys and valuations, conveyancing, current account banking, cheque guarantee cards, unsecured overdrafts and mortgages, stock broking services, pension plans, unit trusts, insurance and other financial services, and to engage in the development of land for residential purposes.

In some circumstances a building society may secure corporate status, i.e. become a public limited company.

No society has plans to exploit all these new freedoms at once, and with most of the smaller societies few obvious changes in their operations will be discernable in the immediate future.

THE NORTH-SOUTH GAP

Average house prices across the nation (including flats, maisonettes and bungalows) reveal the huge difference geographical location can make.

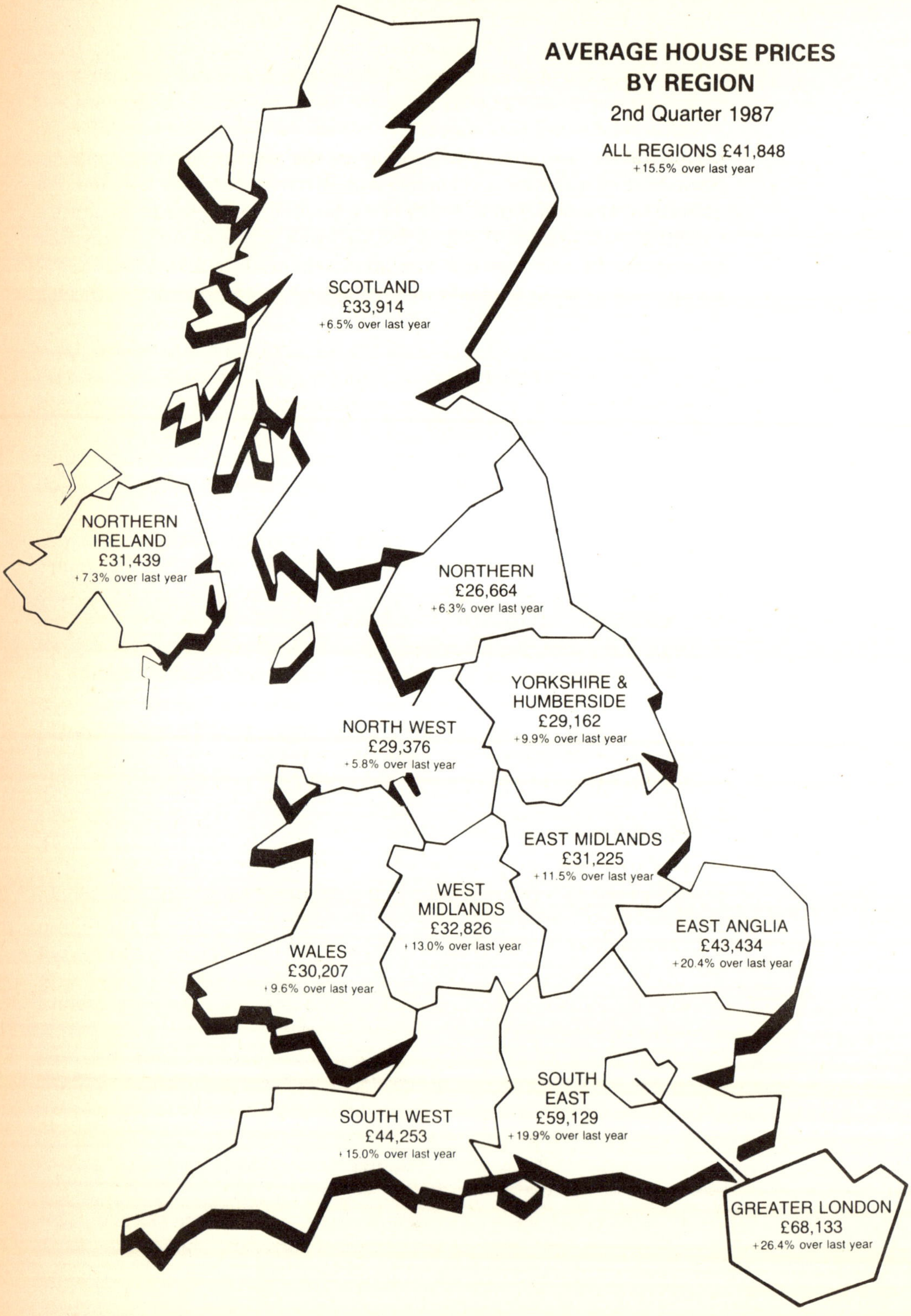

Compiled from mortgage approval statistics supplied by Leeds Permanent Building Society

Weighing Up the Differences

It may well be that in the particular circumstances of the reader none of these points would be a determining factor in deciding whether to ask a building society or a bank for a mortgage. The overriding consideration that controls what terms can be offered is the availability of mortgage funds. When funds are tight there may be little or even no choice. Further, the intending borrower may be influenced by subjective considerations when deciding whether to ask a building society or a bank for a mortgage. For some people, and not only those who do not have a bank account, a visit to a bank can be an intimidating experience.

The banks do not appear to be as well organised in offering peripheral services to the borrower as are the leading building societies. None of the banks has a valuation-cum-survey scheme such as the one offered by Abbey National, but they are generally prepared to facilitate a valuation and structural survey by the same surveyor, or to draw the borrower's attention to the combined scheme offered by the Royal Institute of Chartered Surveyors (R.I.C.S.) and referred to on page 33.

In reply to the question 'What is your attitude if a borrower falls on hard times?' each of the high street banks replied to the effect 'we would be as sympathetic as possible', and most said that a degree of discretion reposed in the branch manager.

Building societies responding to the same question also said they would deal with such cases sympathetically, but appeared to be much more ready to suggest helpful lines of action open to them.

No doubt as a result of their many years of experience in dealing with borrowers, the building societies have already met just about every problem than can face an owner-occupier and can more readily provide help and advice to those whose financial circumstances suddenly worsen through illness, injury, redundancy, etc. The banks, in contrast, are relative newcomers on the mortgage scene and have not yet developed the same degree of expertise in dealing with such eventualities.

This does not mean that when faced with the problem a bank would be any less sympathetic than a building society. It may mean, though, that a building society would have a greater understanding of the problem and exhibit more flexibility.

However, the possibility of being made redundant and unable to keep up the mortgage repayments is a real threat to many nowadays — repossessions by lenders are currently running at an all time high. Some building societies offer a measure of insurance against redundancy, usually in the form of an insurance package which covers the borrower in the event of redundancy, sickness or personal accident. This kind of insurance may well be worth looking into when you are shopping around for a mortgage.

Getting a Mortgage

Although you may arrange your mortgage through one of the banks, in the interest of simplicity in the following pages reference is made to 'your building society' or 'your building society solicitor' since building societies account for most home purchase mortgages. The comments made, however, apply equally to banks.

What Type of Mortgage?

Basically there are three main types of mortgage repayment plans: straight repayment mortgages, endowment mortgages and pension mortgages; endowment mortgages being available with a variety of options.

Straight Repayment Mortgages

A straight repayment mortgage is an arrangement whereby the capital sum borrowed plus interest, is repaid by monthly amounts over the period of the loan. In the early years of the loan, when the outstanding debt is high, the largest part of the monthly repayment will be interest. As the outstanding sum decreases, the amount of interest also decreases, so that in the later years of the loan the capital sum borrowed is reducing rapidly until it is finally repaid, and 'your' house really is yours.

One consequence of this pattern of repayment is that if you decide to sell in the early years of the mortgage you will probably find that you owe the lender almost as much as you borrowed. This is especially so in times of high and fluctuating interest rates.

Mortgage Payments Insurance

To save your family unnecessary anxiety and worry if you should die before the loan is repaid, the loan should be combined with a Mortgage Protection Life Assurance policy. Such a policy would pay off the mortgage in the event of your premature death, i.e. before the end of the mortgage term, thus enabling your family to continue to live in their home. This type of policy is relatively inexpensive.

Endowment Mortgages

Endowment mortgages link the building society loan to an insurance policy. Under this method capital repayments are suspended by the assignment to the lender of an endowment assurance policy, and the borrower pays only interest on the loan. He also pays the premium on the endowment policy direct to the insurance company.

Endowment mortgages can be 'with profits' or 'without profits'. The with profits type is more costly but offers the possibility that the proceeds of the policy at maturity will comfortably exceed the sum borrowed. Without profits endowment is less expensive, and the policy proceeds at maturity just cover or slightly exceed the sum borrowed.

Low Cost Endowment Mortgages

There are myriad options available with the low cost endowment, which is basically a mixture of endowment and life assurance. Under this type of plan only part of the advance is covered by an endowment assurance policy which is assigned to the lender. Repayments of capital are suspended on this part of the loan and the borrower pays interest only on this amount. Repayments of capital and interest are paid on the remaining part of the advance in the usual way. The borrower also pays the premium on the policy direct to the insurance company.

Pension Mortgage

This method is only available to the self-employed or those not in company pension schemes. A pension mortgage involves the borrower taking out two policies:

(1) a pension policy which should repay the mortgage loan on retirement.

(2) a term assurance policy to provide for repayment of the loan in the event of the death of the borrower before retirement.

Both of these policies are held by the building society.

Tax relief under this scheme is usually available at the highest rate paid by the borrower and allowed on both the mortgage interest and on the premiums paid. It is therefore regarded by those who know about these things as being 'tax efficient'. Other advantages of a pension mortgage include:

- You only pay interest to the building society
- The repayment of your original loan is guaranteed in the event of your death before retirement
- You draw a pension for life
- There may be a cash surplus at the end of the mortgage term
- If you move, the policy can be transferred to your new property.

With all these advantages going for it, a pension mortgage is certainly worth looking into.

How Do I Choose?

Under existing tax law, tax relief is allowable on the interest payable on mortgages of up to £30,000. Unmarried couples living together score here because normally each of them can claim tax relief on a joint mortgage of up to £60,000. The present government is committed to continuation of mortgage interest relief, and to an annual review of the upper limit of mortgages eligible for tax relief.

Building societies, banks and other lenders apply this tax relief, known as MIRAS (Mortgage Interest Relief at Source), where appropriate, which means that monthly repayments will be based on the interest rate net of basic rate tax.

If the loan to a married couple is in excess of £30,000 it will not normally be included in MIRAS. In that case you have to pay the interest gross and claim appropriate tax relief from the Inland Revenue.

The majority of borrowers choose the straight repayment mortgage, perhaps because it is easy to understand and straight forward in operation.

The with-profits type endowment mortgage is relatively expensive and the without profits type is generally not regarded as a satisfactory alternative to the straight repayment mortgage.

Among the advantages claimed for the low cost hybrid type schemes may be mentioned the following:

- The mortgage is automatically redeemed in the event of the death of the assured (borrower).
- The policy can be transferred from property to property upon sale and purchase. Thus, as a borrower moves up-market with increasing income and family responsibilities he can transfer the policy each

time a new mortgage is arranged. This does seem to be a positive plus when compared with the straight repayment mortgage.

- Most, if not all, insurance companies will allow the policy sum assured to be increased and the term of the policy to be extended without medical evidence.
- There is a possibility of a tax free cash surplus at the end of the mortgage period. There can be no guarantee that a cash surplus will in fact occur and in my view such possible payments should be regarded as a windfall and not relied upon or taken into account in any comparison that may be made with, for example, a straight repayment mortgage.

Shop Around

Unless you have already made up your mind as to the method by which you will repay the mortgage loan I strongly urge that when considering whether to choose the straight repayment or one of the many variations of endowment plans, you obtain several quotations from an insurance broker who is a member of the British Insurance Brokers' Association. Compare the difference between straight repayment and endowment mortgages in your own circumstances.

Every type of mortgage repayment plan has its advantages and drawbacks. No two borrower's circumstances are identical and it is not possible to suggest the ideal that will suit all. The best advice that I can offer is that if you are in doubt, go for the tried and tested straight repayment mortgage.

As a result of the Building Society Act 1986 and the other developments to which I have referred we may be much nearer to one-stop financial shopping, whereby a complete house buying package — the purchase, the mortgage, the insurances — can be wrapped up by one of the new-look estate agencies or building societies. It may seem very convenient and hassle-free. But if it proves to be one-choice shopping, the convenience may prove to be expensive, and not at all what some of the pundits have predicted.

As always, the golden rule is shop around. You do not have to take the mortgage or insurance package offered if you can get a better deal elsewhere.

The Mortgage 'Promise in Principle'

Whichever sources of funds or type of mortgage repayment plan you decide upon, it is sensible to seek a promise in principle that the amount the source is prepared to lend you will actually be made available.

At the time of going to press several building societies and one or two of the High Street banks will provide such a promise in writing. The Anglia Building Society's Homemaker Mortgage Pledge is reproduced alongside.

Of course you may be seeking a mortgage when funds are scarce and such a promise may not be forthcoming. You may have to go on to a waiting list, but the point remains that enquiries about a mortgage and the amount that will be loaned should be made before you start house hunting or set your heart on a particular property.

HOMEMAKER

Mortgage Pledge

After interviewing

NAME(S) ....

....

of

ADDRESS ....

....

....

and based on information supplied, the Society is pleased to consider a mortgage of

£

for the purchase of a home, subject to a satisfactory valuation of the property and to the Rules and lending policy of the Society.

Signed ....

Branch Manager

FOR ANGLIA BUILDING SOCIETY

This Pledge is valid for 3 months from the date of issue

Your Purchase — Proceeding Up To Exchange of Contracts

Preparations prior to exchanging contracts are faily straightforward, though somewhat time consuming.
Basically, these chores involve a small blizzard of phonecalls, letters, form filling and so on. Your main task is to keep things moving. This means a close eye on detail and regular liaison with the other persons involved.
Each step is explained in detail. If you refer to the flow chart from time to time you may even discern the strange logic of the procedural dance in which you are engaged. Traditionally, four weeks is allotted to this stage, but whether in practice you will need this time depends very much on what is happening to the rest of your 'chain'. Above all, don't be intimidated and do keep cool.

Applying for a Mortgage

By now you have the promise of a mortgage, and have decided on the property you wish to buy, and agreed the price you will pay for it 'subject to contract'. The next step is to complete and send in your mortgage application form. If the property you wish to buy is leasehold the building society will require details of the lease. Usually, the mortgage application form includes a number of questions about the lease, and in some instances you may be asked to provide a photocopy of it.

The Mortgage Valuation

As you will probably have discovered, all sources of mortgage funds require that a valuation of the property be carried out before they will make you a firm mortgage offer. This valuation will be undertaken by a valuer appointed by the building society and the valuation fee is payable by you, the purchaser, on a scale linked to the price of the property. Note that the fee varies according to the selling price of the property and not the amount of mortgage you have asked for. On a property valued at £40,000 the fee would be about £60.

Send the valuation fee with your mortgage application. You can readily work out the fee by consulting the table available from your lender or by telephoning your local branch for the information. Incidentally, the valuation fees vary a little between lenders.

Until relatively recently the building societies would not give the intending borrower any information contained in the valuation report even though he had paid for it. Abbey National was the first of the building societies to provide a copy of the report and other big building societies promptly followed suit or are considering doing so. The banks also make a copy of the valuation report available.

An Independent Survey?

At this stage you should consider whether you require more information on the property than is provided by the mortgage valuation report.

If your building society gives you a copy you may glean a certain amount of information from it. But do remember that the report's sole purpose is to enable the building society to decide whether the property is adequate security for the loan you are seeking.

It is difficult to lay down hard and fast guidelines, but my advice on balance, particularly if older property is involved, is to pay for a report that will give you more information than will be provided by the mortgage valuation report. For examples of the comparative costs of these surveys see the chart on page 120.

A Partial Survey

Two options are available. One is the Report on Condition and Valuation as offered by Abbey National which gives more information. That is to say it incorporates the facts given in the mortgage valuation but also includes concise but comprehensive information on the state of repair and general condition of the property in a six page report prepared by the surveyor. Comments are included on marketability, and on purchase price or fair market value.

The Halifax offers a variation on a similar theme which it calls a Report and Valuation for Homebuyers (other societies have similar schemes). This appears to be an incorporation of the R.I.C.S. scheme of the same name, although the Halifax scheme extends to flats whereas these are excluded from the R.I.C.S. scheme.

Under both of these schemes the purchaser pays only one fee for the extended inspection and valuation report, i.e. he does not pay a fee for the valuation and another fee for the extended report. As an example, under the Halifax scheme the basic Report and Mortgage Valuation fee for a £40,000 property would be about £60, and the fee for their Report and Valuation for Homebuyers would be about £144. These figures include V.A.T.

All the building societies publish pamphlets setting out the rates charged for valuations which can be obtained for the asking.

The R.I.C.S. House Buyers Report and Valuation scheme is operated by many, but not all, chartered surveyors. The scheme excludes flats and period properties, and the fees vary according to the age, size and type of house or bungalow concerned. The objective of this extended inspection scheme is to provide the intending purchaser with the general opinion of a chartered surveyor on the quality and condition of the property, and to assist him in deciding whether or not to buy.

An information leaflet detailing the main features of the scheme is available from most estate agents and firms of chartered surveyors or from the R.I.C.S. at the address listed on page 124.

A Full Survey

The other option available is a full structural survey. The difference between a structural survey and an extended inspection is that a structural survey is a very much more detailed examination of the property and more time consuming than the extended inspection. Further, whilst the surveyor carrying out the structural survey will produce a detailed account on the condition of the property to the extent that he has been able to inspect it, the report does not include a valuation. The Purchaser would have to pay a separate valuation fee as well as a fee for the structural survey. If you decide that you want a structural survey most building societies will arrange for this to be done in conjunction with the valuation. In this way you may achieve some saving in the total cost. You must ensure that the surveyor knows the extent of the survey you wish him to carry out before he makes his inspection and, most important, do agree the fee in advance. A full structural survey of a four bedroomed house in the provinces valued at about £50,000 would cost about £400. In the Greater London area this figure could be 50% higher. Do, therefore, discuss with the surveyor the full extent of the survey you wish him to carry out and do confirm the arrangement in writing, (see page 128).

So, faced with these choices, what should you do? I have already indicated that I would prefer to have more information than is provided by the mortgage valuation report, so I would opt for the Abbey National or Halifax type schemes. Some of the banks and other building societies will accept the R.I.C.S. Report and Valuation for their valuation purposes so if you wish to have something more than just a mortgage valuation report this is something you should discuss with the lender before you apply for a mortgage.

If your lender insists on a normal valuation inspection you can still commission a R.I.C.S. Homebuyers Report and Valuation but in this case you will have to pay both the valuation report fee to the lender and the R.I.C.S. fee to the surveyor you commission.

'Free Surveys'

Whilst on the subject of surveys for which unfortunately you have to pay, it may cheer you up to mention the availability of free surveys! The Yellow Pages carry the names of firms who offer a free survey for woodworm, dry rot, wet rot and rising damp, and who will provide an estimate of any remedial work required. These surveys are intended solely to provide a report only on the specific area of specialisation of the firm conducting the inspection, and should not be confused with the surveys already mentioned.

Whilst undoubtedly there are some 'cowboys' operating in this field, there are also many nationally known and respected firms who value their reputations. I suggest you select three of these firms to report to you.

As a matter of courtesy tell the vendor that you are arranging for these surveys and that the firms will visit the property at a time convenient to him. All you need do then is phone the firms, explain that you are the potential purchaser of the property, give the address and vendor's telephone number and ask them to make arrangements directly. You should normally receive the reports with an estimate of any remedial work required within 7–10 days.

The Cost of Repairs

It is really a matter of judgment what your attitude would be if some remedial work is required. If the cost of this is relatively small I would be inclined to absorb it.

On the other hand, if the cost of treatment is more than, say, £50 or so it would not be unreasonable to ask the vendor to reduce the purchase price by the cost of the treatment or at least by a proportion of the cost. If it is necessary to negotiate a reduction in the purchase price my suggestion is that you hold fire until you have received a copy of the extended inspection report or the structural survey. More on this on page 50.

The Draft Contract

Within a few days of your agreeing, subject to contract, to buy, your vendor's solicitor will usually confirm his client's willingness to sell to you at the agreed price and inform you that he is preparing a draft contract.

A week or so later, the draft contract will arrive. A draft contract is really a proposed contract and it is almost always sent with a carbon copy. There are minor differences between a contract for a registered house and an unregistered house which we will look at a little later.

Registered

If the house is registered you will also receive with the draft contract a copy of the land register of the house. See pages 138-139 for a copy of this register. Each registered house has a separate register with an exclusive title (ownership) number. This register is sub-divided into:

(a) Property Register containing a description of the property and will state whether the property is freehold or subject to a lease.

(b) Proprietorship Register containing, e.g. details of the person(s) presently registered as proprietors of the land, the class of title, any restrictions affecting the land, cautions, and bankruptcy inhibitions.

(c) Charges Register, which lists the rights other people have over or in respect of land, for example mortgages, restrictive covenants or a Notice of a spouse's rights of occupation.

The land register for a leasehold property is basically the same as that for a freehold property. Part A, the Property Register, will state that the property is leasehold and give details of the lease, which you should compare with those set out in the contract.

In practice, the vendor's solicitor may send you either an 'office copy' (official copy) of the register which he gets from the Land Registry, or he can send a photocopy of the Land Certificate which is held by the current owner. Either of these is acceptable as both are copies of the register kept at the Land Registry but the photocopy usually will be kept as up to date as the office copy.

Carefully check the office copy ensure that it is complete and includes a plan of the land. You can check its completeness by reference to the note of the number of pages of which the register consists which appears at the head of page one which will read something like this, 'This register consists of four pages' Check that you have been sent four pages and also a plan of the land on which the property stands. See page 140 for sample plan. Incidentally, blank pages of the register will not be copied but the office copy will state which ones are blank.

Unregistered

If the house you contemplate buying is unregistered you will receive with the draft contract a copy of any restrictive covenants and a plan of the property taken from a previous conveyance. You should also receive a copy of the lease if the property is leasehold.

Form of Contract

The draft contract you receive will most probably be a standard printed form containing a mass of conditions of sale. There are two standard forms in general use by solicitors. One is the 'National Conditions of Sale' form, the other is the 'Law Society Conditions of Sale' form. Of the two, the National Conditions of Sale form is the most commonly used.

The front page of this form is headed 'CONTRACT by reference to the Twentieth Edition of the National Conditions of Sale' and will bear the names and addresses of vendor and purchaser, purchase price, deposit, completion date (left blank), address of the house being sold and title number, if registered.

The remaining provisions are typed on the back page with a host of printed conditions on the two inside pages. But there is, of course, no requirement that either of these forms be used. The contract can just as well by typed (or, as is increasingly likely, word-processed) on plain paper, in which case there will be a reference to the National Conditions of Sale in one of the clauses. See page 134 for a copy of the contract which is included in the forms pack.

Whichever variety of contract the vendor's solicitor has chosen to use you will be comforted to know that regardless of the layout any contract for the sale of a secondhand house is basically the same. Your main concern is to check that the vendor's solicitor has drawn it up correctly — mistakes can and do happen!

Enquiries and Searches Before Contract

If you were planning to buy a car it would not occur to you to consult a solicitor about the purchase details. But you would make some enquiries about the car. For example, has it been used as a hire car and had many drivers? Or by a company rep. and therefore probably been hammered? Is the mileage shown correct? Does the seller truly own the car?

So it is when buying a house. Except that in many respects the enquiries before contract made in connection with a house purchase are simpler than those you would make for a used car.

Searching the Index Map

The first form is probably the simplest of them all, and none of them is difficult. It is the Application for an Official Search of the Index Map (Form 96), a sample is shown on page 129, and is really self-explanatory. Just complete as indicated and post to the appropriate office of the Land Registry listed on the reverse of the form. The result will say whether the house is in an area of compulsory registration, whether the land is registered, (and if so will give the Title Number) and whether it is subject to a lease.

Local Council Searches

The next two forms are sent to the District Council. The forms are LLC1 and Con 29. Form Con 29 will be headed Con 29A England and Wales or Con 29D London, as appropriate. All you have to do is fill in the address of the house you are buying and your own name and address on each of the forms. Both forms have to be completed in duplicate but LLC1 has a duplicate attached so simply insert a sheet of carbon paper.

LLC1 (a completed sample of which appears on page 129) is a search for local land charges. A 'local land charge' is not, as you may reasonably think, another name for the council rates or rubbish collection. Examples of a local land charge include unpaid costs of making up the road when it was taken over by the local council, outstanding charges for sanitary works carried out by the council as a result of an order served on the occupier, restrictions on the use of the land, e.g. under planning law, and so forth.

Form Con 29A England & Wales (or Con 29D London which is basically similar) asks the Council questions on such matters as whether the roadway is maintained by the Council, whether there are any proposals involving the acquisition of land within fifty yards of the boundary of the property, whether a smoke control area order is in force and so on. A completed sample form is on p. 130.

Having completed both LLC1 and Con 29 in duplicate, send them with your cheque to the office of the local Council for the area in which the property is situated. You can find out the current search fees payable by making a phone call to the Council offices. A suggested draft letter for your use in forwarding the forms to the Council is on page 131.

A Personal Visit

If you presently live within reasonable distance of the Council offices or can conveniently get there, I suggest that an alternative to posting the forms is to deliver them personally.

One of the inevitable drawbacks to making enquiries by means of a form is that you will only get a positive answer to a question if the answer already appears on a Council register.

For example, the Council could have been considering proposals for, say, a redevelopment or a new road layout for years but not until the proposal is sufficiently firm to be entered on the register will a local search reveal this. Further, you cannot glean any peripheral information, such as planning applications affecting adjoining or nearby properties, as the search relates only to the house being bought.

So if you can do so, I strongly suggest that you pay a personal visit to the Council's offices. That way you are far more likely to find something of interest about the house you are considering buying (if there is anything to find out) than a solicitor ever will sitting in his office.

Whilst at the Council offices the sort of things you can ask about include:

- Any road-widening proposals in the pipeline or similar developments that could affect the property.
- Any plans to build a new school or extend an existing school or erect council owned dwellings or other buildings. Although not yet on the register the clerk may know if such a development is about to become firm. Ask about any development plans being considered by the Council.
- Any applications for planning permission affecting nearby properties or appeals that are in the pipeline.
- If the road fronting the house is still unmade are there any plans for the Council to take over the road? If so, what is the likely financial

THE TIMES SATURDAY JUNE 21 1986

The home where it all went wrong: David and Elizabeth Holt paid £170,000 for property that will be demolished

Dream house horrors

PROPERTY

What would you do if you had just completed the purchase of your £170,000 dream home, only to find two weeks after you had handed over the money that the local council is publishing proposals which will result in your house being demolished to make way for a new bypass?

This is exactly what happened to David and Elizabeth Holt, who decided at the end of July 1985 to buy a detached house in Wroxham, Norfolk.

The Holts had to get the legal side sorted out quickly. They were able to have access to the local searches dated July 12, 1985, which had been issued to an earlier proposed purchaser.

The searches, which solicitors send out to the local council, are in a standard form. One of the questions is directed to the county council in its capacity as the highway authority. The question asks whether the council

(a) has approved any highway proposals which would involved the acquisition of the property, or

(b) has published for the purpose of public consultation any proposals for a new road within 200 metres of the property.

The council had replied "No" to both these inquiries. The results of the rest of the search were also clear.

The Holts exchanged contracts on August 6 but the date of completion was conditional on their solicitor receiving satisfactory results to their own local searches.

The second standard set of searches was received at the beginning of September. The searches were completely clear and the replies to the road proposal questions were again "No".

Mr and Mrs Holt therefore completed their purchase on September 9. On the September 26 the local council published proposals for public consultation for the proposed routes of the Wroxham bypass. There were, in fact, seven different proposed routes. But the council's planning and transportation committee confirmed earlier this year that it preferred the

'We expected to be here for many years'

eastern route — the one that would run right through Mr and Mrs Holt's property.

Furthermore, Bernard Farrant, a spokesman for Norfolk County Council, said he has no reason to believe that the full council will not approve the committee's recommended eastern route when it meets at the end of July.

Some people may say that Mr and Mrs Holt have been extremely unlucky. If the search had been made just two weeks later, the road proposals would have been published. The reply to the question on the search would have been "Yes", and Mr and Mrs Holt say they would not have bought the property, even though the final route had still to be decided.

They are extremely distraught. Mrs Holt explained: "We bought the property to live in and improve and we have spent £30,000 doing it up. It is a beautiful house and we thought we would be here for many years. Instead the whole of the area will disappear under the tarmac."

The Holt's solicitor said: "The council should consider disclosing the possibility of a road scheme which substantially affects a property as soon as it is 'on the cards'. By sticking rigidly to the strict letter of the law they are perhaps open to criticism."

Bernard Farrant, the council spokesman disagrees: "The sellers' interests have to be looked after as well as those who are buying properties. We have a rolling programme of bypass building, and if we put a note on the searches on all the proposed routes, we would blight hundreds of properties. We have to apply the rules and answer the questions asked."

Could it be then that it is the questions on the search forms that are at fault? A Law Society spokeswoman said: "The wording on searches has given rise to problems in the past and is far from ideal. The main problem is that we work together with the local authorities association and they indicate to us what inquiries they can handle.

" We have also been pressing the local authorities to computerize, but so far the negotiations have come to pretty much nothing."

While the Law Society is battling to change the system, the Holts are asking the council for reimbursement of £5,000 for the legal fees and removal expenses for their purchase over and above any compensation to which they may be entitled if they cannot sell the house or if it is purchased by the council.

Their solicitor explained: "The comments made by the council rather miss the point. A seller compelled to stay put as a result of a comment on a local search will be entitled to compensation. But the Holts have incurred a great deal of additional expense which they may not be able to recover unless the council agrees."

Buyers should make discreet inquiries

The council has intimated that the Holts' request will be considered, but not until September, a whole year after the purchase. Commenting on the likelihood of reimbursement the council's spokesman said: "It would be a major precedent if we were to do it."

The lesson is: Buyer beware. But purchasers of property can frequently help themselves. Discreet inquiries to the neighbours, local newspapers, or the Citizens' Advice Bureau can often reveal road and planning proposals which are still "in the air", and could stop you from making one of the most expensive mistakes of your life.

Susan Fieldman

Reproduced by courtesy of 'The Times'

liability at today's prices bearing in mind that your potential liability increases with inflation.

- Enquire whether there is a public right of way over the unmade road for vehicles. If there is not then there should be a note that a right of way goes with the house, either in a previous Conveyance, where the note should (usually) immediately follow reference to the address of the property, or in Section A of the land register, again immediately after the address. See page 131 for an example from a Conveyance for unregistered property noting a right of way.
- If the property you are interested in has open fires, ask the clerk whether there is a smoke control order in force.
- What are the current rates and check the net rateable value.

If your experience is similar to my own you will find the staff at Council offices helpful and a mine of information. A visit in person will be time well spent. The list of topics above is not meant to be exhaustive, and if any question occurs to you do not hesitate to ask the clerk.

A striking example of the inadequacy of conducting legal searches by post appeared in The Times. In this case, the Council had been considering proposals for a new road layout for some time. But existing procedures nonsensically do not provide any information about plans that are still unofficial. Not until a proposal is sufficiently firm to be entered in the register will a local search reveal it. Unfortunately, you only get a positive answer on a standard search form if the information is in the council register. Furthermore, planning applications affecting nearby properties are also not revealed by standard search forms as these only refer to the house being bought.

It is no help to the unfortunate purchasers to emphasise that their problem could have been avoided by a personal visit to the local Council offices. The proposals would have been known to the clerk, or possibly even by neighbours or the local newspaper.

Pre-Contract Enquiries

Having visited the Council offices and left duplicate copies of LLC1 and Con 29, you can now turn your attention to addressing enquiries of the vendor.

Visit the House

However, before doing so I suggest that you pay another visit to the house you are contemplating buying. As with a visit to the Council offices, a solicitor or conveyancer does not reckon on visiting the house a client proposes to buy. But by paying a visit yourself and using your eyes, ears and common sense you are far more likely to glean some piece of useful information about the property than you will ever obtain from a standard form or questionnaire.

You should, of course, as a matter of courtesy, arrange a convenient time and day with the vendor for your visit to the property. The sort of points you should check include the following:

- What items of furnishing e.g. carpets, curtain runners and pelmets, bathroom cabinets, garden shed, greenhouse and garden ornaments are included in the selling price? I suggest you go through the house, room by room, listing any items that the vendor agrees are to be left. Similarly, go through the garden and garage. This agreed list should be added to the contract as an additional clause. If both parties are quite clear as to what is and what is not included in the sale, the possibilities of a dispute arising are greatly reduced.
- Ask the vendor whether he has made any structural alterations or built a garage, workshop or extension. Your own eyes may also tell you that there have been recent alterations or recently erected out-buildings.
- Did the vendor obtain planning consent and/or building regulations approval? Not all alterations, extensions, garages, etc. need planning consent, but they do need building regulations approval. Your vendor should be able to produce the stamped approval from the local Council building inspector and if you are in any doubt, check with the local Council. If the work has not been approved under the building regulations, pass the problem to the vendor's solicitor to resolve to your satisfaction. Bear in mind that if the necessary consents have not been sought by the vendor, the property may become liable to an increase in rateable value by reason of the improvement that has been made.
- Ask your vendor which fences on his boundaries are his. If some part of the land is unfenced, ask where he considers the true boundary to be. There could be the making of a dispute if, at some time in the future, you erect a fence in what a neighbour considers to be the wrong position, or your neighbour puts up a fence on what you thought was your land. Boundary fences can be a prolific source of disagreement between neighbours, so it is better to try and resolve these matters before they become problems.
- It is surprising how some people seem to think that a given state of affairs will last forever. For example, Mr. A is very friendly with his neighbour Mr. B. Mr. B wishes to build a garage, but to use it would need to drive over part of Mr. A's driveway. "No problem", says Mr. A. "It's all right by me", thereby granting Mr. B a licence to use the driveway. Alas, not long afterwards Mr. A changes jobs and sells his house. The new owner of Mr. A's house revokes permission to use the driveway, so Mr. B has a perfectly good garage but no

means of driving in.

One thing therefore that you can usefully do on your visit to the house is look out for tell-tale signs of a shared driveway. If the driveway between two houses is shared there should be a note in a previous conveyance or in the Land Certificate to the effect that a right of way over this common drives goes with the house. There will almost certainly also be a covenant that you and your neighbours share the cost of maintaining the driveway.

- You can usually see signs that indicate whether a neighbour, or perhaps the general public, have a right of way over the land. Keep your eyes and ears open, and if in doubt ask the vendor and at the Council offices.
- Still on the subject of rights of way, most driveways are within the boundaries of a property, or else access to the garage is gained by a shared driveway. But some older properties have garages at the rear and access is gained over a track at the back of the house. Originally these tracks were used to facilitate the collection of night soil.

  Sometimes access is gained along a track which skirts the outer boundary to the rear, and is shared by a number of houses. Unless the track giving access is a public right of way, there should be a note on a previous conveyance or on the Land Certificate that a right of way over this track goes with the house. If, as is very likely to be the case, the track is a public right of way, you do not need specific authority to use it, for as a member of the public you are automatically entitled to do so. Check with the Council that there is a public right of way over the track.
- It is almost certain that the house has a direct water supply.

  If you cannot locate the stop cock, especially if the house fronts an unmade road or is in the country, check with the local Water Board Inspector. These officials are a mine of information and local knowledge, and in my experience are unfailingly helpful.

Pre-Contract Enquiries (of the Vendor's Solicitor)

Fortified by your visit to your proposed property, you can now send the vendor's solicitor the standard form which traditionally is used to ask enquiries of the vendor. This is one of the forms in the pack — a completed form appears on pages 131-132. It should be noted that on the left side of the form are listed the questions and the vendor's solicitor enters his replies on the right side. Any additional questions are added after Q. 15. Enquiries in respect of leasehold properties follow on the back page. Complete the form in duplicate by entering the address, the names of the purchasers and the vendors, and by signing and dating it. Send it to the vendor's solicitor with a letter along the lines of the draft on page 133.

Questions to Ask Yourself

Is there enough room for all your furniture?

Does the house get direct sun?
Does a neighbour's tree overshadow the property

Do you share a driveway?

Is it expensive to heat?

How much are the rates?

Does it need new wiring or plumbing?

Are there shops or public transport nearby?

Is the garden large enough, is it sunny or shady?

Few people look closely at a house on their first visit. This is understandable. Hence on the second or third visit take the trouble to switch lights on and off, try out the central heating and any domestic appliances you plan to buy, run water taps, open garage doors, ask about insulation and so on. The vendor has every incentive to be cooperative if it helps your decision to buy.

A Little Stocktaking

We have now reached the stage where we can take stock and review progress so far. You have:

- made an offer 'subject to contract'
- applied for a mortgage (and forwarded details of, or a copy of, the lease if leasehold)
- arranged for a structural survey to be done with the valuation or, more possibly, an R.I.C.S. Homebuyers Report
- arranged for a free wordworm, dry rot and wet rot survey
- received the draft contract
- sent off an Application for the Official Search of Index Map (Form 96)
- posted or handed in local search forms LLC1 and Con 29
- visited the Council offices
- visited the house you contemplate buying and made notes of matters of special interest
- sent the vendor's solicitor Pre-Contract Enquiries (Ole Series) form in duplicate

You should carefully file copies of all the letters and forms that you send out and of the replies you receive. I personally use a coloured folder with an envelope flap and I use the cover to keep a record of each transaction. By noting letters sent out and replies received back I can immediately check on my progress.

Examining the Draft Contract

You are now in a position to go through the draft contract which the vendor's solicitor has sent you.

However high-powered (or low-powered for that matter) your vendor's solicitor may be, a contract for the sale of a secondhand house gives little scope for feats of drafting prowess. Every such contract is basically the same as any other contract for the sale of a secondhand house. Therefore, in 'perusing' the draft contract your main concern is that the vendor's solicitor has drawn it up correctly. Have the office copies to hand and carefully check the following:

Stakeholding

1. That the deposit will be held by the vendor's solicitor (or estate agents if the vendor is doing his own conveyancing) as stakeholders and *NOT* as agents. If the clause in your draft contract reads 'Agents' cross it out and substitute 'Stakeholders'. The legal significance is that the stakeholders may not hand over to the seller any of the deposit money without the buyer's agreement, whereas if they held the deposit as agents it could be passed to the seller at any time. If the deposit is held by the solicitor or estate agents as stakeholders they will not be able to release it until Completion. This is standard practice so if your contract does not provide it, insert a clause to cover the point (similar to condition 10 of the sample contracts on page 134 and page 135). Incidentally, make any alterations or additions to the contract in red ink.

Vacant Possession

2. That vacant possession is to be given on Completion.

Beneficial Owners

3. There is usually a clause to the effect that the vendor sells as 'beneficial owner' by which the vendor implies that he owns the property and has the right to sell it. Sometimes, as in the case of a deceased's estate, the vendor sells as 'Executor' or 'Personal Representative' in which case he will produce evidence of his right to sell, e.g. a grant of probate. If a husband and wife are joint owners they will sell as 'beneficial owners' or 'trustees for sale'.

The Property's Description

4. That the house you are buying is correctly described. If the house is registered the description should incorporate a reference to its title number, as in the contract on page 134. Thus, '. . . the freehold dwellinghouse known as 15 Lone Pine Close, Hutton in the County of Wessex as registered at the Land Registry with Title Absolute under Title No. XZ 498031 . . .'

   If the property you are buying is unregistered it would be identified by the postal address and a plan attached to the contract.

   Make doubly certain that if the house, bungalow or whatever that you are buying is freehold this word is incorporated in the description of the property, e.g. '. . . the freehold dwellinghouse known as 15 Lone Pine Close, Hutton . . .'

   If the property is leasehold it should be so described since title will commence with the granting of the lease. Note the term of years granted by the lease, the period unexpired, and the ground rent payable.

Completion Date

5. The completion date is left blank for the present.

Fixtures and Fittings

6. That any items (chattels is the jargon word) which you agreed with the vendor to include in the purchase price are listed in a separate clause, thus:

   'The following items are included in the purchase price:
   1. Venetian blinds to kitchen and bathroom
   2. Carpet as fitted to the lounge and dining room
   3. Garden shed
   and £••• of the purchase price shall be apportioned to these items.'

   Listing such items in a separate clause does two things. It puts beyond dispute what is included in the purchase price, and it ensures that if stamp duty is payable you only pay it on the cost of the house.

Registered Property

7. If the house is registered check the following points against the copy of the register sent with the draft contract:

   (a) That the address recorded under Section A — Property Register — is identical with that of the house you are buying as stated in the draft contract and that the land is described as freehold land.

   (b) That the proprietor (owner) listed in Section B — Proprietorship Register — is your vendor in the contract. If husband and wife own jointly then both names should appear on the contract as vendors. The phrase 'Title Absolute' which should appear under the Proprietorship Register — see copy on page 138 — indicates that the Land Registry guarantees that the person or persons listed as proprietor(s) own the house.

(c) That any reference in any clause in the contract to entries on the Charges Register (Section C on page 139) refers only to restrictive covenants and the like and does not in error include reference to any other charge e.g. a mortgage. Restrictive covenants are dealt with in more detail on pages 47 and 48.

If the Charges Register records a Notice of a spouse's right of occupation under the Matrimonial Homes Act you must insist that the notice will be cancelled before completion. A Bankruptcy Inhibition recorded on the Charges Register would cause me to look elsewhere for a property.

(d) That the title number of the land register is the same as that quoted in the contract, either in a separate clause, or as part of the description of the property you are buying. Thus, '. . . the freehold dwellinghouse known as 15 Lone Pine Close, Hutton, in the County of Wessex as registered at the Land Registry with Title Absolute under title number XZ 498031 . . .'.

If the property you are buying is leasehold you will already have been provided with a copy of the lease and this you should read very carefully so that you are familiar with the terms. Some leases,usually those of fairly high-priced flats, provide that the landlord's consent to the sale must be obtained 'the same not to be unreasonably withheld'. You should make a note to request the vendor's solicitor to confirm that this consent will be forthcoming.

Unregistered Property

8. If the property is unregistered you have no land register to check, and satisfying yourself as to your vendor's title can only occur after exchange of contracts. You will note that clause 3 of the draft contract on page 136 specifies a Conveyance at least 15 years old.

Agreeing Amendments

9. In 'perusing' the draft contract you do not really do any more than a prudent buyer of a car or caravan would do, and none of it needs more than common sense. The most likely amendment will be a clause to list furnishings, carpets and so on which the vendor agrees to leave. You may, as mentioned above, wish to apportion part of the purchase price to these items. Other than that, there should not be any more amendments to make. It is wise, as well as courteous, to telephone the vendor's solicitor with the gist of any amendments so that you can agree to them before writing them into both copies of the contract.

Restrictive Covenants

Together with the draft contract you will have received an office copy of the land register, if the property is registered, and Section C of this is the Charges Register. This section contains any restrictive covenants to which the house you are buying may be subject.

If the house is unregistered you will have received a separate copy of any restrictive covenants or other matters to which the property is subject.

Simply stated, a restrictive covenant is a condition written into a Transfer or Conveyance on the occasion when the owner of a plot of land sells part of it. The covenant controls the use of the land sold, or the buildings erected on it, for the benefit of the land he retains.

Frequently, the sheer mass of verbiage used to spell out these conditions appears menacing to the layman. It may be helpful, therefore, to deal with the subject in a little depth.

Outdated Covenants

In theory, once imposed, a restrictive covenant is enforceable not only against the original purchaser by the original vendor, but by and against their successors, even though the original land may have been further sub-divided. Many ordinary houses today stand on land that was first built on 100 or more years ago when it was commonplace for houses to have large gardens. These gardens have in turn been sold off and built over, but the deeds or Land Certificate will slavishly copy the original restrictive covenants. It is obvious that it would be impossible to trace the person entitled to enforce the original covenant, and even if that were possible, would such a person be interested in enforcing the covenant or able to do so. This grey area arises because in the majority of cases the land intended to benefit by the covenant has not been identified.

I have before me a restrictive covenant which drools on for a complete page of the Charges Register. Other restrictive covenants of a similar nature clutter up a further three pages of the same register. This covenant prevents the fortunate owner of a modest dwelling on the fringe of the London commuter belt from '. . . using the said premises or any part thereof for the purpose of any trade, business or calling whatsoever nor use or suffer to be used the said premises as a Tea Garden or place of public amusement or resort nor for the purpose of a public school, workhouse or police station, nor for the reception of idiots or lunatics . . .'

Thus, you may find that the house you are buying is subject to a covenant that not more than so many houses per acre may be erected without the consent of the landowner or his successors in title who first sold the land. Let's call him Mr. Wiseacre. This covenant will have been imposed by Mr. Wiseacre say fifty years ago. Or the covenant may require you to obtain the approval of Mr. Wiseacre or his successors in title before erecting any buildings. In virtually every case there is just no way you can trace Mr. Wiseacre, and thus no way by which you can know if the covenant has been broken. Nor could a solicitor in some magic way find out.

In practice you can ask the vendor's solicitor for evidence that the plans of the house were approved by Mr. Wiseacre or his agent but the most likely answer you will get is 'there are no approved plans with the deeds but the Vendor has not received notice of any breach of the covenant'. And if the covenant is fifty years old I would leave it at that. Indeed I would also do the same if the house is more than a few years old and no previous objection has been raised.

This is an area of Land Law and Conveyancing that seems to be quite unnecessarily complicated as there is really no good reason why unenforceable covenants should be slavishly copied each time a house changes hands. However, I hope that the foregoing expedition into the morass of restrictive covenants will have reassured you that they need hold no fears for you.

Positive and Negative Covenants

Before we leave this topic, you may find it helpful if we look briefly at 'negative' and 'positive' covenants.

A negative covenant merely restrains the doing of an act or acts, and contrasts with a positive covenant which requires the doing of an act or acts for its performance. If this seems like gobbledegook, bear with me a little longer.

The wording of a covenant does not necessarily determine whether the covenant is positive or negative; what really matters is the nature of the covenant. A usual test that is applied to determine whether a covenant is negative or positive is that if the performance of a covenant requires the spending of money it is positive. A positive covenant is enforceable only as an ordinary contractual obligation, i.e. by and against the persons who originally entered into it and not against a subsequent purchaser.

Common Covenants

So apart from the more esoteric covenants which we have already dealt with, you are most likely to see on the Charges Register (or copy of the restrictive covenants, if the house is unregistered) covenants of a more mundane nature.

Examples of these are:

1. To use the house only for residential purposes and not for any trade or business. Sometimes this is modified to permit the carrying on of a learned or artistic profession. This is pretty straightforward and should present no problems.
2. Not to permit or cause any nuisance. Again, this is quite straightforward and adds nothing to your existing common law obligations.
3. To erect and/or keep a fence or wall in good order and repair. As this requires the expenditure of money, you will recognise this covenant to be a positive one. Unless your vendor has entered into a personal covenant and requires you to give a written undertaking to observe its provisions this covenant is unenforceable.

I have already referred to a covenant stipulating that buildings are not to be erected or altered without the approval of our Mr. Wiseacre or his successors in title. Its variant is the covenant restricting the building of houses of a given value, and density. This sometimes also includes building heights and building lines (a building line being the distance from the centre of a road beyond which houses may not be built).

As I have indicated, unless building work or alterations are fairly recent, if no notice of breach of covenant has been received by the vendor's solicitor I would accept the situation as it is. If the work is fairly recent I would be inclined to spend a few pounds on an insurance policy indemnifying me against the risk. And I would take comfort in the knowledge that every day that passes without notice of breach of covenant reduces the negligible risk even further. Remember, apart from advising you to insure against the risk, if you employed a solicitor there is nothing else he could do either. You will have the satisfaction of saving his fees.

You are likely also to encounter what are described as 'rights and exceptions' in favour of other properties nearby. The sorts of things implied are free passage of water or soil pipes to or from all other property on the estate, i.e. sewerage and drainage pipes, cables running under the land and so on. Whilst this may look fairly ominous staring at you from the Charges Register or the copy of restrictive covenants, there is nothing you can do about them; but equally they present no cause for alarm. Just accept them as part of the system.

Outstanding Mortgages

The Charges Register also contains particulars of any mortgages outstanding on the property. It is usual, of course, for a house that is being sold to be subject to a mortgage which is to be paid off from the proceeds of the sale. As will be seen a little later on, as purchaser you must ensure that any outstanding mortgage has been redeemed before you become the owner. In effect, you hand over the purchase money and get in exchange the charge certificate containing the mortgage and the lender's acknowledgement that the mortgage has been redeemed. We deal with this in more detail a little later.

Approving the Draft Contract

Having visited the property you propose buying and perhaps agreed with the vendor which items are to be left and included in the sale, you will have added a clause to the draft contract along the lines suggested earlier. You may also have agreed to apportion some of the purchase price against items being left, such as carpets, garden shed and summerhouse, venetian blinds and so on. Remember to adjust the purchase price in the contract by the sum agreed.

Having examined the contract and made any amendments that may have been necessary, you are now able to 'approve' the draft copy. By approving you are doing no more than saying in effect, 'if the local searches and preliminary enquiries I am making are satisfactory, and my mortgage application is approved, I would be prepared to do business with you in accordance with the terms of the draft contract, as amended'.

You therefore send the (amended) draft contract to vendor's solicitors with a covering letter along the lines of the draft on page 140.

Checking on Progress

At this point you should refer to your buyer's timetable chart (page 55) and follow up by letter or telephone wherever there is an unexplained holdup along the way. You may of course be asking for a mortgage at a time when funds are being rationed and have to take your turn on a waiting list. Usually, in such a case, the manager of the building society or bank is able to give you a verbal indication that your advance will be made available in, say, two months' time. So long as you have done all you have to do concerning the loan, e.g. paid for the valuation, you will not help matters by telephoning every other day to chase up your mortgage. Unless there is a mortgage famine you will probably receive an offer within 14 days of your application.

Other than this (and mortgage funds have been rationed a few times over the past decade) your main task is to keep the transaction moving.

Accepting a Mortgage Offer

Check the terms of the mortgage offer carefully and make sure that the names of the borrowers, the term of the loan, amount of loan, address of property to be mortgaged and tenure (i.e. whether freehold or leasehold) are correctly stated. Assuming these are all correct and you find the terms acceptable, sign the acceptance copy and return it to the building society. A normal condition is that the offer is open for three months and is subject to satisfactory title.

The building society will employ a solicitor to check this (at your expense) and when you have sent in your signed acceptance they will inform you of the name and address of the solicitor they have appointed to act for them. If may save time if you write to this solicitor at once asking him what he will require of you to enable him to release the loan on the day fixed for completion. A suggested draft letter is on page 142.

The Survey Report

If your lender provides a copy of the valuation report you normally will receive this with the written mortgage offer. If you requested an extended inspection this will normally reach you about the same time as the mortgage offer, as also will a R.I.C.S. Homebuyer's Report.

The valuation report is solely for the purpose of assessing the property as security for the loan you are seeking, but it may yield some useful pieces of information. If so, such information will be more likely to put you on your guard or at least suggest that a full survey is necessary.

The Abbey National/R.I.C.S. type reports can be regarded as a half-way house between a valuation report and a full structural survey. You should study the comprehensive details provided very carefully and, not least, read the report in the light of the qualifications expressed.

If you have commissioned a structural survey bear in mind that most surveyors have their own individual style of writing a report, and many devote an over generous proportion of the text to such matters as the state of decoration, hairline cracks and so on.

Whichever kind of report you have, list all serious faults and if you feel it would help talk to the surveyor about them, either face to face or over the telephone. Obviously it is the degree of seriousness of any fault that will influence you. For example, signs of subsidence would be sufficient to cause me to lose interest, whereas rotting timber window frames can be replaced. So it is up to you to decide where to draw the line.

At the same time consider the reports you will by now have received from the timber treatment specialists. If the cost of necessary remedial work is more than you had expected or can afford, it would not be unreasonable to ask your vendor to meet all or at least part of the costs, in which case it is advisable to make your first approach through the vendor's estate agent and let him have sight of the reports.

In practice, the house you are interested in buying will most likely be structurally sound with little more wrong with it than the odd loose tile and cracked plaster or other minor faults, and there will be nothing to cause you sleepless nights.

Leasehold Property

You may have been asked to send a copy of the lease to the building society with your mortgage application (but will have retained a photocopy for your own use). The lease will prescribe when the ground rent is payable, usually annually in arrear, and it is usual to apportion this on a per day basis. Do you have to give notice of change of ownership? Is there a fee payable to the landlord or his agent? Make a note to check the ground rent receipts on Completion.

Replies from the Vendor's Solicitor

Your vendor's solicitor will by now have returned the form Pre-Contract Enquiries with answers to your questions. Do not be alarmed, surprised or dismayed if you feel that the answers could be a trifle more helpful. Despite the vagueness of some of the answers, you should get sufficient information from the completed form which, together with your own enquiries made during your visit, should satisfy you. It will usually be obvious whether the replies are those of the vendor's solicitor rather than the vendor himself, especially if the subject of the enquiry is within the vendor's knowledge as, for example, the question relating to disputes. If, say, the reply to that question was 'We are not aware of any', you would obviously have to refer back to the vendor's solicitor because surely the vendor knows whether or not there have been or are any disputes. Similarly with any other unacceptable reply.

If, under the question on guarantees (Question 8) the vendor's solicitor replies that there is a National House Building Council certificate or guarantee in respect of timber treatment or wall cavity insulation, I suggest that you ask him to include a clause in the contract to cover this. A suggested draft clause is on page 141.

Results of Searches

You will by now have received back from the Land Registry the Index Map Search (Form 96) with the result of the search endorsed on the reverse of the form. This should confirm what you have been told by your vendor or his solicitor, for example, that the land is registered freehold or leasehold or is not registered. If the search does not correspond with what you have been told you must get a satisfactory explanation from the vendor's solicitor. And do remember that the Land Registry maintains an enquiry department at each District Land Registry Office. You will find the staff to be very helpful and expert in their field. If there is some aspect of the search about which you are not happy, do not hesitate to telephone them with your query or write addressing your letter to the Search of Index Map Department.

Local Search Replies

The time taken by local councils to return the search forms varies from council to council, but a rough guide is about six weeks, except in some London Boroughs where the time taken tends to be somewhat longer. In 999 cases out of 1,000 the searches will show nothing even to cause a slight lifting of an eyebrow, but if yours is the one case in which an answer creates a doubt in your mind, telephone the local council and the clerk dealing with your area will helpfully explain the significance of the answer. By visiting the council offices as suggested, you are far more likely to get details of planning applications or the progress of projected developments that could affect your property.

Exchange of Contracts

You have now completed all the pre-exchange procedures and should be ready to exchange contracts. Before doing so, however, I suggest you make a last check that everything is in order. Here is a check list of the steps you have taken:

- Contract approved — you have 'perused' the draft contract and agreed with the vendor's solicitor any changes to the text or additional clauses.
- The Index Map Search is satisfactory as are the local council searches and enquiries; any queries have been satisfactorily answered.
- You have accepted the mortgage offer.
- You have considered the surveyor's report and the report(s) of the timber treatment specialist and find them to be satisfactory, or have agreed with vendor's solicitors the sum by which the purchase price will be reduced. In the latter case the purchase price shown on the contract has been amended to reflect the reduction.
- Enquiries before contract are satisfactory.

So now you can take the momentous step of exchanging contracts.

Simultaneous Purchase and Sale

If your purchase depends on a simultaneous sale you must hold fire until you have received the signed copy of the contract for your own sale, signed by your purchaser together with the full deposit by banker's draft. Do not accept a personal cheque. The time taken to clear a personal cheque through the system could jeopardise your transaction, especially if it is a simultaneous one.

You can then (and only then) send to your vendor's solicitor your copy of the signed contract for your own purchase, together with the full deposit by banker's draft. If you and your wife are buying jointly, both of you should sign the contract.

Within about three days you should receive the copy of the purchase contract signed by your vendor. Most usually the vendor's solicitor will have inserted a date for Completion about four weeks after exchange. As soon as you receive your vendor's signed contract, post immediately the counterpart of your sale contract and, as it is a simultaneous sale and purchase transaction, insert the same date for Completion as the vendor's solicitor inserted in his contract.

Simultaneous Sale and Purchase

The Vendor's Solicitor	You	The Buyer's Solicitor
		1. Sends contract to buy along with banker's draft for the deposit.
	2. Check deposit is a banker's draft.	
	3. Send your signed contract to buy the new house together with your deposit.	
4. Returns your contract signed by the vendor		
	5. Return your signed contract to sell.	
	6. Take out insurance on the house you are buying.	

The importance of following the correct steps in a simultaneous sale and purchase cannot be over-emphasized. Fail to do so and you could become the unlucky owner of two houses, or else join the ranks of the homeless.

Keeping Your Options Open

If you follow this procedure strictly the contracts in a sale and purchase transaction are exchanged simultaneously. Right up to the moment before exchange something could go wrong, causing either the sale or purchase to fall through. You must ensure that if this does happen you are in a position to cancel, and are not left holding the baby.

So, until you receive the signed contract for your sale do not release the signed contract for your purchase, and until you receive the vendor's signed contract on your purchase do not release the signed contract on your sale.

Purchase Only

If your purchase is not dependent on a simultaneous sale, you can of course send your signed contract and deposit to the vendor's solicitor just as soon as you have checked that all pre-contract steps of the procedure have been satisfactorily performed and your vendor's solicitor indicates that he is ready to exchange.

Suggested draft letters to accompany the contracts being exchanged are on pages 142 and 143.

If you live in the same town or conveniently near to your purchaser it is well worth tying things up by personally exchanging contracts. Go along to your purchaser's solicitor's office with your signed copy of the contract which you hand over in exchange for your purchaser's signed contract and bank draft. It is unlikely that a solicitor will hand you anything other than a banker's draft. A banker's draft is as good as cash so please DO NOT ACCEPT A PERSONAL CHEQUE. Date the contract with the date of exchange. Your contract to sell is binding from the moment of exchange. Then you immediately post your signed contract to buy with the banker's draft for the deposit to your vendor's solicitor and date it with the date of posting. Your contract is binding as from the moment of posting.

Insurance Cover

As soon as you exchange contracts for your purchase, telephone the building society or bank who are providing funds for the purchase and ask them to arrange buildings insurance cover with immediate affect, or if you are not purchasing with the help of a mortgage, i.e. are a cash buyer, arrange immediate cover yourself. From the moment of exchange of contracts the property is at your risk.

Do remember to confirm your telephone call — a draft letter is on page 143.

Double Checking

Just by way of the recap, if yours is a simultaneous sale and purchase transaction, the drill to follow is:

Step 1	You receive your purchaser's signed part of the contract to buy and his deposit.
Step 2	Check that your purchaser's deposit is paid by bank draft or building society cheque and not by personal cheque.
Step 3	You can then send to your vendor's solicitor your signed part of the contract to purchase, together with a deposit or balance of deposit.
Step 4	You should receive within about three days the vendor's signed part of the contract for your purchase. At that point your purchase transaction is binding, so . . .
Step 5	. . . immediately send your purchaser's solicitor your signed part of the sale contract, thus making your sale transaction binding.
Step 6	Arrange insurance cover on buildings by telephone to take immediate effect, then confirm in writing. If you are taking out a mortgage you must arrange the insurance through the building society or bank. Otherwise make your own arrangements, either through an insurance broker or direct with an insurance company.

Buyer's Timetable

The following timetable will give you an idea of the rough timescale involved with the various stages of your transaction and provide you with a progress check sheet.

TYPICAL TIMETABLE — BUYING A PROPERTY
(UP TO EXCHANGE OF CONTRACTS)

Step	Stage	Day
1	Make offer to purchase 'subject to contract.' Vendor or his agent accept offer.	1
2	Receive confirmation of agreement from vendor's agent.	2
3	Apply for mortgage, pay valuation fee. Possibly also instruct surveyor to carry out structural survey.	
4	Receive draft contract from vendor's solicitor	7
5	Send Form 96 Index Map search to District Land Registry.	
6	Visit local council offices and leave search forms, or send local search forms to local council.	8
7	Receive written mortgage offer.	9
8	Receive Form 96 from Land Registry.	10
9	Visit property if possible, then send Enquiries before Contract to vendor's solicitor.	11
10	Consider mortgage offer.	
11	Receive completed Enquiries before Contract from vendor's solicitor.	15
12	Receive Local Search forms (depending on workload of local council)	17
13	Consider results of local searches, valuation report (if disclosed) and structural survey. Also, any free surveys requested.	18
14	Agree Completion date	19
15	Agree any amendments to contract.	
16	Approve draft contract. Send to vendor's solicitor.	21
17	If all loose ends are tied up sign your part of contract and send to vendor's solicitor.	27
18	Receive vendor's part of contract duly signed.	30
	THE CONTRACT IS NOW LEGALLY BINDING ON BOTH PARTIES	

Completing the Purchase — Registered Land

If the property you are buying is unregistered, ignore this section and go directly to Chapter 5. If registered, this chapter will take you through the various steps from exchange of contracts to completion of your purchase.

From Exchange to Completion

You are now ready to prepare for the final set piece of the purchase — the stage known as Completion. At Completion the remaining money will change hands and ownership of the property will finally pass to you.

The first document you must deal with is a form known as 'Requisitions on Title'. In general terms a 'requisition' is legal jargon for a 'question'. The form consists of a set of questions, which you ask the vendor's solicitor, dealing with various details of the completion process.

Most of the documents involved in this stage are prepared by you and are required whether or not you are buying with the aid of a mortgage. As you will see, if you are getting a mortgage you will also be producing the documents for the building society's solicitor. As he is being paid by you one wonders why he doesn't produce them himself. But this procedure is hallowed by time and it is best to swim with the current and just accept it as part of the system.

The 'Requisitions on Title' Form

The Requisitions on Title (Ole series) is an easy form to deal with. You should strike out any questions which do not apply, and as you are dealing with registered land, strike out questions 2B and 3A. Prepare the form in triplicate by filling in the address of the property, the vendor's name, your own family name and by signing and dating the form. Keep one copy in your files and send two copies to the vendor's solicitor. He will send one copy back to you with his replies and retain one copy for his own files. Send your Requisitions on Title with a covering letter along the lines of the draft on page 143. The same letter can be used to accompany the Transfer Form which we deal with next.

Transfer of Ownership

This again is one of the forms in the pack. Although none of them is difficult to fill out, the Form of Transfer is probably the easiest. You will be concerned with either Form 19(JP) Transfer of Whole, which is used for a joint purchase, or Form 19 Transfer of Whole, which is used for a sole purchaser. A completed form 19(JP) is on page 146 and a completed Form 19 on page 145.

Using your copy of the entries on the land register as a guide, fill out the form taking particular care that your spelling of names and places is correct and that the finally agreed purchase price is correctly stated.

If it has been agreed to apportion a sum for carpets, furnishings etc., or by way of contribution towards the cost of remedial work revealed by the survey, deduct the agreed figure to arrive at a net purchase price.

On the reverse of Form 19(JP) at (8) you have to delete 'can' or 'cannot'. This refers to a joint purchase, either as joint tenants as discussed on page 21 or as tenants in common as discussed on page 21. If you are purchasing as joint tenants delete 'cannot', if you are purchasing as tenants in common delete 'can'.

The certificate of value at (9) on the reverse of Form 19(JP) and at (8) on the reverse of Form 19 relates to the stamp duty that may be payable on a purchase, and is primarily aimed at preventing purchasers from avoiding paying stamp duty by taking a transfer in two or more parts, each part at a price below the level at which stamp duty is payable.

Currently stamp duty becomes payable at £30,000. If your purchase is £30,000 or less insert £30,000 and, lucky you, no stamp duty is payable. The rate of stamp duty on property transfers above £30,000 is £1.00 per £100 (i.e. one per cent) on the full purchase price, so if your purchase price is, say, £38,000 the stamp duty payable is £380.

You prepare four copies of the Transfer. Two of these you send to the vendor's solicitor, one copy is for your file, and the fourth copy you send in due course to the solicitor acting for your building society. The vendor's solicitor will treat the top copy (of the two you sent him) as the engrossment, which he will get signed by the vendor in preparation for Completion.

By the way, an 'engrossment' is the actual deed that is executed by the parties, as opposed to a draft of it —sorry about that bit of jargon.

Send the two copies of the Transfer to the vendor's solicitor together with a letter similar to the suggested draft on page 144.

Replies to Requisitions on Title

Within 3 or 4 days of sending these out you should have received back from the vendor's solicitor the answers to your Requisitions on Title. It is very unlikely that these answers will not be satisfactory. The answers that were given to your Enquiries before Contract will be confirmed, any existing mortgage will be agreed to be discharged on or before Completion and, usually, the vendor's solicitor will promise to inform you where Completion will take place and the amounts and names of the recipients of your banker's drafts.

Your Building Society's Solicitor

By this time you will almost certainly have heard from the solicitor who is acting for your building society asking you to send him various documents.

The list of documents comprises the following:

- Contract for Sale signed by vendor
- Enquiries before Contract and replies
- Local search forms and council's replies
- A copy of the Transfer form
- Authority to Inspect the Register (Form 201)
- A copy of the Land Register and plan.

You will recall that you asked the vendor's solicitor to furnish you with two Authorities to Inspect the Register (Form 201) when you wrote to exchange contracts; one in your name and the other in the name of the solicitor acting for your building society. A facsimile of Form 201 is on page 147. I also suggest you have a photocopy made of the Contract for Sale and of the copy of the Land Register before parting with them. Send the documents with a covering letter along the lines of the suggested draft on page 147.

You should hear again from your building society solicitor in about a week, which is about the time he will require to consider the documents you sent him. He will then send you yet more documents, namely:

- A mortgage deed for the signature of you and your wife
- A Requisitions on Title form
- A building society solicitor's statement of the amount that will be available at Completion, after deducting his charges, land registry fees and any stamp duty payable, out of the total sum being loaned.

The Mortgage Deed

Some solicitors when acting for a building society send two identical mortgage deeds, the idea being that one is to be treated as a draft and retained, the other being executed and returned. Other solicitors send only one mortgage deed which is to be signed and returned.

As no variations or amendments of the mortgage deed are permitted it follows that there can be no question of your 'approving' the document. You simply take it as it is.

This fact of life need cause you no concern because whilst the actual documents vary between building societies (and banks and other lenders) in respect of layout, verbiage and so on, all mortgage deeds in general boil down to the same thing. That is to say, the deed is a printed form with blank spaces that the building society solicitor will have filled in as appropriate. A sample deed is on page 148.

There are numerous clauses, some of which may be barely comprehensible, but which you will find commit you to repay the loan with interest, prohibit the subletting of the property without prior agreement and state the period of notice the building society requires prior to your paying off the loan (which will probably be expressed as 'redeeming the mortgage or legal charge'). There will also be a clause dealing with the rights of the building society in the event that you fail to meet the agreed repayments.

None of the clauses of a standard building society mortgage deed need cause you any problems, but you should nevertheless carefully read the document, and if there is something you do not understand ask the building society's solicitor to explain it.

Having read through the document check that the names of you and your wife (if you are buying jointly) are correctly stated, the address of the property is correct and the amount of loan, rate of interest and amount of the monthly repayments corresponds with the mortgage offer. If there are any errors return the deed or deeds to the building society's solicitor for correction, having previously telephoned to notify him.

Documents Required by Your Building Society

Requisitions on Title

This form from the building society's solicitor is not to be confused with the form of the same name which you sent to your vendor's solicitor, although in general, the questions asked are similar to those you asked on your 'Requisitions'.

Solicitors make up their own forms for these requisitions, with their questions in the left hand column and a space for your replies on the right. Just repeat the answers you were given to your own requisitions.

There may also be a question requesting you to confirm that you are providing the full purchase price, less the loan, from your own resources; in other words that you are not taking out a second mortgage on the quiet.

Also there may be a question which relates to subletting, i.e. the building society requires to be satisfied that you have no plans to sublet the property. The point here is that if you sublet, unless the lease was very carefully drafted the tenants would be likely to have a protected tenancy under the Rent Act, and the building society would find it impossible to regain possession.

If the building society wished to exercise its right to sell in the event that you failed to keep up the repayments, they would find that a house in which protected tenants are living is worth appreciably less than a house sold with vacant possession. Thus, upon sale the proceeds might be less than the outstanding loan.

Documents for Completion

The requisitions usually also list the documents required by the building society on Completion. When a mortgage is involved it is the building society solicitor who attends to the Completion formalities and to the post Completion procedures. The documents he requests of you are required to confirm that you (and the building society) are getting 'good title' to the ownership of the property; most of them will also be used in the post Completion procedures.

For registered land the documents are:

- The vendor's Land or Charge Certificate
- The Transfer signed by the vendor
- A Form 53 or an undertaking in respect of any existing mortgage on the property
- Land Registry Index Map Search (Form 96)
- Land Registry Search (Form 94A)
- Mortgage Deed executed by you and your wife
- Form K16
- Stamps L(A) 451 and Stamps 61 duly completed
- Completed A4 form
- NHBC certificate (if applicable)

The Land Certificate, Transfer and Form 53

Now for a few comments on these forms. The first three on the list will be produced and handed over as appropriate by the vendor's solicitor at Completion.

You will note that Form 53 (a sample appears on page 148) is a form used by building societies certifying that an outstanding mortgage (charge) has been paid off (discharged). It is this form that the vendor's solicitor undertakes to send to you within 14 to 21 days. You may wonder, as I do, why building societies cannot devise a means of lodging a sealed certificate with their solicitor in readiness for Completion.

Land Registry Search (Form 94A)

I am sure you will find this form to be self-explanatory. Its purpose is to warn you in the event of any new entry made on the Land Register after the date that you will find stamped at the bottom of each page of the 'office' copy which you were sent at the beginning of your transaction. There is a completed Form 94A on page 149.

This search, usually known as an 'official search', is very important. It is really the only effective way by which a purchaser can ensure that the Land Register has not been changed since the date stamped on his copy. Alternatively, this search will give notice of any entries made on the register since that date.

Incidentally if, instead of sending you an 'office' copy of the register, the vendor's solicitor originally sent you a photocopy of the vendor's Land Certificate, the relevant date must have been written in by him. This date appears on the inside front cover of the Land Certificate, inside a large circular stamp reading 'Compared with register'. Whether you have an office copy of photocopy with the date written in, both serve the same purpose. Just fill this date into the appropriate box on Form 94A.

You complete Form 94A and attach Form 201 'Authority to Inspect the Register' which the vendor's solicitor sent you previously and send both to the appropriate District Land Registry. Thoughtfully, the Form 94A is provided in duplicate so just slip a sheet of carbon paper between the two copies.

If, as in almost all cases, the search form is returned with the certificate on the reverse which is Form 94D endorsed 'Since . . . (the date of your copy) no adverse entry has been made thereon', you can confidently proceed in the knowledge that the certificate is conclusive evidence that nothing on the Land Register has changed. This is a valuable safeguard. A Form 94D is on page 149.

Guaranteed Priority

An equally valuable function of the search is that if a purchaser applies to be registered as the new owner of the property within 30 working days of the date of the search certificate, the State guarantees to give him priority over any other person or body who may apply to register an interest in the land.

The District Land Registries are particularly efficient in the processing of official searches and usually succeed in returning the result of the search within three days. In times of heavy work load, staff shortages and so on, the turn round time may be longer. You can always check the current time scale by telephoning the appropriate District Land Registry.

Timing

If you can, aim to obtain the search no more than about one week before you are due to complete. This will leave adequate time to carry out the post-completion formalities and submit the application to be registered as the new proprietor of the property within the allowed priority period. No charge is made for this search.

It has been assumed above that your experience is similar to that of almost all searches and that you receive a 'clear' search certificate from the District Land Registry, i.e. a certificate that, since the date of your copy of the register, 'no adverse entry has been made thereon'.

An Adverse Entry

But what if yours is one of the fairly rare cases when the search certificate is returned with an adverse entry? Such an entry could be a second mortgage and if so you would immediately contact the vendor's solicitor for an explanation. If this second mortgage is a further mortgage (advance) with the same building society you require the solicitor's written agreement to include this mortgage with his undertaking for the first mortgage. If the second mortgage is to another finance source you must insist upon a form 53 being handed over at completion.

Another kind of adverse entry could be a 'Caution'. This is a procedure that enables a person with an interest in the land, but whose interest is not registered, to lodge a caution against any dealings in the land. You must have the vendor's solicitors written assurance that this Caution will be cancelled prior to Completion before proceeding.

A spouse, not being a joint proprietor, may register a Notice of her/his interest in the matrimonial home. If you should encounter such as entry you should immediately contact the Vendor's solicitor. Do not proceed further unless and until you are provided with a written release of her/his rights in the property which must be identified, signed by the spouse, and that before Completion the solicitor will complete and lodge with H.M. Land Registry Form 202 signed by the spouse.

The example of a notice registered by a spouse under the Matrimonial Homes Act 1983 is cited by way of illustration. There are of course many other interests in the land that may be registered by notice or caution. Therefore, if your search form is returned with the word 'Caution' or 'Notice' with details of the interest registered (or these words were on the office copy you were sent by the vendor's solicitor) immediately contact your vendor's solicitor. Inform him that you will not proceed unless and until you have the solicitor's written undertaking that the caution or notice will be cancelled before Completion, and a certificate vacating it has been signed by the person who registered the caution or notice.

If all this appears to be rather forbidding, do not worry. An adverse entry is rare and I have referred to the subject purely for the sake of completeness.

However, it does underscore the need to obtain a complete copy of the register of the vendor's property when you receive the draft contract referred to on page 34 because in the unlikely event of a caution against dealing being registered you want to satisfy yourself that it will be withdrawn before you proceed any further. Certainly do not sign the contract or enter into exchange of contracts, until you are certain of this.

Land Registry Enquiry Service

Finally, on this topic, mention should be made of the enquiry service provided by District Land Registries. This service is staffed by experts with wide experience of land registry procedure so if by some chance your search is returned referring to an entry on the register whose significance escapes you, ask the experts at the Land Registry Enquiry Section. They will explain its significance, or if they do not know the answer, have recourse to qualified legal colleagues who do. You will find the staff of the District Land Registry to be both knowledgeable and helpful and they will deal with reasonable enquiries without charge but they are not able to act as legal advisers.

Bankruptcy Search (Form K16)

The solicitor acting for your building society will almost certainly require you to make a search in the Land Charges Registry at Plymouth. This Registry is concerned with unregistered land and should be distinguished from the District Land Registries which deal with registered land.

Among other information, the Land Charges Registry holds details of bankruptcy petitions and receiving orders, and the object of the search is to discover whether you or your wife, if you are joint purchasers, have been made bankrupt.

Application for Official Search is made on Form K16. The form is self explanatory and is completed by inserting the full names of yourself and your wife (if you are joint purchasers), your address and the date. Send to the address on the reverse of the form together with the fee which currently is 50p per name searched. A completed Form K16 is on page 150 and below.

Within a few days the Land Charges Registry will send you Form K17 (Bankruptcy). This form incorporates a certificate that there are 'no subsisting entries'. In other words, that you are not bankrupt. A 'clear' bankruptcy search on form K17 is on page 150.

Form K16

Land Charges Act 1972

Payment of fee
(see Note 2 overleaf)
EITHER
Insert a cross (X) in this box if the fee is to be paid through a credit account ☐
OR
affix stamps in this space

APPLICATION FOR AN OFFICIAL SEARCH
(BANKRUPTCY ONLY)

Application is hereby made for an official search in the index to the registers kept pursuant to the Land Charges Act 1972 in respect of the under-mentioned names for any subsisting entries of:
(i) petitions in bankruptcy in the register of pending actions
(ii) receiving orders in bankruptcy in the register of writs and orders
(iii) deeds of arrangement in the register of deeds of arrangement

IMPORTANT: **Please read the notes overleaf before completing the form.**

For Official Use only	NAMES TO BE SEARCHED (Please use block letters and see note 3 overleaf)	
#	Forename(s)	GERALD GEORGE
	SURNAME	FORD
	Forename(s)	JOAN
	SURNAME	FORD
	Forename(s)	
	SURNAME	
	Forename(s)	
	SURNAME	
	Forename(s)	
	SURNAME	
	Forename(s)	
	SURNAME	

Particulars of Applicant (see notes, 4, 5 and 6 overleaf)		Address for despatch of certificate (Leave blank if certificate is to be returned to applicant's address)
Key number	Name and address	
	G.G.FORD, 112 DORSET ROAD, HUTTON, WESSEX	

Applicant's reference:	Date	FOR OFFICIAL USE ONLY
	**	

Stamp Duty

Every sale of freehold or assignment of leasehold land must be reported to the Inland Revenue. This is done by completing a form known as Stamps L(A)451 and a form Stamps 61 both of which are available from Inland Revenue stamp offices. See page 121 for a list of addresses.

If you refer to the completed samples of Stamps L(A)451 and Stamps 61 on pages 151 and 152 you should have no problems in completing them.

If you are buying with the aid of a mortgage, the building society solicitor will attend to their submission to the stamp office, and you need only fill out the forms.

Registering Your New Ownership

Form A4 is the form on which you apply to the District Land Registry to be registered as the new owner. If you are getting a mortgage it is submitted by the building society solicitor, and you need only fill out the form.

There is a completed form A4 on page 152 which illustrates a typical transaction which, it is assumed, is being part financed by a £10,000 mortgage. If we go through that example together, you will see what is required.

On page 1 in box 1 insert the title number of the property.

Box 2 requires you to state the 'Nature of applications in priority order'. This calls for a little explanation. In the example on page 152 there are three applications. First, the removal of the seller's mortgage from the land register. Second, the entry of the new owner's name in place of that of the seller (this is on the Transfer Form 19 or Form 19(JP)), and, third, the name of the building society providing the £10,000 mortgage.

That is the order in which the Land Registry is asked to deal with the applications. Obviously a buyer wants any existing mortgage deleted from the Land Register, his own name substituted as owner and then if there is a mortgage the details of the lender entered.

No fee is payable when a mortgage is paid off (redeemed) and the other figures entered in the column headed 'Value' are self explanatory. That to be entered against 'Transfer' is the sum on the Transfer Form and the figure for 'Mortgage' is the amount of the loan.

The fee scale (column 3 of box 2) for a property already registered is scale 4 and it is based on the price of the house. If, as in this example, a mortgage is involved the building society solicitor will tell you what the fee is for registration.

If you are not getting a mortgage, unless you know a friendly solicitor, phone the District Land Registry and ask. (Of course, in this event, there would be no mortgage to enter as item 3 in column 1 of box 2).

When a Transfer is registered at the same time as a mortgage the Land Registry fee in respect of the mortgage is reduced (abated) to nil and 'abatement' is entered under 'fee scale', as in the example.

In box 3 you list all documents lodged with the application. In the example, these comprise the charge certificate (the entry in respect of which you are applying to be deleted from the Land Register), Form 53 certifying that the mortgage has been paid off (redeemed), the Form 19 or Form 19(JP), the mortgage deed for your loan and a copy (this copy will be certified by the building society solicitor to be a true copy of the original), and Form 94A received from the Land Registry.

(If you are not getting a mortgage there will be no mortgage deed or copy.)

Box 4 is self explanatory. Insert the name and address of the building society solicitor, if you are getting a mortgage, or your own if no mortgage is involved.

You are not likely to give any special directions to the Land Registry, so box 5 is left blank.

Box 6 is on the back page, and again is self explanatory. Enter the full names of you (and your wife as appropriate). If, as usual, you are moving into your new home upon Completion or soon after, that is the address to enter.

Box 7 is completed if you have a mortgage.

Box 8 is answered 'Yes' if you are buying as joint tenants, 'No' if as tenants in common. You will remember that when the property is owned as joint tenants, in the event of the death of one of them, the property passes automatically to the survivor, and if it is held as tenants in common the share of the deceased passes into his estate.

Boxes 9 and 10 you can ignore.

Box 11 is a list of 'reminders'. If you are getting a mortgage, the building society can complete this chore. Otherwise, insert a cross in the boxes as appropriate.

Box 12 is completed by the building society if you are getting a mortgage, otherwise by you.

National House Building Council (NHBC) Certificate

If there is an NHBC certificate in respect of the property, the building society requires that this be handed to them and they keep it with the 'deeds'. You will have been told by your seller whether there is such a certificate when he answered your 'Enquiries before Contract'.

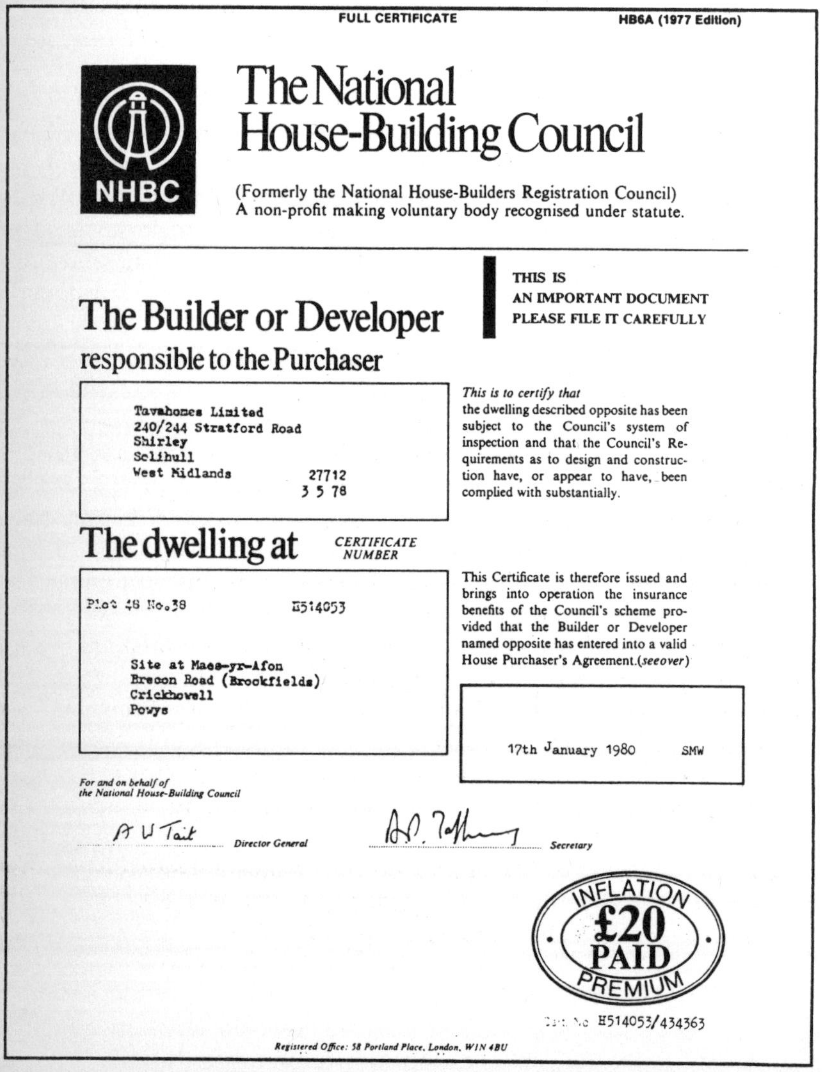
FULL CERTIFICATE HB6A (1977 Edition)

NHBC

The National House-Building Council

(Formerly the National House-Builders Registration Council)
A non-profit making voluntary body recognised under statute.

THIS IS AN IMPORTANT DOCUMENT PLEASE FILE IT CAREFULLY

The Builder or Developer responsible to the Purchaser

Tavahomes Limited
240/244 Stratford Road
Shirley
Solihull
West Midlands 27712
3 5 78

This is to certify that the dwelling described opposite has been subject to the Council's system of inspection and that the Council's Requirements as to design and construction have, or appear to have, been complied with substantially.

The dwelling at *CERTIFICATE NUMBER*

Plot 48 No.38 E514053

Site at Maes-yr-Afon
Brecon Road (Brookfields)
Crickhowell
Powys

This Certificate is therefore issued and brings into operation the insurance benefits of the Council's scheme provided that the Builder or Developer named opposite has entered into a valid House Purchaser's Agreement.*(see over)*

17th January 1980 SMW

For and on behalf of the National House-Building Council

A W Tait Director General

Secretary

INFLATION £20 PAID PREMIUM

Cert No E514053/434363

Registered Office: 58 Portland Place, London, W1N 4BU

Arranging the Finances for Completion

About the time that you received the statement from the building society's solicitor showing the mortgage funds (less his charges) that will be available, you should also have had a completion statement from the vendor's solicitor. If this has not arrived by, say, ten days before you are due to complete, telephone him to hurry things along.

Organizing the finances for Completion looks far more complicated than it really is. In essence it merely involves a few simple sums of arithmetic, and if maths was not your best subject at school, there is no need to worry — someone else does the sums and you need only check to see that the answers are correct.

The Completion Statement

Refer to the vendor's solicitor's completion statement and the building society solicitor's account, both on page 154. Basically, the vendor's solicitor's completion statement details how he has arrived at the sum required at Completion, i.e. the purchase price less deposit, plus any sum agreed for chattels, and in the example, an apportionment of water and sewerage rates.

The balance due at Completion is £27,547.27. You will note that the solicitor has indicated that he wants this sum split into two drafts and has given the amount of each draft. A 'draft', by the way, is shorthand for a Banker's Draft which is a cheque drawn by a bank and as such cannot be stopped, unlike a cheque drawn on a personal bank account.

The building society solicitor's account shows how he arrived at the amount that will be available at Completion. This is the amount of the mortgage you will be loaned less charges for Land Registry fees and the solicitor's fee, which gives a net balance of £14,819.25 that he will pay over at Completion.

You will, of course, have given thought to the financial aspects of the transaction before you agreed to buy, and have a pretty clear idea of your financial resources.

Finding the Funds

As a simple exercise, assuming that you are the purchaser, let us go through the figures below together. In this example, you have to find £27,547.27, i.e. the balance due to the vendor. You will receive £14,819.25 from the building society, leaving you to provide £12,728.02 from your own funds or from the proceeds of a simultaneous sale, or perhaps a mixture of both. For simplicity, we will assume that you are finding this sum from your own funds.

Referring to the vendor's solicitor's completion statement which indicates how the sum due on Completion is to be split into two drafts, you would instruct your bank to issue a draft in favour of the vendor's solicitor for £12,728.02.

You would also ask your building society solicitor to arrange for the mortgage advance to be split into two drafts; one in favour of the vendor's solicitor for £3937.00 and one in favour of the vendor's building society for £10,882.25. (The drafts for £12,728.02 and £3937.00 together satisfy the vendor's solicitor's request for £16,665.02.)

So your simple sums in this example are:

Balance of purchase price	£27,547.27
Net mortgage advance available	£14,819.25
Sum required from other funds (Own funds or simultaneous sale etc.	£12,728.02
Provided as follows:	
Draft on own bank in favour of vendor's solicitor	£12,728.02
Draft from own building society in favour of vendor's solicitor	£3937.00
Draft from own building society in favour of vendor's building society	£10,882.25
	£27,547.27

A suggested draft letter to your building society solicitor is on page 155.

If this looks a little off-putting, bear up, it's really quite straightforward once you have studied it a couple of times.

Preparing for Completion

If you are selling and buying simultaneously your plan should be to arrange for your sale to be completed first, followed by your purchase. It is vital to follow this sequence and only this sequence. Any other and you could run the risk of being caught with two homes on your hands.

The Completion of your sale will be at your building society solicitor's office where the other participants (your purchaser or his solicitor) gather. The whole process takes no more than 10 minutes. Then you will be free to go to the office of your vendor's solicitor or of the vendor's building society solicitor.

Last Chance to Inspect

You should, if at all possible, take the opportunity to visit the property you are about to buy before you proceed to Completion with the vendor and I suggest you arrange for an interval between the two transactions of a couple of hours or so.

If you can possibly arrange to have the keys beforehand from the vendor or the estate agents, then do so. Look around the property to make sure that any items that the vendor agreed to leave are there and, in particular, that there is no-one still in occupation.

If for some reason you are not personally able to do this chore, get your wife or other reliable person to do it for you, and give your representative a telephone number at which you can be contacted if necessary.

Needless to say, you would not complete if the house is not vacant. If chattels for which you have paid, or which it was agreed would be left, have been removed the matter should be raised at Completion before you hand over the money. If the question is left until after Completion you will merely have a virtually useless right of action, whereas if you press for a realistic sum in settlement before you complete there is every incentive for the vendor's solicitor to come up with a solution.

One of the chores to take care of once you have arranged the times of Completion is to ensure that the instructions you gave to your removal contractors are in hand, and that arrangements have been made that will allow the furniture van to drive directly to your new home after collecting its load from the old house. Strictly, the keys should not be available to you until you have completed and your planning should provide for this. Ideally, you should arrange the timing so that you are already at your new house to meet the furniture van when it arrives.

Completion of Your Purchase

When the final hour arrives you present yourself at the agreed venue armed with the documents and the appropriate draft(s). If yours is a simultaneous sale and purchase you will have already attended to the Completion of your own sale.

In the interest of clarity, let's go through the Completion procedure that applies if you are financing your purchase through a mortgage, and then the procedure if you are financing the purchase from your own resources.

Completion With a Mortgage

If you are getting a mortgage, the venue for Completion of your purchase will be either at the office of your vendor's building society solicitor or your vendor's solicitor. (The latter case will apply if your vendor does not have a mortgage to pay off.)

Your own building society solicitor will be there on behalf of your building society, which will eventually retain all the documents relating to your ownership while the loan is outstanding.

Just to remind you, you take along:

- The mortgage deed signed by you and your wife.
- Form 94A
- Form K17 — Result of Bankruptcy Search
- Form A4
- Stamps L(A)451 and Stamps 61
- The bank draft for any balance needed to make up the building society loan to the purchase price.

These documents you hand to your building society's solicitor who will do a quick check to see that they are in order. You receive from the vendor's solicitor the Transfer and Land Certificate (or Charge Certificate if there is a mortgage on the house).

You do a quick check that the Transfer is the one you prepared and is signed by the vendor and his wife (if selling in joint names, which you can check by reference to section B of the register). Their signatures should be witnessed and the address of the witness appended.

You also check that the Land Certificate or Charge Certificate is the same as the office copy or photocopy of the one you received originally and bears the title number that has been referred to throughout.

If, originally, you were sent a photocopy, you check the date stamped on the inside of the cover of the Land Certificate to ensure that this is the date that was written on the photocopy when you received it. You will recall that it was this date that you quoted on Form 94A. Having checked both the Land Certificate (or Charge Certificate) and the Transfer, you hand them to your building society solicitor.

You then date the mortgage deed which will be handed to you by your building society solicitor, and the Transfer (Form 19 or Form 19(JP)) which will be handed to you by your vendor's solicitor, with the same date. Similarly insert the same date on the draft copies of these documents. You now hand to your building society solicitor the Transfer, The Land Certificate or Charge Certificate, and the mortgage deed.

Your vendor no doubt will have a mortgage outstanding on the property he is selling, and this, strictly, should be paid off before Completion, but it is common practice for the solicitor acting for the vendor's building society to give an undertaking that Form 53 will be sent within 14 to 21 days after Completion. A specimen form of undertaking is on page 155.

At this point your building society solicitor produces the bank drafts in the sums you asked for. Check that the amounts and payees are correct. You then produce your own bank draft. These drafts are handed to the vendor's solicitor, who will pass the appropriate draft or drafts directly to your vendor's building society solicitor.

If you paid a small deposit to your vendor's estate agent, you now hand over a letter authorising its release to the vendor's solicitor. A specimen letter is on page 156. Payment of a deposit of £50 or £100 is less usual nowadays than it used to be, although in some parts of the country an estate agent may still ask for a deposit as a sign of good faith.

All that remains is for the keys to be handed over. This usually is arranged by mutual agreement between seller and buyer.

So you are now free to hurry to your new home in time to supervise the unloading of the removal van.

Completion Without a Mortgage

Now let's look at the completion procedures if you are not getting a mortgage.

The venue will be at the office of your vendor's building society solicitor (assuming that he has a mortgage on the property he is selling to you). Otherwise it would be at his solicitor's office. Let us assume that there is a mortgage on the vendor's house.

In effect what is to happen at Completion is that in return for the documents of title (ownership) you will hand over the purchase price.

All that you have to take with you are the drafts split as requested by the vendor's solicitor, plus, if you paid a deposit to the estate agent, a letter authorising its release.

The vendor's solicitor will hand you the Transfer to check that it is the one you and your wife signed, and has been signed by the vendors and properly witnessed. After checking, you retain the Transfer.

The vendor's building society solicitor will then hand you the Charge Certificate, which you check against the office copies to ensure you have been given the correct one. (Some solicitors handle a large volume of conveyancing so it is not unheard of for the wrong documents to be taken to Completion.) After checking, you keep the Charge Certificate.

All the other points regarding the checking of the Transfer and the Charge Certificate made on page 67 apply equally if you are not getting a mortgage. This checking does not take long, but it is a vital part of the procedure.

You date the Transfer and your draft copy identically. Your vendor has a mortgage outstanding on the property he is selling to you, and this, strictly, should be paid off before Completion, but it is common practice for the solicitor acting for the vendor's building society to give an undertaking that Form 53 will be sent within 14 to 21 days after completion. A specimen form of undertaking is on page 155.

You now produce the bank drafts in the sums and in favour of the recipients as requested. You hand them to the vendor's solicitor, who will hand the appropriate draft to the building society solicitor.

If you paid a deposit to an estate agent, (this is becoming less usual) you now hand over a letter authorising its release to the vendor's solicitor. A specimen letter is on page 156.

All that remains is for the keys to be handed over. Arrangements for this are usually made between the vendor and buyer. So having collected the keys you are free to hurry to your new home to supervise the unloading of the removal van.

Completion Does Not Mean it is Over

If your purchase was part-financed by a mortgage, the post-completion administrative formalities will be carried out by the building society solicitor.

However, if you are financing the purchase wholly from your own funds without the aid of a mortgage it may be helpful to run through the post-completion chores you will have to attend to yourself.

Stamp Duty

Your first priority should be to have the Transfer stamped and the procedure varies depending upon whether stamp duty is payable.

The procedure is as follows:

A. No stamp duty payable

1. As a general statement in respect of transactions which do not attract stamp duty i.e. when the consideration (price paid) is £30,000 or less, all the documents are sent to the appropriate District Land Registry and not as in the case of transactions on which stamp duty is payable firstly to the Inland Revenue Stamp Office and then to the District Land Registry.
2. If your transaction does not attract stamp duty complete form Stamps L(A)451 and attach any plan referred to.
3. Send the completed application for registration with supporting documents (refer to the section headed 'Registering as the New Owner' on page 70 for details of what to send) together with form Stamps L(A)451 to the appropriate District Land Registry.
4. This procedure does not apply to transfers which need adjudication e.g. a deed of gift, even if it is thought that no duty will be due.
5. The District Land Registry staff will check that no stamp duty is payable and that form Stamps L(A)451 has been completed correctly and assuming all is correct will stamp the transfer 'Produced' and pass form L(A)451 to the District Valuer.

B Stamp Duty Payable

1. You present form Stamps L(A)451 and the executed Transfer at any one of the stamp duty offices listed on page 121 within 30 days of Completion. An official will impress the Inland Revenue stamp on the Transfer to signify that it has been 'Produced'. The official will calculate the stamp duty payable and accept payment, usually in cash. The Transfer is then stamped with rather impressive seals signifying the sum paid. If the property is leasehold, box 6 of Stamps L(A)451 should be completed thus: 'Assignment of the residue of a lease for a term of 99 years from (date) at an annual rent of £ . . .'.

If the 'consideration' is more than £30,000 and if it is more convenient, you can apply for stamping of the Transfer through the post. Complete Stamps L(A)451 and Stamps 61 and send these with the Transfer and any stamp duty payable by recorded delivery to the designated stamp office listed on page 121. Current rates of stamp duty are on page 119.

Having had your Transfer stamped (it will be returned to you in a few days), you should now apply to register as the proprietor of your new home and for the vendor's mortgage to be taken off the Land Register. As the protection given by the certificate on Form 94A lasts only 30 working days, you should not delay registering the change of ownership.

Registering as the New Owner

If your transaction does not attract stamp duty because the consideration is £30,000 or less, as explained in 'A' above you send the documents required to register your interest as owner in your new property to the appropriate District Land Registry, together with form Stamps L(A)451. The District Land Registry will process the change of ownership and pass form L(A)451 to the District Valuer. This change in procedure only affects transactions in respect of which the consideration is £30,000 or less and eliminates one of the steps, thus speeding up the procedures.

If stamp duty is payable on your transaction the procedure is unchanged as explained in 'B' on page 69. Form Stamps L(A)451 and form Stamps 61 have to be completed and 'presented' to the Inland Revenue. You can do this in person at any of the stamp duty offices listed on page 121 or, if you prefer, you can send the documents by post to the appropriate stamp duty office (it will be returned to you in a few days), you now apply to register as the proprietor of your new home and for the vendor's mortgage to be taken off the land register. As the protection given by the certificate on Form 94A lasts only 30 working days you should not delay registering your change of ownership.

Whether or not stamp duty is payable on your transaction, you send to the appropriate District Land Registry the following:

- Charge certificate
- Search Form 94A
- Transfer document (from previous owner to you)
- A4 — Land Registry Application form
- Copy of Solicitor's undertaking re Form 53
- Cheque for Land Registry fee.

Do not delay sending the forms because you have not yet received Form 53. Instead, get the other documents in the post, and telephone the vendor's solicitor frequently until he sends it to you. You can then send it off to the Land Registry with a covering letter to link the form up with the documents sent earlier. A suggested draft of a covering letter to accompany the original set of documents is on page 147 and addresses of District Land Registries are on pages 122-123.

The period taken to alter the register and issue a new Land Certificate averages about eight weeks. The new Land Certificate will show you as the proprietor (or you and your wife if you bought jointly) and you should check that the details recorded are correct, before you deposit it in a safe place. The most usual repository is your bank. You should bundle up all the relevant documents relating to your purchase together with the Land Certificate, preferably in a strong envelope. When you hand over the documents the bank will give you a receipt, which you should keep in a safe place.

If you bought with the aid of a mortgage the Land Registry will send the new Charge Certificate to your building society solicitor. He will check it and send it on to your building society who will retain it with all the other papers until the mortgage is repaid.

You can, however, obtain an office copy of the updated register by completing Form A44, an Application for Office Copies. Send this form to the appropriate District Land Registry and your office copies will arrive within a few days showing you as the new owner of the property. A completed Form A44 is on page 157. No fee is payable for this service.

So congratulations! Whether you purchased out of your own funds or with the aid of a mortgage you have now completed all the stages of conveying ownership of registered land. I am sure you found the process well within your capacity.

New Owners of Leasehold Property

It is a usual condition of a lease that notice of a change of ownership must be given. Such notice is usually given to the landlord or his agent, and the lease may stipulate that a fee is charged for dealing with the notice. A suggested notice is set out on page 157.

Send a notice along these lines, in duplicate, to the appropriate person, together with any fee payable. Ask the recipient to sign and return one copy of your notice as a receipt. When the receipted copy is returned, unless you have a mortgage on the property, keep the document with the title deed as evidence that this term of the lease has been complied with. If you have a mortgage you should send the receipted copy to the building society solicitor to lodge with the title deeds he holds.

Buyer's Timetable from Exchange to Completion

The following is a typical timetable of the various stages of purchasing a property from Exchange of Contracts to Completion. It follows on from steps 1 to 18 in Chapter 3 that took you as far as Exchange of Contracts.

FROM EXCHANGE OF CONTRACTS TO COMPLETION

STEP	STAGE	DAY
19	Investigate vendor's title	4
20	Prepare your Requisitions on Title (Con 28B)	4
21	Draft the purchase deed	6
22	Consider replies to Requisitions on Title	8
23	Send all relevant documents to building society solicitor.	8
24	Receive building society solicitor's Requisitions on Title and forward to vendor's solicitor	12
25	Receive draft mortgage deed.	12
26	Draft the purchase deed and submit for approval.	12
27	Receive replies to building society's solicitor's Requisi tions on Title and forward to building society's solicitor.	15
28	Receive draft purchase deed 'approved'. Approve the draft mortgage deed.	15
29	Engross and execute the purchase deed	18
30	Send purchase deed to vendor's solicitor.	18
31	Receive engrossed mortgage deed and execute the same.	19
32	Make a pre-completion search.	20
33	Receive Completion statement	21
34	Arrange for bank drafts in specified amounts.	21
35	Receive result of pre-completion search.	24
36	Completion	28

The total time elapsed since your original offer to purchase is now two months.

POST COMPLETION (only applies if buying without a mortgage)

STEP	STAGE	
37	Present purchase deed for stamping	5 days
38	Apply to register change of ownership (registered land)	8 weeks
39	Apply for first registration (if applicable)	3 months

Completing the Purchase — Unregistered Land

If the property you are buying is registered, you should ignore this chapter entirely and turn to Chapter 4 instead. If it is unregistered, then the steps described here will take you from exchange of contracts to completion of the purchase.

From Exchange to Completion

The stages from exchange of contract to Completion for registered and unregistered land have been separated because they are basically different insofar as proving title is concerned. It will make for much easier understanding of what is involved to keep the two apart.

The main difference is that with registered land there is a single document — a Land Certificate (or Charge Certificate) in which the names of the owners and the restrictive covenants, mortgages, etc. are set out. In the case of unregistered land, instead of a Land Certificate there are a succession of deeds or Conveyances which must go back at least fifteen years. Of course, there may be as few as two deeds executed say thirty years ago; one when the land was conveyed to the builder and another when the builder erected the house and the land and premises were conveyed to your vendor.

Whichever it may be, what you are looking for is an unbroken chain of ownership which stretches back at least fifteen years and leads to your current vendor.

The Abstract of Title

After exchange of contracts the vendor's solicitor will send you the Abstract, or 'Epitome', of Title which traces the ownership of the house you are planning to buy for at least the previous fifteen years. The deeds and documents comprising the Abstract will show how your vendor became the legal owner of the property. A typical Abstract of Title and a model Conveyance are on pages 158 and 159. The deeds and other documents you receive with the Abstract will be photocopies; the originals must be handed to you on Completion. The onus is on the vendor to prove his title to the land, and upon receiving the Abstract and accompanying documents, you should carefully check to make certain that he has done just that.

Old time conveyancers used to excel in the extravagant language they used, and well deserved the rebuke that lawyers were paid by the yard. Today, particularly since the Law of Property Act 1969 reduced the period for which a vendor must show title from 30 years to a mere 15 years, Conveyances are much more simply drawn, and you should have no problems in your checking.

Have pencil and paper ready as you go through the documents, and make notes of any points on which you require clarification. Please do remember that the deed which transfers a leasehold property is called an Assignment whereas the deed which transfers a freehold property is a Conveyance.

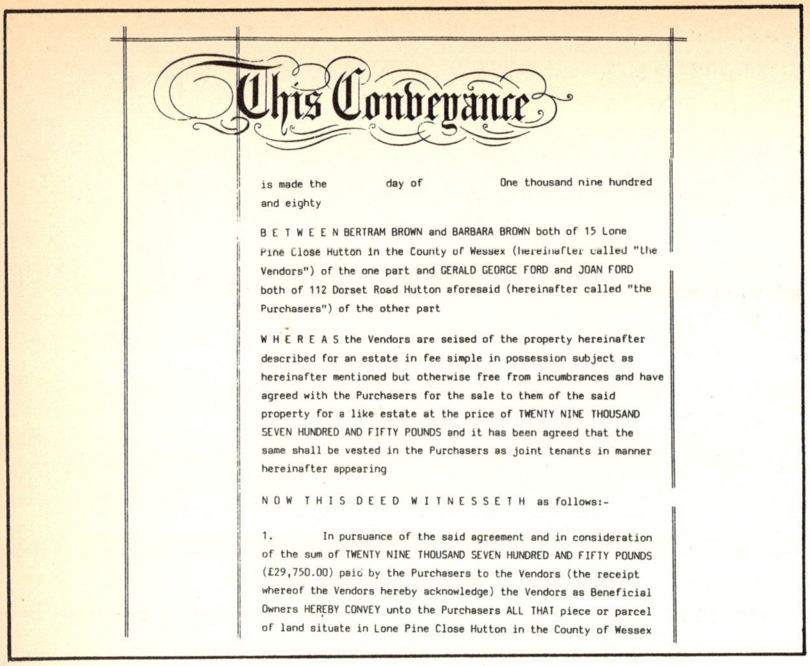

This Conveyance

is made the day of One thousand nine hundred and eighty

B E T W E E N BERTRAM BROWN and BARBARA BROWN both of 15 Lone Pine Close Hutton in the County of Wessex (hereinafter called "the Vendors") of the one part and GERALD GEORGE FORD and JOAN FORD both of 112 Dorset Road Hutton aforesaid (hereinafter called "the Purchasers") of the other part

W H E R E A S the Vendors are seised of the property hereinafter described for an estate in fee simple in possession subject as hereinafter mentioned but otherwise free from incumbrances and have agreed with the Purchasers for the sale to them of the said property for a like estate at the price of TWENTY NINE THOUSAND SEVEN HUNDRED AND FIFTY POUNDS and it has been agreed that the same shall be vested in the Purchasers as joint tenants in manner hereinafter appearing

N O W T H I S D E E D W I T N E S S E T H as follows:-

1. In pursuance of the said agreement and in consideration of the sum of TWENTY NINE THOUSAND SEVEN HUNDRED AND FIFTY POUNDS (£29,750.00) paid by the Purchasers to the Vendors (the receipt whereof the Vendors hereby acknowledge) the Vendors as Beneficial Owners HEREBY CONVEY unto the Purchasers ALL THAT piece or parcel of land situate in Lone Pine Close Hutton in the County of Wessex

The time honoured introduction to a Conveyance is usually printed on fairly stiff ruled 'legal' paper. It is not essential that this form be used but it looks both more professional and intimidating to the layman.

Reading a Conveyance

A Conveyance starts with 'THIS CONVEYANCE is made . . .' and gives the date of execution and the full names and addresses of the parties.

Then follows the 'Recital', commencing with the traditional words 'WHEREAS . . .'. The purpose of the Recital is to explain where necessary the history of a transaction or of the vendor's title.

This is followed by the operative part of the deed, introduced by the formal and time honoured 'NOW THIS DEED WITNESSETH as follows:'. This is the 'Testatum' and sometimes is still referred to as 'the premises'.

It is purely introductory and is followed by the words stating the consideration paid (i.e. the price paid), an acknowledgement by the vendor of the receipt of this sum, the words of grant, e.g. 'the Vendor as Beneficial Owner hereby conveys' which expresses the capacity in which the vendor sells, and a description of the property comprised in the Conveyance (known as the 'Parcels' clause).

This may be followed with a statement of any easements or other rights passing with the land introduced by the words 'TOGETHER WITH'.

Then follows the 'Habendum' clause, the usual form of which in the case of freehold land 'TO HOLD the same unto the Purchaser in fee simple . . .' describes the estate being conveyed.

Frequently a builder or someone who has sold off part of his land will limit what a purchaser takes by an 'Exceptions and Reservations' clause. An 'Exception' enables a vendor to retain some specified right over the land, e.g. mining and mineral rights, whereas a 'Reservation' describes some new right which the vendor's retained land is to enjoy.

An Exceptions and Reservations clause usually follows either the

Parcels clause or the Habendum with, e.g. the words 'Subject to the Exceptions and Reservations contained in Schedule Four hereof'.

Any restrictive or other covenants attaching to the land will appear at this point.

The Conveyance also includes a certificate of value if the price paid does not exceed the stamp duty threshold which currently is £30,000.

The Conveyance concludes with the 'Testimonium' clause. This normally reads 'IN WITNESS whereof the parties hereto have hereunto set their hands and seals the day and year first before written'.

The 'Execution and Attestation' by the parties to the deed follows and normally appears thus (the vendor signs first):

SIGNED SEALED AND DELIVERED by:
the said JOHN VENDOR
.... Seal
in the presence of:
Name ....
Address ....
Occupation ....

SIGNED SEALED AND DELIVERED by:
the said PERCIVAL PURCHASER
.... Seal
In the presence of:
NAME ....
ADDRESS ....
OCCUPATION ....

All this may appear wildly byzantine the first time you read it, but if you go through this potted explanation in conjunction with the model Conveyances on pages 158-160, you will quickly become familiar with the standard layout.

Note that if the tenure of the property is freehold, the appropriate words used are 'fee simple'.

If the property is leasehold, the assignment of a lease would be worded, e.g. 'TO HOLD the same unto the purchaser for the residue now unexpired of the term of . . . years created by the lease'.

Whereas a conveyance of a freehold (fee simple) will read 'hereby conveys', an assignment of a lease (a leasehold assignment) would read 'hereby assigns'.

Check List

As you read through the documents look out for the following:

- Check that any mortgages have been vacated (paid off or redeemed).
- Check that all Conveyances are dated.
- Check that the vendor is the same person who took title by a previous Conveyance. Make sure the names are spelt identically.
- Check that the property is described identically in all Conveyances.
- Check that all Conveyances have the 'Produced' stamp of the Inland Revenue, and that correct stamp duty (if applicable) was paid.
- Check that any plans are correct.
- Check that all documents are signed and witnessed.

The produced stamp indicates that the record of a transfer of property has been presented to the Inland Revenue. If the consideration attracted stamp duty there should be stamps to the value of the duty paid.

Queries

If you have any queries about the documents raise them with the vendor's solicitor in the Requisitions on Title which you attend to next. It is for him to satisfy you on the queries you raise, and you should not be put off by unsatisfactory or non-committal replies.

A building society mortgage is shown to be vacated (paid off) by a statement on the reverse of the mortgage deed which usually reads 'XYZ Building Society hereby acknowledge to have received all moneys intended to be secured by the within-written deed' and bears the date, the society seal, and the signature of an authorised officer of the society. An example of a vacating receipt is on page 88.

(You will note that the Abstract on page 158 lists 2 mortgages that have been vacated (redeemed or paid off), and photocopies of these would be sent to you with the Abstract.)

If you are getting a mortgage, you could ask your building society solicitor to check that the correct stamp duty has been paid on the Conveyances abstracted, i.e. shown on the Abstract of Title. He probably will do so anyway. If you are not getting a mortgage, telephone the Stamp Office for the correct scale of stamp duty applicable. This may appear to be a niggling point to make, but the simple fact is that a Conveyance which is not properly stamped is defective and cannot form a link in a chain of ownership.

In an average transaction, there wil not be more than 2 or at most 3 Conveyances to check; the procedures sounds more arduous than they actually are in practice.

Your Requisitions on Title

If you are buying with the aid of a mortgage, complete the form in triplicate. You will recall that I explained that I have drafted a form of Requisitions on Title which does the same job as the Oyez form, Conveyancing 28B, and you will find a copy in the forms pack. If you are buying with the aid of a mortgage, complete the form in triplicate. A completed sample form of Requisitions on Title is on page 144 for your guidance.

If you had any queries when checking the Abstracted documents, you put them to the vendor's solicitor on this form and at the same time you ask more general questions of him.

You fill in the address of the property, the vendor's name, and in question 3 delete part B which refers to registered land.

Raise the queries that arose from your checking of the documents on a separate piece of paper (in triplicate) and staple to the form. Strictly, any queries on the vendor's title deeds should be raised within 6 or 11 working days of receipt of the Abstract of Title, depending on the contract made, so Requisitions on Title is a form you should send off to your vendor's solicitor without delay. The Law Society contract provides a time limit of 6 working days after receipt of the Abstract in which to raise requisitions. The National Conditions contract specifies 11 working days after receipt of the Abstract in which to raise requisitions. So this is a chore you must deal with promptly.

Of the three copies you prepare, keep one copy in your file and send two copies to the vendor's solicitor. He will send one copy back with his replies and retain one copy for the files. Send the copies with a covering letter along the lines of the draft on page 143.

This suggested letter is also used for sending the draft Conveyance which we deal with next.

Your Draft Conveyance

Having checked the documents of title, you now have to prepare the draft Conveyance of the property to yourself. There usually is no reason why you should not use the Conveyance that conveyed the property to your vendor as a model. The important point is to make sure that the name of the vendor of the property, which you will insert in the Conveyance to yourself, is identical with the name shown in the previous Conveyance when he was the purchaser.

You must also ensure that the address of the property is correctly stated, and that the purchase price is as agreed. Do not forget to adjust the purchase price if you have agreed with the vendor that a certain amount of the total price is to be apportioned to carpeting, curtains, greenhouse etc., which you will be taking over. Finally, the certificate of value which is required for stamp duty purposes must be included if the selling price is £30,000 or less.

You prepare the draft Conveyance on ordinary paper, in triplicate, and send two copies to the vendor's solicitor for approval. Send the draft Conveyance with a letter along the lines of the one on page 162. He will retain one copy for his own use and return the other copy to you with any suggested amendments in red. If there are any amendments, they are likely to be quite minor and will present no problems to you in incorporating them.

If, though, some alteration or additional clause is proposed with which you are unhappy, ask the vendor's solicitor just why he wishes this to be done. If his answer does not satisfy you, telephone the building society solicitor and explain the situation to him (the reasons for doing so are explained more fully below).

If, for some reason, you do not wish to use the Conveyance to your vendor as a model, the sample Conveyances on pages 158-160 will be perfectly acceptable to your vendor's solicitor.

However, if the property is leasehold, refer to the model Assignment on page 163.

The Building Society Solicitor

By this time you will have heard from the solicitor who is acting for your building society asking you to send him various documents. These are:

- The Abstract of Title you received from the vendor's solicitor
- A copy of the draft Conveyance which you have prepared
- Local search forms and replies
- Enquiries before Contract and replies
- The Contract for Sale signed by the vendor

Now you will remember that I urged that you do not delay raising your Requisitions on Title with the vendor's solicitor as questions on title should be raised within a few working days of receipt of the Abstract, as explained on page 77. You may possibly come across something when checking the deeds that you think gives pause for thought, or you feel doubtful as to the wording of a requisition. In this case my suggestion is that you send the complete Abstract on Title, the local searches and replies together with your Requisitions on Title as soon as you possibly can to the building society solicitor. Ask him to vet your proposed requisitions and, if necessary, add to or amend them. He shares your interest in you getting good title and if you ask him to check the Requisitions on Title as a matter of urgency you should have them back within a couple of days with his comments. You can then send the form on the vendor's solicitor, suitably amended if necessary, for his attention.

As soon as you receive the vendor's solicitor's replies to your Requisitions on Title send a copy to the building society solicitor. Do this without delay as he will want to compile his own requisitions on title. (Keep a photocopy in your file.)

About a week or so after receiving the various documents from you the building society solicitor will send you the following:

- Draft mortgage deed
- Building society's Requisitions on Title
- Building society solicitor's statement of his fees and of the money available at Completion.

The Draft Mortgage Deed

Some solicitors acting for building societies send two identical mortgage deeds, the idea being that one is to be treated as a draft copy and retained, the other being executed and returned. Other solicitors send only one mortgage deed to be executed and returned (a sample deed in on page 148).

As no other variations or amendments of the mortgage deed are permitted it follows that there can be no question of 'approving' the document. You simply take it as it is.

This need cause you no concern because whilst the actual documents vary as between building societies (and banks and other lenders) in respect of layout, wording and so on, all mortgage deeds boil down to the same thing. That is to say, the deed is a printed form with blank spaces that the solicitor for the building society will have filled in as appropriate.

There are numerous clauses, some of which may be barely comprehensible, but you will find they commit you to repay the loan with interest, prohibit the subletting of the property without prior agreement and state the period of notice the building society requires prior to your paying off the loan, (which will probably be expressed as 'redeeming the mortgage or legal charge'). There will also be a clause dealing with the rights of the building society in the event that you fail to meet the agreed repayments.

None of the clauses of a standard building society mortgage deed need cause you any problems but you should, nevertheless, carefully read the document and if there is something you do not understand ask the building society's solicitor to explain it.

Having read through the document check that your name and those of your wife (if you are buying jointly) are correctly stated, that the address of the property is correct and that the amount of the loan, rate of interest and amount of the monthly repayments correspond with the mortgage offer. If there are any errors return the mortgage deed or deeds to the building society's solicitor, having previously telephoned to notify him.

If all is well, you and your wife sign the mortgage deed with your usual signature, alongside the seals, in the presence of a witness who signs with his name, address and occupation.

The Building Society Solicitor's Requisitions on Title

Solicitors make up their own forms for these Requisitions with their questions in the left hand column and a space for the answers on the right. If you sent a copy of your Requisitions on Title with replies to the building society's solicitor as suggested, his requisitions will reflect your questions and the answers you received, as well as any other questions that the building society solicitor may wish to put.

It may be that he is not satisfied with one or more of the answers you received from the vendor's solicitor, and will put further questions designed to extract a more satisfactory reply. Any such questions should be immediately passed to the vendor's solicitor as should any other questions which you yourself cannot answer. Other than requisitions relating to the title deeds, the questions posed by the building society's solicitor should be quite straightforward and present no difficulties in answering.

He will ask you to confirm that you are providing the full purchase price, less the mortgage loan, from your own funds. In other words, that you are not taking out a second mortgage on the quiet. He will ask you to confirm that the property will be occupied by you for your own use. Building societies need to be satisfied that an intending borrower has no plans to sublet the property. The point is that if you did sublet, unless the lease under which you sublet was carefully drafted the tenants would be likely to have a protected tenancy under the Rent Act, and the building society would find it impossible to regain possession. If at some future time the building society wished to exercise its right to sell, in the event you failed to keep up the repayments, they would find that a house with protected tenants in residence is worth appreciably less than a similar property sold with vacant possession. Thus upon sale the proceeds might be less than the outstanding mortgage loan.

The Building Society Solicitor's Statement
The solicitor acting for the building society will send you a statement of the money available to you at Completion. A typical statement is on page 154. You will note that this, basically, is the loan less Land Registry Fees and the solicitor's charges. The stamp duty will also be deducted if the selling price exceeds £30,000. The sum left after such deductions is the amount that the building society will make available at Completion.

Returning the Building Society Solicitor's Requisitions
Within three or four days you should have received replies from the vendor's solicitor to any requisitions of the building society solicitor which you felt necessary to refer to him. You should make every effort to complete your part of the form and post it to the building society solicitor the same day you receive it. If no requisitions were referred to the vendor's solicitor then do ensure, if at all possible, that you complete the form and send it back to the building society solicitor the very same day.

Engrossing the Conveyance

'Engrossing' the Conveyance consists of preparing the actual document which the vendor and purchaser will sign in due course.

You will recall that the Conveyance is first typed on ordinary plain paper and two copies are sent to the vendor's solicitor for approval. One of these copies is returned, marked 'agreed', or perhaps with a minor suggested amendment in red ink, which you find acceptable.

The Conveyance is then typed out incorporating those amendments which you have agreed on a fairly stiff formal looking sheet of paper. Use the 'engrossing' paper, headed in printed copper plate 'THIS CONVEYANCE', which is included in the forms pack.

One red wafer seal is affixed for each person who is to sign (see example on page 159). Four of these seals, which are used today instead of the wax of bygone days, are to be found in the forms pack.

After typing, the Conveyance must be very carefully proof read, word by word. Any minor corrections should be made as neatly as possible and MUST be initialled in the margin by all the signatories. Any serious typing errors may necessitate retyping.

Send the engrossed Conveyance, duly executed, to the vendor's solicitor for him to obtain the signature of the vendor in readiness for Completion.

The Conveyance is executed by you signing alongside the seal in the presence of a witness who signs with his usual signature, address and occupation. If the purchase is in joint names, both of you must sign in the presence of a witness. He may witness both signatures, but you and your wife must not witness each other's signature.

You will have noted that the Attestation clause in the example on page 159 reads 'Signed, sealed and delivered'. 'Signed' is self-explanatory; 'sealed' refers to the red wafer seal which replaces the wax seal of bygone days; and 'delivered' indicates that the signatory, having signed in the presence of a witness, said 'I deliver this my act and deed'. Most people take the last act as read, though it is a delightfully theatrical moment in the transaction.

A suggested draft letter for sending with the engrossed Conveyance is on page 162.

Pre-Completion Search

About a week before the completion date you must make a pre-completion search.

In the case of registered land a search is made, prior to completion, against the title number of the land, using Form 94A which is sent to the District Land Registry.

In the case of unregistered land a search is made against the names of the vendor in the registers (there are in fact five registers) of miscellaneous interests that are maintained by the Central Land Charges Registry in Plymouth.

The Central Land Charges Registry should not be confused with the Plymouth District Land Registry which deals with registered land nor with the Local Land Charges register kept by local authorities.

The Central Land Charges Register is NOT a central register of unregistered houses, but of a wide range of interests which third parties may have in unregistered property and which are registered against the name of the owner of the property.

The Central Land Charges Register comprises five registers, each of which is searched when you apply on Form K15. The most important register for our purpose is the Land Charges register, which is sub-divided into 6 classes — A, B, C, D, E and F. Classes C and D are sub-divided further.

The other four registers are:

- Register of Pending Actions. Examples include a dispute about the ownership of a piece of land and a wife's claim in divorce proceedings for a transfer of property order. Importantly, a bankruptcy petition is registerable as a pending action. Registration is only effective for 5 years and must then be renewed.
- Register of Writs and Orders. Examples include writs and orders made by a court for the purpose of enforcing judgement and receiving orders in bankruptcy. Registration is only effective for 5 years and must then be renewed.
- Register of Deeds of Arrangement. An example is an agreement whereby a debtor agrees to hand over his property for his creditors to administer in an effort to avoid bankruptcy proceedings.
- Register of Annuities. You are not likely to encounter such an animal.

It is not proposed to go into more detail with these four registers. If you are interested in studying this area of Land Law further I suggest you obtain Megarry & Wade 'The Law of Real Property' from your library.

Land Charges Search

Although there are five registers of miscellaneous interests, traditionally the search is known as a 'land charges search'. You will appreciate that the purpose of making a search before Completion is to establish that no adverse interests have been registered. This you do by completing Form K15 and sending it to the Land Charges Department of the Central Registry in Plymouth (the full address is on the form) having affixed the appropriate Land Registry stamps for the search fee. These can be obtained from any head post office and most Crown post offices. A completed sample of Form K15 is on page 164.

The pre-completion Land Charges search is very important because having made it a purchaser will take the property free from all other interests save those which have been registered, and of which he will be given notice by the result of his search.

Further, you are given a measure of protection for a period of 30 working days from the date of the search. This 'protection period' appears on the face of the certificate — see sample on page 165. Provided that completion takes place before the expiry of the protection period, a purchaser will have priority and will not be bound by any entries that may appear on the register within the protection period.

If, between the dates of the search and Completion an adverse entry is made on the Central Land Register, a purchaser has priority and is not bound by them.

Computerised Search

The search procedure is computerised which makes for speed in getting the results back, but it also means that you must be extremely careful to search the correct names of the vendor. This cannot be too strongly stressed.

For example. If one of the names you are searching is John James Jones the computer will also search J.J. Jones but it will not search John Jones or John J. Jones. If a name is changed upon marriage you should search both names. Similarly, if someone is known by more than one name, e.g. John and Jack, search both names.

The Abstract of Title will reveal the names of the previous owners and there should be a search certificate in respect of each. If a search certificate for one of these is missing you will have to do the search again, and thus also include the names of the former owners as well as your present vendor.

Before sending off the form ask your friendly building society solicitor if he wishes any other name to be added, and you should add your own name if this was requested in his requisitions. The Form K15 provides for six names to be entered. If you wish to search more than six names, use a second form.

When filling out Form K15 it is important to state the correct name of the county. County boundaries were changed as from 1 April 1974. It may therefore be necessary to give the name of the county and the former county. Obvious examples are the Metropolitan counties, such as West Midlands, which absorbed parts of Warwickshire, Worcestershire and Staffordshire; and poor old Rutland which ceased to exist.

It is not normally necessary to give a description of the land.

At this point, also send Form K16 (Banktuptcy only) if this is requested by your building society solicitor.

Results of Pre-Completion Searches

Within a few days of sending off Form K15 you will receive the results of the searches against the names you listed. If these are on Form K17 you need take no action, as the form incorporates a certificate that there are 'no subsisting entries' against the names listed. This means that no-one has registered any interest against the names on the form.

To obtain the protection of the priority period, Completion must take place within the dates stamped on Form K17. A sample of Form K17 is on page 151. Thus the 'Certificate Date' is the date of issue and the box headed 'Protection Ends' is the date of expiry of protection. If, between the date of the certificate and Completion an entry is made on the Central Land Register it will not bind a purchaser provided Completion of the purchase takes place within 30 working days of the date of the certificate. This period of 30 working days is known as the 'protection' period or the 'priority' period because if during that period a purchaser completes his purchase he will not be bound by any entries that may be made on the register, i.e. he has priority. Always provided, of course, that the purchaser has searched the correct name(s). If for some reason Completion is delayed beyond the priority period the search must be repeated, otherwise the protection given within the priority period will lapse.

The purpose of the search of the Land Charges Register is to discover whether any interests have been registered affecting the property you are buying of which you are not aware and which will be binding on you if you buy.

Any entries against the names searched are reported to you by the Land Charges Registry and each type of registerable interest has a code. As the register is maintained by name, there could possibly be several persons of the same name in the same area, so the search could relate to a person other than your vendor.

What You Do If an Adverse Entry is Revealed

If an adverse entry is revealed you should immediately ask the vendor's solicitor what it relates to and how he proposes to deal with it.

The vendor's solicitor may say that the entry does not relate to the vendor, in which case ask him to endorse Form K18 accordingly, and to sign and date his certificate. Before you go any further inform the building society solicitor and take his advice before proceeding. In normal circumstances you would not be prepared to proceed unless you have the written undertaking of the vendor's solicitor that the adverse entry will be removed before Completion.

Let us use our two examples by way of illustration. If the Official Search reveals a Class C(i) charge, i.e. a second mortgage, you would not be prepared to purchase unless you have the written undertaking of your vendor's solicitor that the entry will be removed before Completion and that you will be handed the mortgage deed endorsed with the lender's receipt of the loan repaid.

If your bankruptcy search reveals a Class F charge, i.e. a spouse's statutory right of occupation under the Matrimonial Homes Act, do not proceed unless and until you are provided with a letter signed by the spouse registering the interest, stating that he or she agrees to the sale and to the cancellation of the charge, and that before Completion you will be sent a completed Form K13, duly signed by the spouse. Form K13 is an application for cancellation of registration.

If, in the earliest days of your negotiations to purchase, you have cause to think that your vendor and spouse may not be on the best of terms, you would be wise to make a search there and then. Better face such problems early on before the contracts have been exchanged.

I emphasise that the chances of these problems arising tend to be fairly remote.

The code for restrictive covenants is D(ii). You will already know whether the property is being sold subject to a restrictive covenant as this was disclosed in the contract or was apparent from the Abstract. If D(ii) appears on the official search certificate, then all you need do is to satisfy yourself that the entry relates to a restrictive covenant of which you already have notice. You do this by asking the vendor's solicitor to certify this on Form K18 and to sign and date the certificate.

Notify the Building Society Solicitor

If any entries are reported under codes not referred to above, do not proceed any further unless the vendor's solicitor is prepared to certify that the entries do not relate to the property you are buying. In any event, notify the building society solicitor.

Now for a final recap. In general, the only entries you should be prepared to accept are Class D(ii), i.e. restrictive covenants. If the search reveals a Class F or Class C(i) or any other entry you must obtain a signed undertaking from the vendor's solicitor that this entry has been or will be cancelled before you even consider proceeding.

Let me stress that if any adverse interests were revealed by the search send the results to your building society solicitor without delay.

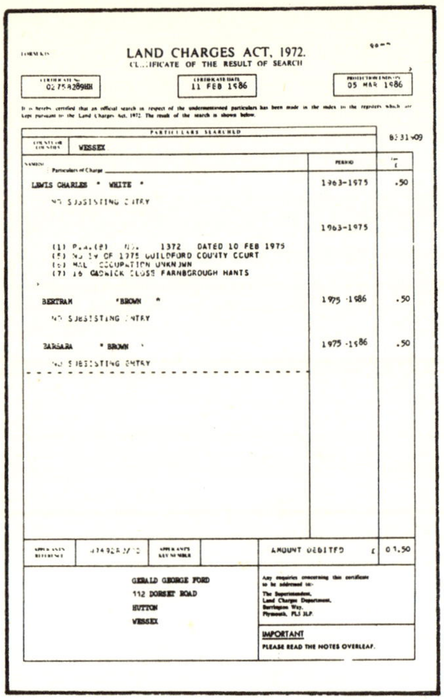
LAND CHARGES ACT, 1972.
CERTIFICATE OF THE RESULT OF SEARCH
0275B289HH
11 FEB 1986
05 MAR 1986
PARTICULARS SEARCHED
WESSEX
LEWIS CHARLES * WHITE * 1963-1975 .50
NO SUBSISTING ENTRY
1963-1975
(1) P.A.(B) NO. 1372 DATED 10 FEB 1975
(5) NO 19 OF 1975 GUILDFORD COUNTY COURT
(6) NIL OCCUPATION UNKNOWN
(7) 16 CADWICK CLOSE FARNBOROUGH HANTS
BERTRAM *BROWN * 1975-1986 .50
NO SUBSISTING ENTRY
BARBARA * BROWN * 1975-1986 .50
NO SUBSISTING ENTRY
AMOUNT DEBITED £ 01.50
GERALD GEORGE FORD
112 DORSET ROAD
SUTTON
WESSEX
Any enquiries concerning this certificate to be addressed to:-
The Superintendent,
Land Charges Department,
Burrington Way,
Plymouth, PL5 3LP.
IMPORTANT
PLEASE READ THE NOTES OVERLEAF.

This example of an 'adverse entry' on a Land Registry search form refers to a County Court judgement which may or may not relate to the person whose name is being searched.

The Building Society's Requisitions on Title (Continued)

The building society solicitor's requisitions, which you have already dealt with, list the documents which he requires for Completion. In the case of unregistered land these are:

- The vendor's title deeds
- The Conveyance signed by the vendor
- A written undertaking by the vendor's building society solicitor to forward a sealed receipt for the money secured by the vendor's mortgage within 14–21 days. The receipt is endorsed on the mortgage deed and an example is found on page 148.
- A mortgage deed signed and sealed by you (and your wife if you are buying in joint names).
- Results of Land Charges searches.
- Completed Stamps L(A) 451 and Stamps 61.

(Every sale of freehold land or assignment of leasehold land must be reported to the Inland Revenue. This is done by completing a form Stamps L(A)451 and a form Stamps 61, both of which are included in the forms pack. If you refer to the completed Stamps L(A)451 and Stamps 61 on pages 151 and 152 you should have no problems filling them in.)

The first three of these documents will be produced by the vendor's solicitor, the others by you.

Arranging the Finances for Completion

About the time that you received a statement of the mortgage funds that will be available to you from the building society's solicitor, you should also have had a completion statement from the vendor's solicitor. If this has not arrived by, say, ten days before you are due to complete, telephone him to hurry things along.

Organising the finances for Completion looks far more complicated than it really is. In essence it merely involves a few simple sums of arithmetic, and if maths was not your best subject at school, there is no need to worry — someone else does the sums and you need only check to see that the answers are correct.

The Completion Statement

Refer to the vendor's solicitor's completion statement and the building society solicitor's account, both on page 154. Basically, the vendor's solicitor's completion statement details how he has arrived at the sum required at Completion, i.e. the purchase price less deposit, plus any sum agreed for chattels and, in the example, an apportionment of water and sewerage rates.

The balance due at Completion is £27,547.27. You will note that the solicitor has indicated that he wants this sum split into two drafts and has given the amount of each draft. A 'draft', by the way, is shorthand for a Banker's Draft which is a cheque drawn by a bank and as such cannot be stopped, unlike a cheque drawn on a personal bank account.

The building society solicitor's account shows how he arrived at the amount that will be available at Completion. This is the amount of the mortgage you will be loaned less charges for Land Registry fees and the solicitor's fee, which gives a net balance of £14,819.25 that he will pay over at Completion.

You will, of course, have given thought to the financial aspects of the transaction before you agreed to buy, and have a pretty clear idea of your financial resources.

Finding the Funds

As a simple exercise, assuming that you are the purchaser, let us go through the figures on page 86 together. In this example, you have to find £27,547.27, i.e. the balance due to the vendor. You will receive £14,819.25 from the building society, leaving you to provide £12,728.02 from your own funds or from the proceeds of a simultaneous sale, or perhaps a mixture of both. For simplicity, we will assume that you are finding this sum from your funds.

Referring to the vendor's solicitor's completion statement which indicates how the sum due on Completion is to be split into two drafts, you would instruct your bank to issue a draft in favour of the vendor's solicitor for £12,728.02.

You would also ask your building society solicitor to arrange for the mortgage advance to be split into two drafts; one in favour of the vendor's solicitor for £3937.00 and one in favour of the vendor's building society for £10,882.25. (The drafts for £12,728.02 and £3937.00 together satisfy the vendor's solicitor's request for £16,665.02.)

So your simple sums in this example are:

Balance of purchase price	£27,547.27
Net mortgage advance available	£14,819.25
Sum required from other funds (Own funds or simultaneous sale etc)	£12,728.02
Provided as follows:	
Draft on own bank in favour of vendor's solicitor	£12,728.02
Draft from own building society in favour of vendor's solicitor	£3937.00
Draft from own building society in favour of vendor's building society	£10,882.25
	£27,547.27

A suggested draft letter to your building society solicitor is on page 155.

If this looks a little off-putting, bear up, it's really quite straightforward once you have studied it a couple of times.

Preparing for Completion

If you are selling and buying simultaneously your plan should be to arrange for your sale to be completed first, followed by your purchase. The whole sale process takes no more than 10 minutes, then you will be free to go to the venue agreed for the Completion of your purchase.

You should, however, take the opportunity to visit the property you are about to buy before you proceed to the Completion and I suggest that you arrange an interval between the two transactions of a couple of hours or so if possible.

If you can arrange to have the keys beforehand from the vendor or the estate agents, then do so. Look around the property to make sure that any items that the vendor agreed to leave are there, and in particular, that there is no one still in occupation. If, for some reason, you are not personally able to do this chore, get your wife or other reliable representative to do it for you, and give them a telephone number at which you can be contacted if necessary.

Needless to say, you would not complete if the house was not vacant. If items (chattels) for which you have paid or which it was agreed would be left have been removed, the matter should be raised at Completion BEFORE you proceed. If the question is left until after Completion you will merely have a virtually useless right of action, whereas if you press for a realistic sum in settlement before you complete there is every reason for the vendor's solicitor to find a solution.

One of the administrative tasks that you must finalise once you have agreed the times of Completion, is to make sure arrangements are in hand which will allow the removals van to drive directly to your new home after collecting its load from your 'old' house. Strictly, the keys should not be available to you until you have completed and your timing should allow for this. Ideally, you should arrange the timing so that you are already at your new home to meet the removals van when it arrives.

Needless to say you would not complete if the house was not vacant.

Completion of Your Purchase

When the great day and hour for Completion at last arrives you present yourself at the agreed venue armed with the documents. If yours is a simultaneous sale and purchase you will have already attended to the Completion of your own sale.

In the interest of clarity let's go through the Completion procedure that applies if you are getting a mortgage, and then the procedure if you are financing your purchase from your own resources.

Completion With a Mortgage

If you are getting a mortgage, the venue will be either at the office of your vendor's building society solicitor or your vendor's solicitor. (The latter case will apply if your vendor does not have a mortgage to pay off (redeem), or his solicitor is also acting for the vendor's building society.)

Your building society solicitor will be there on behalf of your building society, which will eventually retain all the documents relating to your ownership while the loan is outstanding.

Just to remind you, you take along:

- Mortgage deed already signed by your wife and yourself.
- Completed Stamps L(A)451 and Stamps 61
- Your bank draft(s) for the balance of the purchase price
- If you paid a deposit to the estate agent, take along a letter authorising its release. A specimen letter is on page 156.

So far you have seen only an abstract or photocopies of previous Conveyances. At Completion you will compare the originals of the deeds with the Abstract and duly certified photocopies you were sent. Check that the originals of all documents abstracted are produced to you, and that these span a period of at least 15 years.

That is the usual case. However, if the property you are buying was sold off from a larger area of land, the original deeds are held by the owner of the larger area. The purchaser of the land sold off would have received a Conveyance to himself and duly certified photocopies of the previous deeds for the larger area. In this event, you may not have original Conveyances of your plot going back at least 15 years, but merely the original Conveyance from the date it was sold off, say 10 years ago, and copies of previous Conveyances of the larger area of land.

Sorry if this seems complicated, but it is not really as bad as it sounds if you stop and think about it.

You can hardly fail to recognise the original of a Conveyance, as it is on fairly stiff paper and will have been signed, sealed and delivered by the parties to it. It will also have a 'P.D' stamp of the Inland Revenue and probably also duty stamps which are quite imposing.

A 'Vacating Receipt'

In the case of a mortgage on unregistered land (called a Legal Charge) when the mortgage loan is paid off (redeemed) the building society endorses the mortgage deed with a receipt signed by an authorised officer of the society and sealed with the society's official seal. This receipt is known as a 'vacating receipt' i.e. because the mortgage has been vacated or paid off. (This is also referred to as 'redeeming' the mortgage.)

Check that all mortgages paid off (vacated) have vacating receipts and, if a building society was the lender, that the society's seal and authorised signature are in place. If there is an existing mortgage on the property, you MUST receive the vendor's solicitor's written undertaking to discharge the mortgage. An example of such an undertaking is on page 155.

Assuming that these documents pass your scrutiny, you hand them to your building society solicitor, who will also check them.

You will now be handed the Conveyance from your vendor which his solicitor will pass to you. Check that this is indeed the Conveyance which

VACATING RECEIPT

Leeds Permanent Building Society hereby acknowledge to have received

all moneys intended to be secured by the within written deed

In Witness whereof the Seal of the Society is hereto affixed

this__________________ day of____________

by order of the Board of Directors in the presence of

____

by authority of the Board of Directors

When a mortgage loan is repaid the 'vacating receipt' is filled out and signed by an official of the building society. It acknowledges that the mortgage has been redeemed.

you have typed out so impeccably, and that the vendor has signed alongside the seal. The vendor's solicitor will hand you his written undertaking to discharge the mortgage, and this you pass to your building society solicitor together with the Conveyance.

You should now receive an N.H.B.C. certificate, if appropriate, and any guarantees that have been assigned to you such as timber treatment, cavity wall insulation and so on. You pass these documents to your building society solicitor who will keep them with the deeds. See page 141 for an example of an assignment of the benefit of guarantees.

The vendor's solicitor has now given you all the documents of title and in exchange you give him the purchase price. First you date the mortgage deed and pass this to your building society solicitor together with the Stamps L(A)451 and Stamps 61 forms.

He will produce the bank drafts in the sums you asked for. Check that the amounts and payees are correct. You then pass these drafts and your own bank draft to the vendor's solicitor, who will pass the appropriate draft to the vendor's building society solicitor.

If you paid a deposit to your vendor's estate agent, you now hand to your vendor's solicitor a letter authorising its release, see page 156 for an example. Payment of a deposit is less usual nowadays than it used to be, although in some parts of the country an estate agent may still ask for a deposit as a sign of good faith.

To recap. You have received all the old deeds and the Conveyance to you; in other words, your title to the property and any guarantees. In exchange you have given over the purchase price made up of the loan from your building society and your own money, perhaps from the sale of your last house.

All that remains is for the keys to be handed over. This usually is arranged by mutual agreement between seller and buyer.

A bank draft is a cheque drawn on bank and signed by an authorised signatory. A bank draft cannot be stopped, unlike a personal cheque, and is therefore regarded as the equivalent of cash.

Some solicitors have access to CHAPS. Not to be confused with the leather over-trousers worn by cowboys of the Golden West CHAPS stands for Clearing House Automated Payments System, the system for the electronic transfer of funds which enables completion monies to be transferred safely and quickly. It is not available to ordinary members of the public.

Completion Without a Mortgage

The procedure for Completion if you are not getting a mortgage is little different from that we have just run through.

The venue for Completion will either be at your vendor's solicitor's office if he has no mortgage on the property, or at the office of the vendor's building society solicitor. In practice, the vendor's solicitor may also act for the building society, and if so the venue will be his office.

As you are not getting a mortgage, there will not be a solicitor representing the building society present; you yourself retain the documents passed to you.

You only need take the bank drafts and, if you paid a deposit to an estate agent, a letter authorising its release (see page 156).

You check the deeds handed to you exactly as explained above and when you are satisfied, you retain possession of them. Similarly you check the Conveyance from the vendor to you, and when satisfied, retain possession. You also retain an N.H.B.C. certificate and any guarantees there may be affecting the property. You should be handed a letter from the vendor's solicitor assigning the benefit of the guarantees to you.

Having received the documents of ownership, you now exchange these for the purchase price by handing over the bank drafts the vendor's solicitor requested.

All that remains is for the keys to be handed over.

So there you are, you've done it! Congratulations. Not too bad, was it? And the next time you will be able to tackle it like a veteran.

After Completion

If you purchased with the aid of a mortgage your building society solicitor will attend to the post-completion formalities. If the land is an area of compulsory registration, the solicitor will apply for first registration. After about 10 or 12 weeks you can obtain an office copy of the land register by completing Form A44 Application for Office Copies (see page 157 for a sample form) and sending this to the appropriate District Land Registry.

As a matter of interest, when the property is first registered the District Land Registry sends not a Land Certificate but a Charge Certificate to the building society solicitor for transmission to the building society. An example of a Charge Certificate is on page 167.

If you purchased without a mortgage you yourself must deal with the various post-completion formalities.

Stamping the Conveyance or Assignment

The Conveyance (or Assignment, if leasehold) should be presented at any of the Inland Revenue stamp duty offices listed on page 121 within 30 days of Completion, together with a completed form Stamps L(A)451 (for a sample see page 151). When filling in Stamps L(A)451, if the property is leasehold complete box 6 thus: 'Assignment of residue of lease for a term of 99 years from (date) at an annual rent of £ . . .'. This task should be treated as a first priority. An official will impress the Inland Revenue stamp on the deed to indicate that it has been 'produced'. The official will calculate how much, if any, stamp duty is payable and will accept payment only in cash. The Conveyance is then stamped to indicate the amount of stamp duty paid. Do please bear in mind that the original copy of the Conveyance MUST be presented, whether or not stamp duty is payable. If it is more convenient you can do all this through the post. Complete Stamps L(A)451 and Stamps 61 and send these with the Conveyance and any stamp duty payable by recorded delivery to the designated stamp office listed on page 121.

Current rates of stamp duty are on page 119.

If the land conveyed is not in an area of compulsory registration, you have reached the end of your stint as a conveyancer, having now completed all the steps involved in securing the transfer of ownership of the property from the vendor to yourself.

If, however, the property is within an area of compulsory registration, it is your responsibility to apply for the first registration of unregistered land. The procedure is quite straightforward and is described in the section which follows.

First Registration of Unregistered Land

When applying for first registration of unregistered land, you are required to submit all the deeds and documents relating to the land to the appropriate office of H.M. Land Registry serving the area in which the land is located.

There the documents are examined, and provided that they show you are the legal owner of the land, the Land Registry will issue you a Land Certificate with its own unique title number.

The first step is to collect all the deeds and documents relating to the land and list them in chronological order. Form A13 'List of Documents sent to H.M. Land Registry' is included in the forms pack and a completed sample is on page 165. You require four copies, three of which accompany the documents to the District Land Registry, the other copy which is retained by you. Send the documents by recorded delivery. The Land Registry will return one copy of Form A13 as a receipt, and will insert the time likely to be taken to complete the registration. Note that a certified true copy of the deed by which the property was transferred to you and the original of this deed must be included in the documents. You 'certify' the copy deed, having dated it with the date of the execution of its original, by writing at the head 'I certify that this is a true copy of the original deed', and signing and dating it. If you are buying jointly with your wife, she must also sign the certificate, which should then read 'We certify . . .'

You also complete Form 1A (if leasehold Form 2A) on which you apply for first registration. As you will see from the completed Form 1A on page 166 or Form 2A on page 168, there is nothing difficult about this. H.M. Land Registry have produced Explanatory Leaflet No. 2 'Application for First Registration Made By An Owner' which you may find useful. It is available from any District Land Registry free of charge.

Checking the Documents

When all the documents are gathered together, do another check to satisfy yourself that they agree with the chronological list on Form A13 before sending them to the District Land Registry by recorded delivery, together with Form 1A (or 2A), which we have just discussed, and your cheque for the fee payable.

To recap, your final pile of documents should include:

- Form A13 in triplicate listing all documents being forwarded
- All the documents listed on Form A13 in chronological order
- The original property transfer document
- Certified true copy of property transfer document
- Form 1A (or 2A) Application for First Registration
- Cheque for Land Registry fees in favour of H.M. Land Registry
- Solicitor's undertaking in respect of discharge of mortgage

When you receive the Land Certificate check all the details carefully but if you spot any errors do not attempt to correct them. You must return the certificate to the District Land Registry with a note of explanation.

Check that your names (and your wife's names, if appropriate) are spelled correctly, the address of the property is correct and that there are no apparent errors on the certificate.

As was explained on page 90, if you have a mortgage the District Land Registry will send a Charge Certificate to the building society solicitor to send on to the building society. The building society will retain the Charge Certificate and all the old deeds, searches, etc, relating to the property until the mortgage loan has been paid off.

Obtaining a Copy for Yourself

You can, however, obtain an office copy of the Land Register by completing Form A44 Application for Office Copies. I suggest that you make contact with the building society's solicitor, say, 10 weeks or so after Completion and enquire whether he has received the Charge Certificate, and if so ask for the title number. You insert this title number in the appropriate box on Form A44, which you then complete and send to the District Land Registry. No fee is payable for this service. Your office copies will arrive within a few days of application showing you to be the new owner of the property. A completed form A44 is on page 157 and there is a blank form for your use in the forms pack.

Leasehold Property

It is the usual requirement of a lease that notice of a change of ownership must be given to the landlord. Such notice is usually sent to the landlord's agents, and the lease may stipulate that a fee is payable for dealing with the notice. You may recall that Q6 of the Requisitions on Title asked 'to whom should notice of any dealings with the property be given?'. A suggested notice is set out on page 157. Send a letter along these lines, in duplicate, to the appropriate person together with any fee payable. Ask the recipient to sign and return one copy of the notice as a receipt. It usually helps things along if you enclose a stamped and self-addressed envelope as well. When the receipted copy is returned, unless you have a mortgage on the property, keep the document with the title deeds as evidence that this term of the lease has been complied with. If you have a mortgage you should send the receipted copy to the building society solicitor to lodge with the deeds they hold.

Well Done!

Having finally reached the end of your purchase I hope you will agree that conveyancing procedures are not so much difficult as long-winded. It is largely a matter of becoming familiar with the forms, the terms and the legal jargon.

One last thing you should remember is to cancel your previous insurance; and if the property was mortgaged make a note to ask for a refund from the building society in case you paid your premiums in advance.

Buyer's Timetable From Exchange to Completion

The following is a typical timetable of the various stages of purchasing a property from Exchange of Contracts to Completion. It follows on from steps 1 to 18 in Chapter 3 that took you as far as Exchange of Contracts.

FROM EXCHANGE OF CONTRACTS TO COMPLETION

STEP	STAGE	DAY
19	Investigate vendor's title	4
20	Prepare your Requisitions on Title (Con 28B)	4
21	Draft the purchase deed	6
22	Consider replies to Requisitions on Title	8
23	Send all relevant documents to building society's solicitor.	8
24	Receive building society solicitor's Requisitions on Title and forward to vendor's solicitor.	12
25	Receive draft mortgage deed. Receive statement of amount available.	12
26	Draft the purchase deed and submit for approval.	12
27	Receive replies to building society solicitor's Requisitions on Title and forward to building society's solicitor.	15
28	Receive draft purchase deed 'approved'. Approve the draft mortgage deed.	15
29	Engross and execute the purchase deed.	18
30	Send purchase deed to vendor's solicitor.	18
31	Receive engrossed mortgage deed and execute the same.	19
32	Make a pre-completion search.	20
33	Receive Completion statement.	21
34	Arrange for bank drafts in specified amounts.	21
35	Receive result of pre-completion search.	24
36	Completion	28

The total time elapsed since your original offer to purchase is now two months.

POST COMPLETION (only if buying without a mortgage)

STEP	STAGE	
37	Present purchase deed for stamping	5 days
38	Apply to register change of ownership (registered land)	8 weeks
39	Apply for first registration (if applicable)	3 months

Selling the Roof Over Your Head

Finding a buyer for your home is the tricky bit — the part that calls for a nerve wracking combination of practice and sheer good luck. Compared with the exhilaration of reaching a verbal agreement on the price, the legal steps of selling are a pretty pedestrian piece of work.

Selling is Easier

As you followed the legal steps involved in buying a house, described in the preceding pages, you will no doubt have concluded that a domestic conveyancing transaction is, as I have suggested, well within the capacity of anyone of average intelligence and common sense.

Selling a house is even easier.

Whereas when you were buying you investigated the vendor's title (ownership), and satisfied yourself that he indeed owned the property, checked various matters with the local Council, e.g. possible planning approvals that could affect your use of the property, and made enquiries regarding such matters as fences and boundaries, disputes, and so on; when selling you have only one concern — to receive the agreed purchase price from your buyer on a given date.

Finding a Buyer

The methods used to find buyers tend to vary with the state of the housing market. This market has fluctuated violently over the past decade. There have been times when demand for houses has exceeded the supply; prices soared and a new word 'gazumping' found its way into common use.

At other times the market has been flat, with very little activity discernible.

Of course, when houses are in short supply and sell readily many sellers are able to find buyers by advertising their house themselves. Others, regardless of the state of the market, instruct an estate agent or (quite often) several estate agents.

Sell-It-Yourself

Certainly if you can sell the house yourself you will save a considerable sum in estate agent's commissions. The rate charged by agents tends to vary considerably, depending on the area in which the property is situated and how successfully the seller haggles with the agent.

Unless you are desperate to sell, it may be well worth while to try one or two insertions of a well-written, informative advertisement in the press, put up a 'For Sale' board and tell your friends.

On the other hand, estate agents have a network of contacts and may even have someone on their books requiring just such a property as yours.

Estate Agents' Commissions

As a rule of thumb, the commission rate charged in much of the South of England is around 2½% of selling price, in the London area the rate can be as high as 3½%, whilst in the Midlands and further North about 2% plus the cost of advertising is usual.

The granting of a 'sole agency' for a limited period should reduce the rate of commission by ½% or ¾%. Personally, I think there are advantages in granting a sole agency for a period of say six to eight weeks, as a sole agent will naturally do all he can to make the sale and earn all the commission for himself.

The major associations to which bona fide estate agents belong are the Royal Institution of Chartered Surveyors with around 14,000 members, the Incorporated Society of Valuers and Auctioneers who have about 7,000 members and the National Association of Estate Agents with a membership of just under 4,000. Each of these bodies has an indeminity or bonding scheme which safeguards deposit money. Their addresses are listed on page 124 and they will provide a list of members in your region.

One major defect of the Estate Agents Act 1979 is that virtually anyone without a criminal record can set up shop as an estate agent. No mimimum level of competence is required and, since only 70% of estate agents belong to a recognised body with a code of professional conduct, you can find a very varied quality of service.

A forest of estate agent's boards can mean one of two things; an up and coming area (wiuth rubble-filled skips also in view) or a property that is particularly difficult to sell.

Instructing an Estate Agent

If you decide to instruct an estate agent ensure that he is a member of one of the recognised bodies. You would be wise to compare the charges of other agents, bearing in mind that cheapest rates do not necessarily provide best results. A good yardstick is local reputation, for just as the 'cheapest' is not necessarily the best, so the 'biggest' may not provide the degree of personal service that is required to sell your house quickly.

In many parts of the country the rates of commission quoted are much the same between one agent and another; the principal factor distinguishing agents is the quality of service provided.

Before instructing an estate agent, therefore, you should shop around; make enquiries as to the services offered and the total cost, and satisfy yourself that the agent will get the best price for your property. You should thoroughly discuss the terms of any agency agreement with the estate agent you propose to instruct and he should confirm the agreement in writing.

A number of estate agents are at long last emerging, albeit hesitantly, from the old fashioned ways of doing business and quite substantial amounts of capital now back some of them. In general, estate agents rank low down in public esteem and the vast majority of people with a house to sell simply do not believe that agents provide the services or efficiency to justify their relatively high rates of commission. Not all estate agents deserve these strictures, but undoubtedly there is too little competition, too little real service and too many cosy arrangements between agents as to fees.

New Wave Estate Agents

Prudential, the insurance giant has reported that they have 225 estate agents in their Prudential Property Services chain and there are plans to increase this to 500 by the end of 1987. The size of such a chain is vast when compared with the standard traditional estate agency, but both the Lloyds Bank Black Horse chain of estate agents and the Hambro Countryside chain are claimed to be bigger still.

More moves to link up with estate agents are afoot. Nationwide Building Society (Britain's third largest) plans to have a network of 350 estate agents by the end of 1987, and Halifax has already made a cautious move into the estate agency field by buying up 18 estate agents. No doubt there are other, as yet unannounced, plans by insurance companies, building societies and financial groups to enter the estate agency field.

But the injection of investment capital referred to, the entry of cash-rich outsiders into the business and other developments in train can be expected to act as catalyst for sweeping changes of attitude among the more staid estate agents. All of which is to be welcomed.

One other development that is having an impact is the use of computer technology to match a seller's property with a buyer's requirements. A number of companies offering this service are established throughout the country. One thing they have in common is that the fees charged are very much lower than those of a typical estate agent. Examples quoted as 'typical' include, in London, a fee of £70 charged to the seller of a £35,000 house compared with an estate agent's estimate of £1,000 and, in the provinces, £60 as against a £700 fee to an estate agent. Most of these computer property shops offer a whole range of services; valuations, surveys and mortgage brokerage.

Proceeding With the Sale

Let us assume that you now have a prospective buyer who has made you an offer for your property. If the offer is a realistic one, i.e. not such that you would reject it out of hand, you should then try to determine the likelihood of the deal going through. Is he a cash buyer? Is his property already on the market? If 'yes' what sort of interest has been expressed? Has he been promised a mortgage? When could he complete?

A Token Deposit

By this sort of questioning you can decide whether the offer is truly serious. Perhaps the best test of this is his willingness to make a deposit of, say, £100 as a token of good faith. In return you agree to take your property off the market. This is perfectly fair, so do not be shy about asking for a deposit which, of course would be refundable if for some reason the sale did not go through.

Let us assume, therefore, that you have a serious prospective purchaser who has paid a token deposit and that you have agreed to proceed 'subject to contract'. You should tell your prospective purchaser that you will be doing your own conveyancing and obtain from him his:

1) Full name (and that of his wife if they are buying jointly)

2) Postal address
3) Telephone number
4) Solicitor's or conveyancer's name, address and telephone number.

If you instructed an estate agent, you should telephone him with particulars of the arrangement you have agreed and give him the details of your buyer and his solicitor.

If you did not instruct an estate agent, then write to the buyer confirming his agreement to purchase and send a copy of your letter to his solicitor. A suggested draft letter is on page 170.

One other thing you should do at this stage, if you have not already done so, is either call at his office or write to the solicitor who acted for you when you bought the house you now intend to sell, asking him to let you have the file of that transaction. The file may be useful, so do not be shy about asking the solicitor for it — after all, the documents it contains are yours. See the sample letter on page 172. The file contains copies of the solicitor's pre-contract enquiries, Requisitions on Title, old searches, plans, correspondence and so on, all of which could be useful to you.

Preparing to Repay Your Mortgage

As soon as possible after you decide to put your property on the market you should write to your building society telling them of your intention to sell and to discharge the mortgage. Ask them to tell you how much is required to pay off the mortgage on the anticipated Completion date.

If the land is registered land, ask them to supply you with the title number, and in the case of leasehold land, a copy of the lease.

If the land is unregistered, ask them to send the title deeds to a solicitor on their panel who is located conveniently to you, and to give you the solicitor's name and address when they have done so. If you do this before you have a purchaser, you can press on without delay once someone makes a serious offer. See the draft letter on page 171.

If your property is registered land, you will only need the following forms in connection with its sale:

2 Contract forms
1 Form A44 Application for Office Copies

If the land is unregistered, you need only:

2 Contract Forms

All these forms are to be found in the blank forms pack.

Preliminaries Before Drafting Your Contract

Your first step is to send the purchaser's solicitor a draft contract.

In order to do this you need the title deeds for the property. Bear with me for a few moments while I briefly explain the concept of 'deeds'. A deed is a written document, 'signed, sealed and delivered', and in practice, so far as landed property is concerned, the term is used to embrace Conveyances, mortgages, assignments and so on. 'Title' is the term used to denote ownership and 'title deeds' are the deeds which prove ownership of freehold or leasehold property.

In the case of freehold *unregistered* property, the title deeds will usually consist of conveyances which show how you, and any person(s) who owned the property before you, became the legal owner of the property. For a fuller discussion refer to pages 73-76.

If your property is *registered* a 'Land Certificate' takes the place of Conveyances and other title deeds used in conveyancing. When registered property is mortgaged instead of a Land Certificate a 'Charge Certificate' is issued by H.M. Land Registry which is held by the building society, bank or other lender which made the loan.

Title Deeds
Now to return to the preliminaries before drafting your contract. If your property is registered land, you need a copy of the Land Register, and if it is unregistered land you need to 'have sight' of the title deeds.

If you do not have a mortgage on the property, then you will already have the title deeds, either in your actual possession or in the custody of, usually, your bank.

If like most owner-occupiers you have a mortgage on your property, the deeds, i.e. the Charge Certificate in the case of registered land or the title deeds (Conveyances and other documents) in the case of unregistered land will be held by the building society, bank or other lender who provided the loan.

If the property is registered land you can obtain an 'office copy' (office copy means official copy) of the Land Register by filling out Form A44 Application for Office Copies. The Form A44 is a simple form (an example is found on page 173) and when completed should be sent to the appropriate District Land Registry. A list of District Land Registries is on pages 122-123. In a few days you will receive the office copies of the Land Register.

Covenants
If the house is unregistered, your building society will have sent the title deeds as you requested to their solicitor. You must go to his office to inspect the deeds. From these documents you 'extract' the restrictive covenants and other matters affecting the land and also a plan of the land. For just exactly what 'extracting' involves, please bear with me a little while longer.

Frequently the restrictive covenants are set out in a schedule towards the end of a Conveyance, if not they will most certainly be set out in the body of the document. In either case it is a simple matter to make a note of where they are in a Conveyance. What you are trying to do is ascertain what covenants affect the property and where they are in the Conveyance or Conveyances which you are examining. Generally, you will not find this difficult, but if occasionally you run into problems, this will most likely be because you are handling unfamiliar documents rather than the nature of the task.

To take an easy example. Let us assume that the Conveyance to you is dated sixteen years previously and reads in part '. . . the Vendors as Beneficial Owners hereby convey unto the Purchasers ALL THAT (followed by a description of the property conveyed) *TO HOLD* the same unto the Purchasers in fee simple Subject to the restrictive and other covenants set out in Schedule Four thereof'. In this simple example you need only obtain a copy of the Conveyance and extract the covenants contained in Schedule Four.

Now let us take things a stage further. Assume the Conveyance to you is dated sixteen years earlier, but this time reads in part '. . . Subject to the restrictive and other covenants conditions and other matters contained mentioned or referred to in a Conveyance dated the First day of March One thousand nine hundred and fifty nine (hereinafter called "the Conveyance") and made between Eric Brown of the one part and

John Smith and Mary Smith of the other part'. In this case you will require sight of the 1959 Conveyance which may contain the covenants to which the land is subject or which will refer to one or more earlier Conveyances. You have to continue with your detective work until you locate the Conveyance in which the covenants are spelled out in detail. You will also be looking for a plan of the land. You may strike it lucky and find this is annexed (stapled) to the Conveyance to you. If not, the Conveyenace to you will refer to an earlier Conveyance to which the plan is annexed or on which it is drawn. So whichever it is, you should have little difficulty in locating the plan.

Now that you know what you are looking for, and in which Conveyance(s), it may be that there are spare copies (there frequently are). If you draw a blank and there are no spare copies in either file, ask the building society solicitor to have photocopies run off for you. You will, of course, have to pay him for this service.

Documents to the Buyer's Solicitor

You will be sending either the office copy of the Land Certificate or the photocopy of the restrictive covenants and other matters affecting the land and the plan of the land (if it is unregistered) to your purchaser's solicitor together with a draft contract. One important point needs to be mentioned. If the spare plan, which you found in the file or was photocopied for you, is not coloured to indicate the boundaries of the land you are selling colour the boundaries by edging them red. Before sending the office copy, it is permissable and normal practice to cut out any reference to the price paid which may appear in section B after your name. And so to the contract.

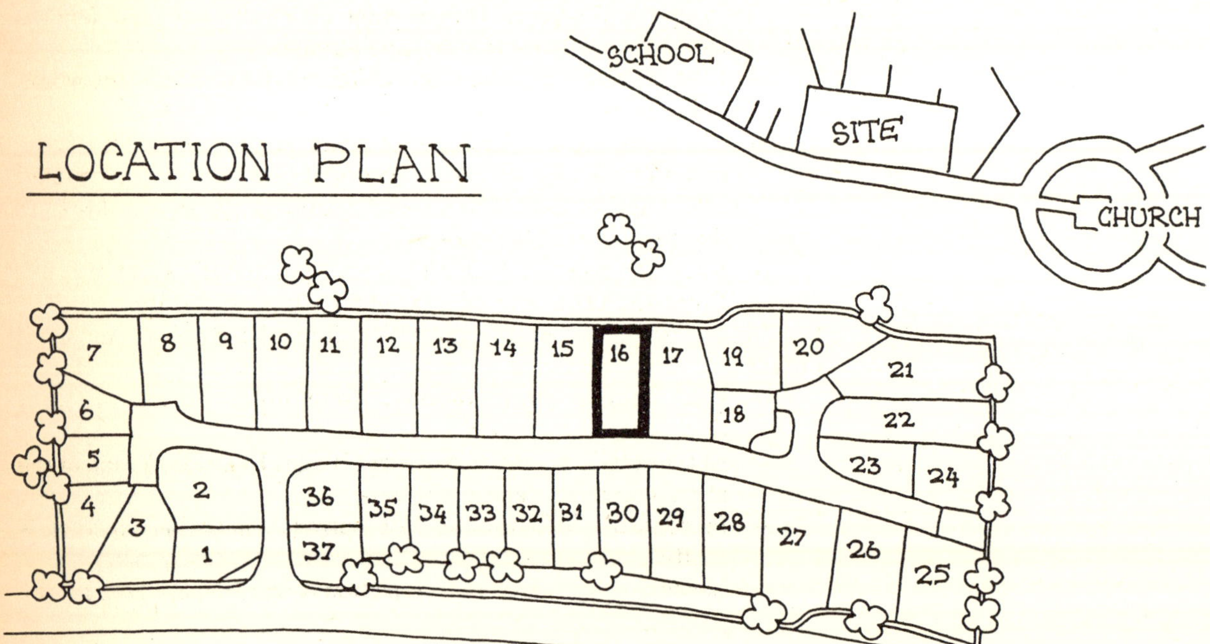

The typical location plan of an unregistered property is annexed to the conveyance. It identifies the property by marking its boundaries — usually in red. This plan shows the plot in relation to other properties and also highlights prominent local features.

Your Contract to Sell

This is the document which, when signed and exchanged by the parties, will commit both sides to go through with the deal. It is prepared by the person selling. Some solicitors use a standard contract form, either the 'National Conditions of Sale' or 'The Law Society Conditions of Sale' form. Both of these forms are copyright and you may find it difficult to purchase a copy. However, there is absolutely no requirement that either of these forms be used and in fact, with the increased usage of word processors many solicitors now produce their own form of contract. I have drafted a simple Form of Contract for you to use. For your guidance, on pages 176 and 177 I have reproduced contracts for the sale of freehold registered land and freehold unregistered land, and on pages 178 and 179, drafts for the sale of registered and unregistered leasehold land.

Armed with your office copy of the Land Register, or copy of restrictive covenants and the Conveyance to you, you should have no difficulty in filling out the appropriate contract. (If your property is leasehold, you will also need a copy of the lease.)

Contracts for Registered Freehold Land

If we go through the registered freehold contract on page 176 together, you will see that there is nothing difficult to it. On the front page of the form headed 'Contract for Sale' work through in order:

- Insert your full name as the vendor and, if your wife is co-owner, her full name.
- Insert the full name of the purchaser(s).
- Enter the address of the property as shown in Section A of the Property Register. This section also tells you the land is freehold and gives you the title number.
- Enter agreed purchase price, in figures and words — the words in brackets.
- The usual deposit is 10% of the purchase price. Enter the name and address of your estate agents. If you have not instructed estate agents, insert the name of a bank that is prepared to hold the deposit as stakeholders.
- Enter the name and address of your purchaser's solicitor.
- Enter the name and address of your local authority.

On the reverse of the form headed 'Conditions for Sale' in numerical order:

- Enter details in condition 2 from office copies or Land Certificate.
- Enter details in condition 4 from Charges Register section of the office copies or Land Certificate.
- In condition 5 enter the rate current when the contract is drafted.
- Leave the date fixed for Completion (Condition 5) blank for the present.
- By expressing your capacity as 'Beneficial Owner' you imply four covenants (condition 8).

  These are:

  (a) That you have full power to convey the property, i.e. the right to sell it.

  (b) That the purchaser may enjoy quiet possession of the property, known as a covenant for quiet enjoyment

(c) That the property shall be conveyed to the purchaser freed from or indeminfied against all incumbrances. Although most usually treated as a separate covenant in text books (b) and (c) are really one covenant. For example, the purchaser's 'quiet enjoyment' may be affected by an undisclosed easement.

(d) That you will do anything reasonably necessary if requested by the purchaser to fully vest the property in him. This is known as a covenant for further assurance.

In Plain English

If you are not too dizzy after all that gobbledegook stay with me and I will try to explain Condition 8 in ordinary language.

(a) Is fairly straight forward.

(b) 'Quiet possession' is a difficult concept to try to convey but in essence it means that you assure your purchaser that you own the property and there is no one who can come along and assert a legal right to it.

(c) 'Incumbrances' is a term that covers all rights that others may have in or over the property. Examples include leases, mortgages, easements and restrictive covenants.

An 'Easement' is a right possessed by a man over his neighbour's property. Examples of easements are rights of way, rights of light, the right to draw water, the right to run water, gas and drainage pipes on, over or under a property and the right to enter on to the property to repair them, the right to enter on to an adjoining property to repair or maintain one's own property, e.g. say a garage erected on the boundary, and so on. There are many other examples but I hope this gives you a general picture.

So, incumbrances of which you have knowledge should be disclosed to your purchaser before he signs the contract. You are in effect promising your purchaser that apart from incumbrances entered on the Land Register (and the purchaser has been provided with office copies) there are no undisclosed incumbrances affecting your property.

(d) You are saying that you will do everything necessary to put right any defect there may be in your title (ownership) of the property. A recent example of this within my experience relates to the sale of a property described as freehold but in respect of which, in the office copies, was recorded a lease still apparently in force. The owner of the property had bought it as a leasehold property 30 years ago and 10 years ago had bought the freehold. By that time the area in which the property was situated had been declared an area of compulsory registration and so on purchase of the freehold interest the owner was required to apply for 'first registration' at H.M. Land Registry.

Now for a bit more legal jargon. As both the freehold interest and the leasehold interest were both owned by the same person, the lease merged and was extinguished in the freehold. The property became freehold and no longer subject to a lease. 'Merger' in these circumstances is easily accomplished by completing the relevant paragraph of the form of application for first registration (Form 1B if a solicitor makes the application, Form 1A if the owner applies). In effect this paragraph, when completed, asks the Land Registry not to enter the lease on the Land Register. When the solicitor applied for 'first registration' he forgot to complete this paragraph, no one noticed his omission until the owner came to sell ten years later. The 'problem' was easily resolved by the owner agreeing to sell both the freehold and the leasehold interests, and when the new purchaser applied to H.M. Land Registry to record the change of owner he also applied for the entry relating to the lease to be deleted.

This little anecdote explains, I hope, what 'a covenant for further assurance' means in ordinary English.

Selling as 'Personal Representative'

Please note that if you are an executor of the Will of the person who owned the property and have obtained a grant of probate, you will be selling as 'personal representative'. If the deceased owner died without leaving a Will, you will also be selling as 'personal representative' by virtue of the Letters of Administration granted by the District Probate Registry of the High Court.

And that is your draft contract for the sale of registered land drawn up.

You type this out, using the blank contract forms from the forms pack, with your own two fingers (or someone else's two hands), and produce a top copy and two carbon copies. Send the top copy and one carbon copy, together with the office copy of the Land Certificate and filed plan to your purchaser's solicitor, making sure that you have snipped out any reference in the office copy to the price you paid. Send a covering letter along the lines of the suggested draft on page 172 and do remember to use the magic words 'subject to contract'.

Contracts for Unregistered Freehold Land

On the front of the form of contract headed 'Contract for Sale' work through in order:

- Insert your full names as the vendor, and if your wife is co-owner, her full names.
- Insert full names of your purchasers.
- Extract the details from the Conveyances to you and insert in the box headed 'Particulars'.
- Enter agreed purchase price, in figures and words — the words in brackets.
- The usual deposit is 10% of the purchase price.
- Enter the name and address of your purchaser's solicitor.
- Enter the name and address of your local authority.

On the reverse of the form headed 'Conditions of Sale':

- Condition 3 starts 'The abstract of title shall begin with'. As you know, in the case of unregistered land, the owner does not have evidence of his title (ownership) conveniently recorded in one document (i.e. a Land Certificate) as does the owner of registered land, but in a Conveyance or Conveyances stretching back at least fifteen years. These Conveyances record the changes in ownership over a period of years, thus:

  1 April 1952 Conveyed by White to Smith
  30 June 1964 Smith conveyed to Brown
  18 May 1979 Brown conveyed to vendor

  Your condition 3 of the draft contract would therefore read: 'The abstract of title shall begin with a conveyance on sale dated 30 June 1964 between Henry Smith of the one part and John Brown of the other part'.
- Condition 4 of the draft contract refers to restrictive covenants

and other matters to which the property is subject and here you refer to the Conveyance or Conveyances in which these are spelled out in detail. It is a copy of these covenants which you will be sending to your purchaser's solicitor with the draft contract.

Contracts for Leasehold Land

In the case of leasehold land, whether registered or unregistered, you proceed as explained above but in addition you also send a copy of the lease. Your covering letter should be modified accordingly, e.g. 'I also enclose copy of the lease'.

Purchaser's Enquiries Before Contract

Within about two weeks of sending the draft contract to your purchaser's solicitor you will receive from him a form listing a series of questions relating to your property. Almost invariably the form used will be the Oyez Publishing standard form Conveyancing 29 (Long). This runs to four pages, the fourth page containing enquiries specifically referring to leasehold properties, and space that is provided for 'additional enquiries'.

Some of the questions are very wide and incapable of a precise answer, but the only advice I can offer is to answer the questions truthfully and as helpfully as possible. Remember that if you have obtained the file from the solicitor who acted for you when you purchased the property you are now selling you will see how he answered the questions. If a question is clearly worded and you know the answer, then give it. If a question is posed in woolly verbiage (e.g. Q.7 on 'Shared Facilities'), unless you know that pipes and drains serving neighbouring properties pass over or under your land, you can give the standard response, 'Not to the Vendor's knowledge but the property is sold subject to any there may be'.

In any event, do not lose any sleep over the form. So long as your answers are honest and preferably helpful, if the purchaser's solicitor is dissatisfied with a particular answer you have given, e.g. because the question was not understood, the worst he can do is ask you to be more specific. You can justifiably reply, courteously, 'If you will ask me precisely what it is you want to know, I will do my best to give you the information if it is within my knowledge'. In practice, solicitors and clerks who handle the paperwork are so accustomed to using stereotyped phrases as answers themselves and receiving the same sort of stock replies from other solicitors that you not likely to encounter any problem. There is a completed Ole Series form on pages 180 and 181 which may help you fill in your answers, and a draft letter to cover their return to the solicitor is on page 182.

The Draft Contract — Approved

Around a week or so after you returned the form Conveyancing 29 (Long), you should receive from the purchaser's solicitor a copy of the draft contract you sent him. This will either be 'approved', or the purchaser's solicitor may suggest one or more changes to the draft. These suggested changes will be written in red and it is both usual and courteous to discuss these with you beforehand.

The suggested draft contract is perfectly fair and reasonable and the only change you should normally agree to would be to provide a clause if some items in your house are to be included in the sale price.

The wording of such a clause and the apportionment for stamp duty purposes is discussed in section 6 on page 44.

If you agree to the addition of such a clause you must make quite certain that both your copy and your buyer's copy of the draft contract are amended with identical wording.

You will remember that originally you sent to the purchaser's solicitor two copies of the draft contract, i.e. one top copy and one carbon copy, for his use. He has now sent you the carbon copy, marked 'approved' (or with an acceptable amendment), and you now await the top copy of the approved contract signed by the purchaser.

Exchange of Contracts

After your purchaser has approved the contract, some little time may elapse before he is able to exchange contracts with you. He may be tying up his own finance or his own sale may be delayed; it could be any of a number of reasons.

In practice, it is usual for the purchaser's solicitor to telephone his opposite number to indicate that he is now ready to exchange and to obtain confirmation that the other side is also ready to exchange. As between solicitor and solicitor, they will exchange contracts verbally relying on professional integrity that each will act as agreed over the telephone. Solicitors are usually not prepared to extend their confidence in the same manner when dealing with a lay person, so that in most cases the solicitor will telephone simply to discuss 'exchange' and 'Completion'. Providing that you are ready to exchange and to agree a Completion date, a day or so later you should receive the contract signed by the purchaser. *Make sure that the deposit has been paid as provided by the contract.* Insert the agreed Completion date in both copies of the contract (for you are now holding both copies) and sign and date the copy you will send to your purchaser's solicitor 'in exchange'. If you are selling jointly, both co-owners should sign.

Send the copy of the contract you have signed with a covering letter along the lines of the suggested draft on page 182.

If the property is registered land and you are using the contract blank provided in the forms pack, Clause 12 of this is an authority to inspect the Land Register so you do not need to also send a form 201. If however you have bought a contract blank from a law stationer you should send a completed form 201 'Authority to Inspect the Register'.

In the case of unregistered land, you also send an Abstract of Title — see page 183 for example. You photocopy the Conveyance or Conveyances that trace title (ownership) to you over at least the previous fifteen years and send these together with the Abstract which you have typed up to the purchaser's solicitor.

Exchange of Contracts is a very important stage in a conveyancing transaction because from the moment of posting your copy of the contract, both parties are legally bound.

Synchronising Your Sale and Next Purchase

If yours is a simultaneous sale and purchase do, I beg you, re-read the procedure outlines on pages 52-53 and carefully follow the steps set out in that section.

The importance of this cannot be over emphasised. Remember, right up to the moment of exchange of contracts something could go wrong which causes either the sale or purchase transaction to fall through. You must make doubly sure that in the unfortunate event of this happening you are in a position to call things off and are not left high and dry.

Redeeming Your Mortgage

Now that contracts have been exchanged, you should contact the solicitor who is acting for your building society or bank to ascertain the amount required to pay off your mortgage on the date agreed for Completion. Ask also what daily rate of repayment the building society or bank will require in the event that Completion is delayed for a few days.

Do this preferably by writing to the solicitor — a suggested draft letter is on page 184. If Completion is delayed for some reason, as does occasionally happen, this daily rate multiplied by the number of days delay must be added to the sum required to pay off your mortgage. Condition 5 of the suggested contract on page 176 provides for the payment of interest by the purchaser if Completion is delayed slightly. By 'slightly' I am thinking in terms of a delay of, say, four or five days. Whilst such delay may prove inconvenient and involve you in having to make various re-arrangements, providing you are told in good time it is usually possible to take such a setback in one's stride.

Leasehold — Notifying the Landlord

If your property is leasehold, the lease probaby provides that you are to give notice of your intention to assign the benefit of the lease. If this is the case, write to the landlord or his agents, i.e. the person or firm to whom you pay the ground rent, along the lines of the suggested draft letter on page 184, together with any fee that may be payable for handling your notice. Enclose a self-addressed and stamped envelope in which the receipted duplicate copy of the letter may be returned to you.

Your Purchaser's Requisitions on Title

Quite soon after you exchanged contracts, you should receive from the purchaser's solicitor a form containing a number of questions known as 'Requisitions on Title'. These may be on an Oyez Publishing form (Con 28B) or on a form that the solicitor himself has devised. Whichever form is used none of the questions posed should present you with any difficulty, and they can be expected to be quite straightforward. If you have obtained your file from the solicitor who acted for you when you bought the property you are now selling, you can see how he replied to the questions. For illustrative purposes I have reproduced the Ole series Requisitions on Title page 161 and as you can see none of the questions is difficult to answer.

It may, however, be helpful to comment on Question 4. This is concerned with mortgages. Naturally the purchaser's solicitor wishes to ensure that if your property is mortgaged, this mortgage will be discharged at or before Completion. The answer, therefore, to Q4(a) is 'Agreed'.

Form 53 — Registered Land
Next the solicitor asks in Q4(B)(1) whether the 'discharge of a registered charge' will be handed over on Completion. In the case of registered land this is given on Form 53 'Discharge of a Registered Charge'. Form 53 was discussed briefly on page 59. It is a form used to certify that an outstanding mortgage (charge) has been paid off (discharged). Rarely, if ever, do building societies lodge a signed and sealed Form 53 with their solicitor in readiness for Completion. Instead, the solicitor acting for them will give an undertaking (i.e. they will guarantee) to forward the sealed Form 53 within 14–21 days of Completion, which of course is after the building society has received the money required to pay off the mortgage.

Unregistered Land
In the case of unregistered land the procedure is similar except that there is no special discharge form such as Form 53. The mortgage deed itself is endorsed with a receipt for the money received, and sealed by the building society, see page 88. The lender's solicitor gives an undertaking to forward the sealed (discharged) mortgage deed within 14-21 days (see page 155).

Nothing else on Con 28B calls for comment. Just complete it and send it back to the purchaser's solicitor.

Draft Purchase Deed

The purchase (or Transfer) deed is prepared by the purchaser's solicitor.

Registered Land
In the case of registered land most solicitors use a standard Form 19 or, if the purchase is in joint names, Form 19(JP). Most usually the form is sent to the vendor with a carbon copy for his own use, the top copy or original becoming the 'engrossment' after the vendor has approved it. An engrossment is legal jargon for the fair copy of a deed. That is to say, it is the document which is actually to be signed, in contrast to an earlier draft of it.

Either with the Requisitions on Title, or perhaps a day or so later, you will receive the draft purchase deed and copy from the purchaser's solicitor. There really is very little for you to do in 'approving' Form 19 or Form 19(JP). You merely check that the information is correct, i.e. the title number, address of property, selling price is as agreed, and the names are as stated in the contract.

Indemnity Covenant
When you purchased the property you are now selling you may have given what in jargon terms is called 'a covenant and for indemnity'. This means that you may have given an undertaking to observe and perform the covenants relating to the property which are set out in the Charges Register, and in the event that you failed to observe and perform the covenants you agreed to indemnify your then vendor if a claim was made against him in respect of your breach. If you did give such a covenant there will be a note in the office copies in Section B of the Proprietorship Register. Such a note will read something like this 'NOTE: The Transfer to the proprietors contains a purchaser's personal covenant. (Copy of covenant in land certificate)'.

You in turn will require your purchaser to give you a similar undertaking to observe and perform the covenants and to indemnify you against any claims that may be made in the event that your purchaser fails to observe and perform these covenants. The form of words usually used for this indemnity is as appears at the foot of Form 19 and Form 19(JP) on pages 186 and 187. So check that this clause has been included on the draft form of the Transfer. And if it has been omitted insist that it be added.

Providing all is correct, you now 'approve' the draft Transfer by writing to the purchaser's solicitor accordingly, along the lines of the suggested draft letter on page 188.

Unregistered Land

In the case of unregistered land, the draft purchase deed is a Conveyance and is prepared by the purchaser's solicitor. Conveyances were considered in some detail on pages 73-75 and you may wish to refresh your memory by referring to that section. There also is a model Conveyance on page 189 which will help you recognise what you are looking for.

'Approving' the Conveyance involves checking it to ensure that all the details are correctly stated, e.g. the names of the parties, the price agreed and the description of the property. These details should also accord with the contract you exchanged with the buyer. For example, if the contract specifies that your property is being bought in the names of the buyer and his wife, these should be the names of 'the purchasers' in the Conveyance. And so on. I am confident you will handle this chore with aplomb as it sounds far more involved when committed to writing than it really is.

If the draft Conveyance passes your scrutiny, you return it to the purchaser's solicitor with a letter indicating your approval; a suggested draft is on page 188. He will then have the Conveyance re-typed on rather impressive-looking stiffish paper usually headed in bold black copperplate script 'THIS CONVEYANCE', which he will send to you (and your wife, if appropriate) to 'execute', i.e. to sign, seal and deliver. It will have already been executed by your purchasers.

You may recall that we briefly discussed the execution of a deed on pages 80-81.

The Completion Statement

We have already discussed on pages 65 and 85 the completion statement that is sent to a purchaser or a purchaser's solicitor in readiness for Completion, and you may find it helpful to refer to these comments again.

Essentially a completion statement sets out the balance due from a purchaser on Completion with, if appropriate, a breakdown of this sum into two banker's drafts.

The starting point is the purchase price, less deposit paid. To this is added any payments made in advance for, e.g. water rates and sewerage charges. If any items of furnishing or other chattels were purchased, the sum agreed is added.

Do not bother apportioning general rates. Tell your local authority the date you will be vacating and they will work out what sum they will refund to you or you must pay to them. They will also provide a receipt on request, which you will need to produce on Completion.

Leasehold Property

In the case of a leasehold property an apportionment is made in respect of ground rent, insurance, maintenance and so on. If payment is made in arrear, as for example ground rent, a deduction is made in respect of the relevant period; if payment is made in advance, e.g. water rates, a sum is added.

So your next task, which is quite as simple as any of the others required of you, is the preparation of the completion statement. You can clearly see what is involved by referring to the statement on page 192.

If you have a mortgage on the property you are selling, the building society's solicitor will by now have told you the amount required to pay off the mortgage. In the example on page 194 I have assumed the amount required to redeem the mortgage is £8,961.50 and you will note that the purchaser is asked to provide a draft for this sum and another draft in your favour for the balance due to you on Completion.

Send the completion statement to the purchaser's solicitor with a covering letter along the lines of the suggested draft on page 194 and keep a copy in your file.

Last Minute Panic

To avoid a last minute panic do remember to cancel banker's standing orders for general rates, water rates and sewerage charges and to notify the Rating Department of your local authority that there will be a change of ownership of your property as from the date of Completion. Similarly, you should ask for your gas and electricity meters to be read and notify British Telecom of your impending departure. Each of these services will send their final accounts to your new address, but it will help if you give them reasonable notice.

Preparing for Completion

You have now sent your completion statement to your purchaser's solicitor; he should have this not later than about eight days before the date fixed for Completion so that he has adequate time to make the necessary arrangements.

You will probably have booked removal contractors so you need to maintain contact either with your purchaser personally (which is to be preferred) or with his solicitor in case the date of Completion has to be put back a day or two for some reason or other.

However, as almost always is the case there should be no delays that affect Completion; the only question is where Completion is to take place?

If you have a mortgage on the property, it will be at the office of your building society solicitor. If your sale is part of a simultaneous sale and purchase transaction, refer to the brief discussion on page 86 about staggering the times of the two Completions to enable you to attend both. In practical terms, you will wish to complete your sale first and then complete your purchase because presumably your sale is part financing your purchase.

If you do not have a mortgage on the property then you yourself can specify the venue for Completion. Whether you have a mortgage or not, it is important that the arrangements for Completion suit all participants.

If you and your wife are selling as co-owners both of you execute the purchase deed prior to Completion and bring it with you when the actual ceremony occurs.

If you do not have a mortgage you also take the documents of title (i.e. the conveyance to you) and other deeds if the property is unregistered land or the Land Certificate if the property is registered land. If there is a mortgage on the property the documents of title will be produced by the building society's solicitor.

You will need the last receipts for general rates, water rates and sewerage charges to show these are paid off; and in the case of leasehold property the receipt for ground rent. Nowadays receipts for these services are not required to be given unless asked for, so if you are in the position of having paid but do not have a receipt, you should explain the situation to the local authority, water board or landlord and obtain a letter confirming the amount paid and date of payment.

You will also have to produce your N.H.B.C. Certificate (if applicable) and any 'guarantees' e.g. cavity wall insulation, timber treatment and so on. Finally, you should make arrangements to hand over the keys to your property.

The ideal situation is to give up possession and all the keys upon Completion. This may not always be possible for one reason or another, so you may perhaps ask the purchaser to allow you a little time to actually vacate. Any such agreement by the purchaser is a concession on his part and should be seen as such. If there is a duplicate set of keys held by an estate agent or neighbour, you must ensure that they are given to the purchaser.

So now you are prepared for Completion, and it's 'all systems go'.

Completion of Your Sale

There is very little for you to do. This is an occasion of relative calm for you as the vendor. You just stand back and when the documents of title have been quickly vetted you hold out your hand (or both hands if you feel so inclined) to receive the banker's draft or drafts you indicated on your completion statement.

Getting the Money

At Completion you are going to hand over the title documents in exchange for the purchase money. Usually, the process is set in motion by your building society solicitor who will hand to you the Charge Certificate if the property is registered land, or the title deeds if unregistered. He will also give you his undertaking in respect of Form 53 if the property is registered or a vacating receipt if it is unregistered as appropriate.

You are now in possession of the title documents, which you exchange for the balance of the purchase money. You check that the banker's drafts are in order, (DO NOT ACCEPT A PERSONAL CHEQUE), and hand all your documents of title to the purchaser's solicitor, at the same time passing to your building society solicitor the draft drawn in favour of the building society. You hand over any guarantees such as cavity wall insulation and the like, and the executed purchase deed. Date this, and

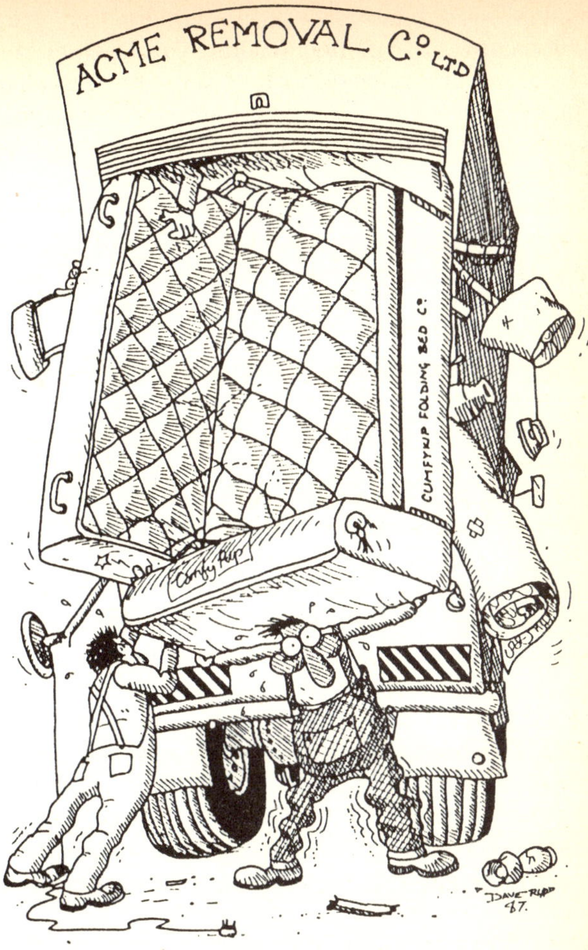

The nerve-wracking job of loading up the moving van at least marks the end of the entire conveyancing process.

your copy, with the date of Completion and pass it to the purchaser's solicitor.

Do remember to obtain from the purchaser's solicitor a note addressed to the estate agents who acted for you authorising the release to you of the deposit paid to them by the purchaser. Of course, if you did not employ an estate agent, and the deposit was held by a bank, the note would be addressed to the manager of the bank.

Only two more points remain. The keys have to be made available to the purchaser either at the time of Completion by handing them to his solicitor or, if the purchaser has allowed you a little time to vacate, at the time and place you agreed.

Finally, once you have vacated do remember to cancel the insurance on the house and its contents. And that is it. Just think of the money you have saved!

Selling was not at all difficult was it? And next time round, I promise you, it will be easier still!

TYPICAL TIMETABLE SELLING PROPERTY: UP TO EXCHANGE OF CONTRACTS

STEP	STAGE	DAY
1	Accept purchaser's offer to buy 'subject to contract'. Obtain details of purchaser and his solicitor.	1
2	Receive written confirmation of agreement to purchase 'subject to contract' from Estate Agent	3
3	If the property is mortgaged, request lender to send title deeds to a building society solicitor on their list located conveniently to you.	4
4	Draft contract and send to purchaser's solicitor.	7
5	Receive purchaser's Enquiries before Contract.	12
	Answer purchaser's Enquiries before Contract.	14
7	Agree Completion date	19
8	Receive draft contract approved by purchaser's solicitor	22
9	Exchange contracts and receive deposit.	28
	THE CONTRACT IS NOW LEGALLY BINDING ON BOTH PARTIES	

FROM EXCHANGE TO COMPLETION

STEP	STAGE	DAY
1	Receive purchaser's Requisitions on Title. Ask building society amount required to redeem your mortgage.	5
2	Receive draft purchase deed from purchaser's solicitor.	13
3	Approve and return draft purchase deed.	14
4	Prepare completion statement and send to purchaser's solicitor. Arrange venue and time of Completion.	20
5	Completion. Receive draft(s) for purchase price and hand over title deeds.	28

The total time elapsed since your original agreement to sell is two months.

Notes on Insurance and Mortgages

Mortgage repayments may be a burden you cheerfully assume, but one of the less obvious costs of home ownership is insurance. You will obviously wish to insure the bricks and mortar, and the contents — carpets and furniture and other possessions — as well. But have you considered a mortgage protection policy if you are buying with the help of a mortgage?

One of the less apparent costs involved in home ownership is that of insurance.

Mortgage Assurance

Reference has already been made on page 28 to the desirability of obtaining mortgage protection life assurance in conjunction with a straight repayment mortgage.

The premiums are relatively modest, especially if related to the peace of mind that such cover brings.

When Mortgage Protection Life cover is taken out it is usual for the life assured to be that of the husband. This provides that the outstanding mortgage will be repaid if he dies during the term of the policy.

But what of the financial problems that could arise if the wife dies? Frequently, a wife's income is essential in meeting the mortgage repayments. Even if the wife is not in paid employment, the cost of paying someone to perform the hundred and one tasks she undertakes in running the home would be considerable. And of course, if the wife is a young mother, the burden is even greater.

One common solution is to have the policy written in joint names so that the benefits would be payable if either dies during the term of the policy. The additional cost of this valuable protection is relatively small and is certainly a feature I would strongly commend intending borrowers to consider seriously.

Buildings Insurance

All building societies require that the borrower is insured against loss or damage to the buildings which are security for a mortgage. The term 'buildings' includes the house, bungalow, etc, and any outbuildings used for domestic purposes, walls, gates, fences, garden pool or swimming pool, paths, patios, drives and, if leasehold, landlord's fixtures and fittings. If the property is a flat the usual practice is for the landlord to take out a policy for the whole building and the interest of each leaseholder is 'noted' on the policy. Mortgage lenders always insist that the amount of cover is adequate for each flat and for the building as a whole. They take out a policy with an insurer from whom they receive a hefty commission.

Policies issued by insurers differ in the extent of cover offered, but all protect against the more common causes of loss or damage such as fire, theft, storm and flood, subsidence, water and oil leakage and impact by vehicles, aircraft or animals.

Many policies are subject to 'excess' clauses whereby the insured pays the first £15 or similar sum of each claim in respect of certain perils, e.g. flood, storm, falling trees. In the case of subsidence, heave or landslide, the first 3% of the cost to fully rebuild your home, subject to a maximum of £500, is usually not covered, but a few insurers impose a somewhat lower excess.

Is it most important that the property is insured for the full reinstatement cost. That is the estimated cost of demolition and removal of debris in the event of a complete loss, plus professional fees, and the cost of rebuilding.

Most lending institutions insist that buildings policies are index-linked, i.e. the amount insured is automatically adjusted each month to reflect the House Rebuilding Cost Index published by the R.I.C.S.

How Much Insurance?

If you are buying with the aid of a mortgage the building society's valuer will estimate the sum to be insured. If you are a cash buyer you have to estimate this figure yourself, and if you had a structural survey carried out the surveyor can give you guidance. A useful guide to buildings insurance is published by the British Insurance Association and is available from the address listed on page 123 or from most building societies and banks. Do bear in mind that unless the sum insured is adequate from the outset no amount of index linking will bring it into line with rising costs. If you make improvements or extend your home, do remember to tell your building society or bank, or, if you arranged the insurance yourself, the insurance company.

The large volume of buildings insurance placed by the building societies and banks gives them considerable bargaining strength in their dealings with the insurance companies, and this 'muscle' is available on behalf of the borrower in appropriate cases.

Some of the biggest building societies have claims sections within their own insurance departments, and provide a speedy and efficient claims settlement service.

There is, of course, a very large sum of commission (as much as 40%) involved which the building societies have a vested interest to protect.

As already mentioned on page 23, the Halifax Building Society will allow a borrower to place the buildings cover with an approved insurer, but charges an administration fee. This concession is only likely to be worthwhile for the borrower who has an existing connection with an insurer with whom he is placing other insurance business. The majority of borrowers will prefer the present arrangement which works well in practice.

Incidentally, for a property of standard construction, the premium charged for buildings cover is usually about £1.50 to £1.90 per thousand insured, but varies between insurers so if you are buying without the aid of a mortgage, shop around. Most building societies offer a limited choice of Insurer from which you can choose.

Contents Insurance

Contents insurance is really a 'must', and most lending institutions will arrange a policy to suit your requirements. The term 'Contents' includes furniture, household goods, clothing and the personal possessions of yourself and family who normally reside with you. The insurance is against loss or damage to the contents from any of the perils referred to under 'buildings' on page 113, e.g. fire, theft, flood, etc.

The extent of cover available is extremely wide with many optional extensions on offer and index linking is virtually standard procedure. As with buildings cover, it is essential that the amounts insured are adequate from the outset and are kept under review.

The Geography of Insurance Costs

Greater London provides considerable problems for Insurers as the number and values of claims rises inexorably. In general, rates vary with postal districts, but are, in any event, much more than the rest of the country.

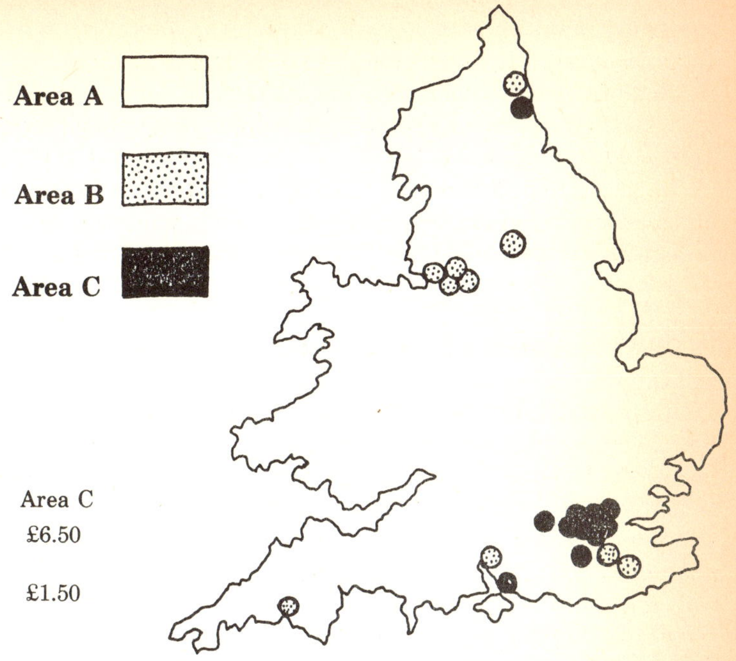

Per £1000

	Area A	Area B	Area C
CONTENTS INSURANCE	£3.20	£4.00	£6.50
BUILDINGS INSURANCE	£1.50	£1.50	£1.50

Where you live has more bearing on your insurance premiums than who you are. The map shows price regions for contents insurance from one typical firm, but all insurers operate on the same general basis.

Most insurers increased their rates substantially in 1986, having recently suffered heavy losses on buildings and contents insurance. Policy holders in large conurbations were hardest hit and the indications are that rates are likely to go on rising.

Contents policies are normally written on either a 'market value' or 'new for old' basis.

The market value basis usually provides, in respect of contents under three years old (other than clothing), for the full cost of replacement as new. In respect of contents more than three years old, and also clothing, the full cost of replacement is reduced by an allowance for deterioration.

The 'new for old' basis provides for the full cost of repair or replacement as new of contents other than clothing, without any reduction for wear and tear and irrespective of the ages and of the items.

A usual condition applied to this type of cover is that if an item is a total loss, the new replacement article shall be substantially the same, but not better, than the original item when new. Usually, the 'new for old' basis attracts a higher premium rate.

Premiums are fixed by reference, primarily, to the location of the property, the insurers having divided the country geographically into Rating Areas which reflect the insurance risk. In some instances the premium required by the insurance company could also be affected by the profession or occupation of the proposer and/or spouse. Rates vary from around £2.90 per £1000 of cover in a rural area to £10.00 per £1000 of cover in parts of Greater London, and also vary as between insurers.

So do shop around, or ask an insurance broker to do so for you, and compare exactly what is being offered. Remember, too, that building societies and banks would be delighted to arrange your cover!

Financing a Mortgage

On pages 28-29 the various ways by which a mortgage could be financed were outlined.

In these times of fluctuating interest rates and intense competition in the mortgage market it would not be helpful to quote specific examples of the costs of the various endowment plans on offer, as the figures would quickly become out of date. An analysis of quotations issued by many of the leading insurance companies shows that the price of a 'low cost' endowment for a £10,000 mortgage to a male aged 30 years next birthday is generally no more per month than the cost of a straight repayment mortgage with mortgage protection.

Typically these hybrid endowment plans combine low cost, the possibility of an excess over the sum required to redeem the mortgage and life cover guaranteeing repayment of the mortgage in the event of death before the policy matures. However, any bonus that may be paid at maturity which results in the assured receiving a sum greater than the original loan should be regarded as a windfall. Projections of terminal bonuses that exceed the loan whilst made in good faith by insurers, should not be relied upon but treated as a safety margin in case the insurer has to reduce the rate of bonus in the future.

Of the various endowment plans discussed on pages 28-29, the 'without profits' type is generally regarded as a poor deal. The 'with profits' endowment offers attractive returns although in practice it is too costly for most borrowers. The 'low cost' hybrid type endowment plans are preferred by some borrowers as such plans may be transferred from property to property upon sale and purchase. The plan will pay off a known sum on a certain date regardless of how many times the borrowers change house.

I strongly advise that you obtain several up to date quotations for your particular circumstances. Do study them carefully — particularly the small print and 'assumptions' on which the quotations are based. If you choose the straight repayment mortgage do consider taking out a mortgage protection policy and have it written in your joint names.

Shopping for a Mortgage

The building societies and the banks are continually producing a wide variety of mortgage schemes specially aimed at particular groups. but these change so frequently that it would not be helpful to refer to any one around at the time of printing as it will almost certainly be quickly superseded.

Several of the schemes available to borrowers are variations on the same theme, but the very multiplicity of home loan schemes serves to emphasize that an intending borrower should talk to more than one source of finance. Make an appointment to see the manager of the building society or bank to discuss your circumstances and requirements. The manager may have a scheme that exactly fits your needs.

Using Your Home to Produce an Income

Although in the early years of a mortgage you may feel that you will be paying forever, so long as you are able to keep up the repayments one glad day the house really will be yours. You will have an asset that will have been appreciating in value and will, most likely, continue to rise.

There are tens of thousands of elderly citizens living in their own properties who long ago paid off their mortgages. Some of them find it difficult to pay for the upkeep of the property, others would find an extra monthly income very useful in helping to maintain a decent standard of life. Whatever the need may be, for the person or couple who own their home extra income can be made available by taking out a loan and using the bricks and mortar that they own as security.

Abbey National have such a scheme which they call the Home Income Plan, and the advantage of this type of scheme over some others is that the ownership of the property still remains with the borrower. This means that the borrower can still leave his property in his/her will.

The Abbey National scheme provides a loan of up to 65% of the current value of the property up to a maximum of £30,000 secured by a mortgage on the property; up to 10% of the loan can be taken in cash to pay for such things as repairs or improvements to the property. The mortgage loan provides an annuity from Royal Life Insurance from which the interest on the loan is paid, leaving a useful sum over as a regular monthly pension.

Of course, the older you are when you buy an annuity the greater will be the sum you receive. For this reason you must be aged 70 years or more, and if a couple, both must be 70 years or older and their combined ages total at least 150 years. And, of course, you must own your own house.

If a couple use this plan the annuity is payable so long as either of them lives. On the death of the survivor, as in the case of a sole annuitant, the annuity ceases and the loan has to be repaid by those inheriting the property.

Similar plans are available from a few of the other building societies and financial institutions but appear to compare unfavourably with the Abbey National scheme. There are other apparently similar schemes, usually called 'reversionary schemes', which involve the sale of part, or all, of your home but frankly I would not recommend them.

Annuity rates fluctuate and it would not be helpful to quote figures. Far better to ask for a quotation based on your circumstances, if the idea interests you.

This type of scheme may be attractive to those senior citizens who prefer not to move to a smaller, cheaper place or away from friends and relatives.

Whilst this type of scheme is strictly outside the ambit of this book, brief details have been included both for general interest and to illustrate the range of activity of the lending institutions, particularly the building societies, across the whole spectrum of house ownership.

Costs, Useful Names and Addresses

The true cost of buying a house or flat is not simply a matter of its asking price. By no means! As the following table reveals you will most likely have to spend a small fortune in related costs as well.

Example of Costs in a Typical Transaction

Selling at £30,000 Purchasing at £40,000 Mortgage of £20,000

Solicitor's fees:	
Sale £275.00 plus VAT = £316.45	
Solicitor's fees:	
Purchase £350.00 plus VAT = £392.50	
Total Solicitor's fees	£708.95
Stamp Duty at 1% on full purchase price	£400.00
Lender's Valuation fee*	£ 55.00
Land Registry fee	£ 60.00
Structural Survey (£425.00 in Greater London area)	£325.00
Lender's solicitor's fee	£ 78.00
Estate Agent's fee — £600 plus VAT	£690.00
Total	**£2316.95**

Selling at £50,000 Purchasing at £75,000 Mortgage of £30,000

Solicitor's fees:	
Sale £480 plus VAT = £552.00	
Solicitor's fees:	
Purchase £700.00 plus VAT = £805.00	
Total Solicitor's fees	£1357.00
Stamp duty at 1% on full purchase price	£ 750.00
Land Registry fee	£ 125.00
Lender's valuation fee*	£ 76.00
Structural survey fee—£480 plus VAT*	£ 552.00
(£700 ± in Greater London area)	
Lender's solicitor's fee	£ 86.00
Estate Agent's fee — £1000 plus VAT	£1150.00
Total	**£4096.00**

Selling at £70,000 Purchasing at £100,000 Mortgage of £50,000

Solicitor's fees:	
Sale £500 plus VAT £75 = £575.00	
Solicitor's fees:	
Purchase £750 plus VAT £112.50 = £862.50	
Total Solicitor's fees	£1437.50
Stamp Duty at 1% on full purchase price	£1000.00
Land Registry fee	£ 175.00
Lender's Valuation fee*	£ 92.00
Structural Survey £600 plus VAT*	£ 690.00
(£800 ± in Greater London area)	
Lender's solicitor's fee	£ 90.00
Estate Agent's fee — £1400 plus VAT	£1610.00
Total	**£5094.50**

Notes:
1. Solicitors scale fees were abolished in 1973 and solicitors may charge what is "fair and reasonable".
2. The Arrangement fee charged by some Banks, Brokers and Finance Houses should be added to these figures.
3. Some building societies offer advantageous rates if the Valuation survey and the structural survey are carried out at the same time.
4. Estate Agents' fees vary throughout the country.
5. Removal contractor's charges, gas, electricity and telephone reconnection charges should be added to these figures.
6. The costs of structural surveys vary considerably depending on the extent of the survey required.
* The Valuation fees vary slightly as between Lenders. Both Valuation and structural surveys may be (and usually are) subject to a surcharge for travelling expenses of the Valuer.

Current Rates of Land Registry Fees

Price Paid	Already Registered	First Registration
£25,001-£30,000	£40	£35
£30,001-£35,000	£50	£40
£35,001-£40,000	£60	£50
£40,001-£45,000	£70	£60
£45,001-£50,000	£80	£70
£50,001-£60,000	£90	£80
£60,001-£70,000	£100	£90
£70,001-£80,000	£125	£100
£80,001-£90,000	£150	£110
£90,001-£100,000	£175	£120

Current Rates of Stamp Duty

Up to £30,000 purchase price:	Duty NIL
£30,001 upwards purchase price:	1% of full purchase price

Examples of Valuation Fees

When an application for a mortgage loan is accepted in principle, the typical building society obtains a valuation of the property which is to be pledged as security for the loan. Borrowers can arrange for this inspection to be "extended" and include a report on the property's condition. This is NOT a structural report. Examples of the fees charged are set out below and these have to be paid by the borrower whether or not a loan is subsequently offered or accepted.

The fees are charged on the selling price of the property not on the size of the loan.

Purchase Price	Valuation Fee	Extended Report
Up to £25,000	£46	£115
Up to £30,000	£52	£132
Up to £60,000	£63	£161

Building Society Solicitor's Charges

If you carry out your own conveyancing, the building society will appoint a solicitor to check the documentation you have prepared, and to 'draw up' the mortgage deed. As it is a standard form this is obviously not a very onerous task.

The following fees are typically charged by solicitors:

Mortgage Loan	Charge
£10,000	£91
£12,000	£97
£15,000	£107
£17,000	£112
£20,000	£116
£25,000	£126
£30,000	£129
£35,000	£132

This is not the end of the story. If the mortgage includes the assignment of a life policy for collateral purposes, the above fees may be increased by a further 25%.

Some solicitors add 'disbursements' and what are described as 'out of pocket expenses' to the above fees. The figures quoted are intended to be no more than a guide, and you should ask the solicitor to specify what his charges will be. Their fees are required to be 'fair and reasonable' so involved. A Licensed Conveyancer's fee would be in the register of £50 or less.

Table of Addresses for Payment of Stamp Duty by Direct Post Application

Send to:

Applicants from:	Birmingham Edmund House Newhall St B3 3DU	Bristol The Pithay All Saints St BS1 2NY	Cardiff Companies Hse Crown Way CF4 3UR	Leeds 42 Eastgate LS2 7LD	Liverpool Tower Bldg Water St L3 1AE	Manchester Alexandra Hse The Parsonage M60 9BT	Newcastle Aidan House All Saints Office Centre NE1 2BG	Nottingham Lambert House Talbot St NG1 5NN
Avon		●						
Bedfordshire	●							
Berkshire				●				
Buckinghamshire				●				
Cambridgeshire					●			
Cheshire					●			
Cleveland							●	
Clwyd			●					
Cornwall		●						
Cumbria							●	
Derbyshire						●		
Devon		●						
Dorset		●						
Durham, County							●	
Dyfed			●					
Essex								●
Gloucester	●							
Gwent			●					
Gwynedd			●					
Hampshire and IOW	●							
Herefordshire	●							
Hertfordshire	●							
Humberside				●				
Kent				●				
Lancashire						●		
Leicestershire	●							
Lincolnshire						●		
London, Postal Dists							●	
Manchester, Greater						●		
Merseyside					●			
Middlesex								●
Mid Glamorgan			●					
Norfolk							●	
Northamptonshire					●			
Northumberland							●	
Nottinghamshire								●
Oxfordshire						●		
Powys			●					
Shropshire					●			
Somerset		●						
South Glamorgan			●					
Staffordshire					●			
Suffolk							●	
Surrey						●		
Sussex					●			
Tyne and Wear							●	
Warwickshire	●							
West Glamorgan			●					
West Midlands	●							
Wiltshire		●						
Worcestershire	●							
Yorkshire				●				

District Land Registries

The Birkenhead District Land Registry,
76 Hamilton Street, Birkenhead, Merseyside L41 5JW
(Telephone No. 051 647-5661)
Areas served: Counties of Cheshire and Merseyside

The Croydon District Land Registry,
Sunley House, Bedford Park, Croydon CR9 3LE
(Telephone No. 01-686 8833)
Areas served: Greater London south of the River Thames (including the London Borough of Richmond upon Thames).

The Durham District Land Registry,
Southfield House, Southfield Way, Durham DH1 5TR
(Telephone No. (0385) 66151)
Areas served: Counties of Cleveland, Cumbria, Durham, Humberside, Northumberland, North Yorkshire, and Tyne and Wear.

The Gloucester District Land Registry,
Twyver House, Bruton Way, Gloucester GL1 1DQ.
(Telephone No. Gloucester (0452) 28666)
Areas served: Counties of Berkshire, Gloucestershire, Oxfordshire, Warwickshire and West Midlands.

The Harrow District Land Registry,
Lyon House, Lyon Road, Harrow, Middx. HA1 2EU.
(Telephone No. 01-427 8811)
Areas served: Greater London north of the River Thames, but excluding the London Boroughs of Barking and Dagenham, Havering, Newham, Redbridge, Richmond upon Thames and Waltham Forest.

The Lytham District Land Registry,
Birkenhead House, Lytham St. Anne's, Lancs. FY8 5AB
(Telephone No. Lytham (0253) 736999)
Areas served: Counties of Greater Manchester and Lancashire.

The Nottingham District Land Registry,
Government Buildings, Chalfont Drive, Nottingham NG8 3RN
(Telephone No. Nottingham (0602) 291111)
Areas served: Counties of Derbyshire, Nottinghamshire, South Yorkshire, Staffordshire and West Yorkshire.

The Peterborough District Land Registry,
Aragon Court, Northminster Road, Peterborough PE1 1XN
(Telephone No. Peterborough (0733) 46048)
Areas served: Counties of Bedfordshire, Cambridgeshire, Leicestershire, Lincolnshire, Norfolk, Northamptonshire and Suffolk.

The Plymouth District Land Registry,
Plumer House, Tailyour Road, Crownhill, Plymouth PL6 5HY
(Telephone No. Plymouth (0752) 701234)
Areas served: Counties of Avon, Cornwall, Somerset and Wiltshire.

The Stevenage District Land Registry,
Brickdale House, Danastrete, Stevenage, Herts. SG1 1XG.
(Telephone No. Stevenage (0438) 314888)
Areas served: London Boroughs of Barking and Dagenham, Enfield, Hackney, Haringey, Havering, Newham, Redbridge, Waltham Forest. Counties of Buckinghamshire, Essex and Hertfordshire.

The Swansea District Land Registry,
37 The Kingsway, Swansea SA1 5LF
(Telephone No. Swansea (0792) 476677).
Areas served: Counties of Hereford and Worcester, and Shropshire. All counties in Wales.

The Tunbridge Wells District Land Registry,
Curtis House, Tunbridge Wells, Kent TN2 5AQ
(Telephone No. Tunbridge Wells (0892) 26141)
Areas served: Counties of East Sussex, Kent and Surrey.

The Weymouth District Land Registry,
1 Cumberland Drive, Weymouth, Dorset DT4 9TT (Telephone No. Weymouth (03057) 76161)
Areas served: Counties of Hampshire, Isle of Wight, Dorset and West Sussex.

Note:
H.M. Land Registry issue a useful Explanatory Leaflet No. 9 which sets out a list of all the counties and administrative areas in England and Wales which is available on request from all district land registries free of charge. Also available from district land registries free of charge are Local Area suplements to the leaflet which shows in greater detail the operative date of compulsory registration of districts and London Boroughs.

Useful Names and Addresses

ORGANISATION	INFORMATION PROVIDED
British Insurance Association, Aldermary House, Queen Street, London EC4N 1TU Tel: 01-248-4477	Register of member insurers
Building Societies Association, 3 Savile Row, London W1X 1AF Tel: 01-437-0655	Register of member societies
British Gas Corporation, 326 High Holborn, London WC1Y 7PT Tel: 01-242-0789	Gas equipment and advice
Corporation of Mortgage, Finance and Life Assurance Brokers, 24 Broad Street, Wokingham, Berks. RG11 1AB Tel: 0734-785672	Register of mortgage brokers
Electricity Council, 30 Millbank, London SW1P 4RD Tel: 01-834-2333	Inspectahome scheme Electricity equipment and its use
House Builders Federation, 82 New Cavendish Street, London W1M 8AD Tel: 01-580-5588	Register of house builders

Incorporated Society of Valuers and Auctioneers, 3 Cadogan Gate, London SW1X 0AS Tel: 01-235-2282	Register of estate agents
Institute of Plumbing, Scottish Mutual House, North Street, Hornchurch, Essex RM11 1RU Tel: Hornchurch 040-24-45199	Register of approved plumbers
National Association of Estate Agents, Arbon House, 21 Jury Street, Warwick CV34 4EH Tel: Warwick 0926-496800	Register of estate agents
National Home Enlargement Bureau, P.O. Box 67, High Wycombe, Bucks. Tel: 0494-711649	Home extensions
National Home Improvement Council, 26 Store Street, London WC1E 7BT Tel: 01-636 2562	Home improvements
National Inspection Council for Electrical Installation Contracting, 237 Kennington Lane, London SE11 5QJ Tel: 01-582-7746	Register of approved electrical contractors undertaking inspections
National House-Building Council, Chiltern Avenue, Amersham, Bucks. HP6 5AP Tel: Amersham 024-03-4477	Housebuilders register and 10-year warranty
Royal Institution of British Architects, 66 Portland Place, London W1M 3DE	List of architects experienced in housing and house extension
Royal Institute of Chartered Surveyors, 12 Great George Street, London SW1P 3AD Tel: 01-222-7000	List of surveyors List of estate agents

Moving Checklist

Fix the actual date for moving and complete contract Notify your Rating Authority Insurance Company Water Board Electricity Company Gas Board Start reducing the contents of your deep freeze Arrange with the Post Office to redirect your mail Arrange for the telephone to be disconnected and connected at the new address on removal day	1 month before moving
Send change of address cards Make travel plans and removal Ensure that your new house will be empty and ready for the estimated delivery time Arrange to disconnect utility services and any specialist attention for washing machines, refrigerators, etc.	2 weeks before moving
Close unwarranted accounts, newspapers, magazines, etc, and return all borrowed goods — library books etc. Collect all cleaning and repairs Start packing items which you wish to personally handle	1 week before moving
Take down curtains that you are taking with you plus the fittings Empty and defrost the fridge and freezer, and finish packing all personal belongings	day before
Inform removal foreman what they must pack and point out the fragile items Make sure access and keys are available at the new house Make a final check, particularly of cupboards etc. to ensure that the house has been cleared Have cash or cheque book available Clean the empty house	moving day
Additional Reminders for those moving overseas	
Prepare an inventory for Customs purposes Complete your Insurance Proposal Form, showing the replacement value of the items at destination. Supply removal firm with a contact address and telephone number, both in the U.K. and at your overseas destination Finalise your banking arrangements here and overseas	3 weeks before moving
Separate the items that are to travel with you Keep to hand passports, vaccination certificates, marriage and birth certificates, purchase receipts and keys to any locked items, such as suitcases or trunks Keep some spare cash for your journey Ensure that friends and relatives have your forwarding address	moving day

Sample Forms and Draft Letters

Samples of all the conveyancing forms and all the letters mentioned in the text are collected here into a single reference chapter. They occur in much the same sequence as in the text, although those dealing with buying a property have been separated from those to do with selling.

Each form has been filled out so that it serves as a model of what you are required to do. (In addition to these completed examples, blank forms for your own use are available, see page 207 for details.) In the same way the sample letters are models of the ones you will have to write.

Dramatis Personae

In the event that you become confused by all the names that appear in the sample forms which follow, here is the cast of the leading characters in 'Our Drama'.

Sellright Estate Agency, 10 High Street, Hutton	The Vendors' Estate Agent
Bertram Brown and Barbara Brown, 15 Lone Pine Close, Hutton	The Vendors
Gerald George Ford and Joan Ford, 112 Dorset Road, Hutton	The Purchasers
Dodson & Fogg, Lloyds Bank Chambers, High Street, Hutton	The Vendors' Solicitors
Best Building Society, High Street, Hutton.	The Purchasers' Building Society (Local Office)
Best Building Society, Best House, 97-99 Lombard Row, Rancaster, West Yorkshire RG1 2HX	The Purchasers' Building Society (Head Office)
Brown & Green, 44 High Street, Hutton	Solicitors acting for the Purchasers' Building Society
Brown & White, 49 Hendon Way, Hutton	Surveyors Instructed by the Purchasers
Hutton District Council, Wendover Way, Hutton	The Local Authority

LETTER TO ESTATE AGENT CONFIRMING PURCHASE OFFER

The Manager Sellright Estate Agency, 10 High Street, Hutton	Your Name Your Address Today's Date

SUBJECT TO CONTRACT

Dear Sirs,

Re: 15 Lone Pine Close, Hutton.

I confirm our * (telephone) conversation of today when I informed you that Mr. and Mrs. Brown have accepted my offer to purchase the above property at the price of £29,750 (twentynine thousand, seven hundred and fifty pounds) subject to contract.

You promised to send me confirmation of this agreement and the full names of the vendors, and the name and address of the firm of solicitors who will be acting for them.

As mentioned, I shall be carrying out my own conveyancing and would be grateful if you will ask the vendor's solicitor to send me a draft contract so that the matter may proceed.

I have sent a copy of this letter to Mr. and Mrs. Brown.

Yours faithfully,

Your Signature

* Omit if inapplicable

N.B. Also send a copy of this letter to the vendor.

ESTATE AGENT'S SALES SHEET

ESTATE AGENT'S SALES SHEET

SELLRIGHT ESTATE AGENCY

10 HIGH STREET, HUTTON, WESSEX   Telephone Hutton 2649
4 lines

AUCTIONEERS ESTATE AGENTS SURVEYORS VALUERS MORTGAGES ARRANGED

==

DETAILS OF SALE, SUBJECT TO CONTRACT
OF
15 LONE PINE CLOSE, HUTTON.

==

VENDOR(S)   Mr. BETRAM BROWN and Mrs BARBARA BROWN
Telephone : Hutton 2494
In residence

VENDORS SOLICITORS   Dodson & Fogg,
Lloyds Bank Chambers,
High Street,
Hutton   Telephone Hutton 2555

PURCHASERS'   Mr GERALD GEORGE FORD and Mrs. JOAN FORD,
112 Dorset Road, Hutton   Telephone Hutton 2999

PURCHASERS' SOLICITORS   Mr. Ford will conduct his own conveyancing.

Tenure :   Freehold

Purchase Price : £29,750.00.

Deposit :   10% of purchase price to be paid to the Vendors' solicitors as stakeholders, upon or before exchange of contracts.

FIXTURES/ FITTINGS :   Full list to be agreed and incorporated in contract.

MORTGAGE: Through Best Building Society Hutton Branch. Tele. Hutton 2343

LOCAL AUTHORITY : Hutton District Council, Wendover Way, Hutton.
Telephone Hutton 2111

REMARKS

For SELLRIGHT ESTATE AGENCY

....Date

SUGGESTED LETTER TO REQUEST STRUCTURAL SURVEY

Your Name
Your Address

Today's Date

Messrs Black and White,
Chartered Surveyors,
49 Hendon Way,
Hutton.

Dear Sirs,

Re: 15 Lone Pine Close, Hutton

I confirm our telephone conversation of today when I requested you to carry out a structural survey of the above property at the same time as the valuation survey you are carrying out for the Best Building Society.

I agree your fee for this survey of £••• and look forward to receiving your report as soon as possible.

Yours faithfully

Your Signature

APPLICATION FOR LAND REGISTRY SEARCH

Application
for an
Official Search of the Index Map (1),(2)

HM Land Registry

Form 96

(Rule 286 Land Registration Rules 1925)

(1) Please send this application to the district land registry serving the area in which the land is situated. This information is contained in Explanatory Leaflet No 9 obtainable free of charge from any district land registry.

(2) **Please complete white boxes in typescript or in BLOCK LETTERS and in ink.**

For official use only

(3) **Please provide as much of the following information as is available.**

Postal number or description
Name of road
Name of locality
Town
Post code
District or London Borough
Administrative County
Ordnance Map Reference or Title Number

Property description (3)

15 LONE PINE CLOSE,
HUTTON
XYZ 123
HUTTON
WESSEX

For official use only

(4) **Any attached plan must contain sufficient details of the surrounding roads and other features to enable the land to be identified satisfactorily on the Ordnance Map. However, a plan is normally unnecessary if the land is situated in an area where registration of title is compulsory on sale and the property can be identified by postal description. Nevertheless, the Chief Land Registrar reserves the right to ask for a plan to be supplied where he deems it necessary.**

I/We apply for an official search of the Index Map and Parcels Index, including the list of pending applications for first registration, in respect of the land referred to above and shown edged/coloured RED **on the attached plan** (4)

Signed | **Date**

Solicitor's name and address including postcode (5),(6)

GERALD GEORGE FORD and JOAN FORD,
112 DORSET ROAD,
HUTTON,
WESSEX XYZ322

Telephone number: Hutton (0200) 2999

(5) **If no solicitor is acting please enter the name and address (including postcode) of the applicant.**

(6) **N.B. The result of the search will be sent to this address.**

Solicitor's/Applicant's reference

APPLICATION FOR SEARCH OF LOCAL LAND CHARGES

Form LLC1. *(Local Land Charges Rules 1977 Schedule 1, Form C)*

Official Number ______________
(To be completed by the registering authority)

The duplicate of this form must also be completed: a carbon copy will suffice

For directions, notes and fees see overleaf

Insert name and address of registering authority in space below

Register of local land charges

Requisition for search and official certificate of search

fold

Requisition for search
(A separate requisition must be made in respect of each parcel of land except as explained overleaf)

An official search is required in XXXXX ______________ X⁴ⁿ the register of local land charges kept by the above-named registering authority for subsisting registrations against the land [defined in the attached plan and][2] described below.

Description of land sufficient to enable it to be identified

ALL THAT land and dwellinghouse erected thereon situate and known as Number 15 Lone Pine Close, Hutton, Wessex as the same is delineated and edged red on the plan annexed hereto.

Name and address to which certificate is to be sent

GERALD GEORGE FORD,
112 DORSET ROAD,
HUTTON,
WESSEX XYZ 123

Signature of applicant (XXXXXXXX)

Date

Telephone number
Hutton 2999

Reference

Enclosure
Cheque/Money Order/Postal Order/Giro

To be completed by authorised officer

Official certificate of search

It is hereby certified that the search requested above reveals no subsisting registrations.[3]

or the ________ registrations described in the Schedule hereto[3] up to and including the date of this certificate.

Signed ....
On behalf of ....
Date

1 Delete if inappropriate. Otherwise insert Part(s) in which search is required.

2 Delete if inappropriate. (A plan should be furnished in duplicate if it is desired that a copy should be returned.)

3 Delete inapplicable words. (The Parts of the Schedule should be securely attached to the certificate and the number of registrations disclosed should be inserted in the space provided. Only Parts which disclose subsisting registrations should be sent.)

4 Insert name of registering authority

LETTER TO LOCAL COUNCIL ENCLOSING SEARCH FORMS

The Hutton District Council
Council Offices
Wendover Way,
Hutton.

Your Name
Your Address

Today's Date

Dear Sirs,

Re: 15 Lone Pine Close, Hutton

I enclose herewith Forms LLC1 and Con. 29 duly completed together with the appropriate fees. I would be grateful if you would let me have the search certificate and replies to enquiries as soon as possible.

Yours faithfully

Your Signature

LOCAL SEARCH FORM (Front Page)

1982 EDITION

To be submitted in duplicate

ENQUIRIES OF DISTRICT COUNCILS

(NOT LONDON BOROUGHS)

NAME AND ADDRESS OF DISTRICT COUNCIL (IN BLOCK LETTERS) TO WHICH THIS FORM IS TO BE SENT

Hutton District Council,
Council Offices,
Wendover Way,
Hutton, Wessex

Description of the Property

RE 15 Lone Pine Close,
Hutton,
Wessex
(Dwellinghouse)

Relevant roadways, footpaths and footways (see Enquiry 1) in addition to those specified in the above address, on which information is sought.

Fees of ** ** are enclosed, including fees for an Official Search.

Signed Your Signature

Dated XX/XX/XXXX Purchasers

HEADNOTES

(1) This Form of Enquiry is approved by the Law Society, the Association of County Councils, the Association of District Councils and the Association of Metropolitan Authorities and is published by their authority.

(2) Under the arrangements made between the District Council and the County Council the Replies below to certain Enquiries cover knowledge and actions of both the District Council and the County Council. References to "the Council" are intended to include reference to a predecessor Council and to a Committee or Sub-Committee of the Council or of a predecessor Council acting under delegated powers, and to any other body or person taking action under powers delegated by the Council or a predecessor Council.

(3) The Replies below are furnished after appropriate enquiries and in the belief that they are in accordance with the information at present available to the officers of the respective Councils, but on the distinct understanding that neither the District Council nor the County Council, nor any officer of either Council, is legally responsible therefor, except for negligence. Any such liability for negligence shall extend not only to the person by or on whose behalf these Enquiries are made but also to a person (being a purchaser for the purposes of Section 10(3) of the Local Land Charges Act 1975) who or whose agent had knowledge, before the relevant time as defined in the said Section, of the Replies to these Enquiries.

(4) It is pointed out that so far as the Replies may relate to proposals they may yet change.

(5) References to the property concerned in the Enquiries and Replies are intended to include reference, where appropriate, to any part of the property.

(6) References to any Act, Regulation or Order are intended to include reference to (i) any statutory provision replaced thereby and (ii) any amendment or re-enactment thereof.

(7) References to any Town and Country Planning Act, Order or Regulation are abbreviated, e.g. "T&CP Act 1971".

(8) Where no plan of the property is furnished with the Requisition for Official Search or this Form of Enquiry, neither the District Council nor the County Council can be expected to know the boundaries of the property, and the Replies are given on the basis of the information as to these available to the Councils in their offices. The furnishing of a plan in duplicate will help the Councils to give accurate replies and may save time. The Councils must reserve the right in any particular case to call for a plan in duplicate sufficient to enable the boundaries of the property to be identified on the ordnance survey map before furnishing Replies.

CURRENT FEES

It should be noted that the following fees are liable to change during the currency of this edition. Enquiries submitted on a form which is up-to-date apart from the information concerning fees will be answered provided the current fees are tendered.

PART I ENQUIRIES –

(a) Where relating to one parcel of land only, as defined in Rule 2(2) of the Local Land Charges Rules, 1977 .. .. ..

(b) Where relating to several parcels of land (which a single Requisition for Official Search would cover) and delivered on a single form: –
For the first parcel of land .. .. ..
For each additional parcel of land .. .. ..
provided that where the fee on that basis would exceed £100, the amount is to be fixed by arrangement between the solicitors and the proper officer of the District Council.
The above fees cover all the Enquiries in Part I.

PART II ENQUIRIES: –
Where relating to one parcel of land only or to several parcels (as above-mentioned) and delivered on a single form: –
For each printed Enquiry numbered in the form .. .. ..
For any and each further Enquiry added by solicitors and which the proper officer of the Council is willing to answer ..
No maximum fee.

NAME AND ADDRESS (IN BLOCK LETTERS) TO WHICH THIS FORM IS TO BE RETURNED

GERALD GEORGE FORD,
112 DORSET ROAD,
HUTTON,
WESSEX XY4 322

SOLICITORS' REFERENCE

TELEPHONE NUMBER Hutton (0200) 2999

TELEX

TYPICAL RIGHT OF WAY APPEARING IN A CONVEYANCE

N O W   T H I S   D E E D   W I T N E S S E T H as follows :-

1. In pursuance of the said agreement and in consideration of the sum of TWENTY FIVE THOUSAND POUNDS (£25,000.00) now paid to the Vendors by the Purchasers out of monies belonging to them on a joint account (the receipt whereof the Vendors hereby acknowledge) the Vendors as Beneficial Owners hereby convey unto the Purchasers ALL THAT piece or parcel of land situate on the south side of Fir Tree Close Croftown in the County of Wessex having a frontage to the said road of forty seven feet or thereabouts and with a depth therefrom of one hundred and sixty feet or therebouts as the same is for the purposes of identification only delineated on the plan annexed to a Conveyance (hereinafter called "the said Conveyance") dated the 27th day of February 1968 and made between Frederick Jones of the one part and John Taylor of the other part and thereon edged red TOGETHER WITH the dwellinghouse and garage erected thereon or on some part thereof situate and known as Number 43 Fir Tree Close aforesaid TOGETHER ALSO WITH the right for the Purchasers and their successors in title owners or occupiers for the time being of the land hereby conveyed and their undertenants and servants and all other persons authorised by them in common with the Vendors and all other persons lawfully entitled thereto or having the like right at all times and for all purposes with or without horses cars or other vehicles mechanically propelled or otherwise to pass and repass over and along the road delineated on the said plan annexed hereto and thereon coloured brown which said road leads from the property hereby conveyed to the highway known as Wentworth Road aforesaid TO HOLD the same unto the Purchasers in fee simple UPON TRUST for themselves as beneficial joint tenants Subject to the covenants exceptions and reservations stipulations and conditions contained in the said Conveyance

Ole SERIES PRE-CONTRACT ENQUIRIES Page One

PRE-CONTRACT ENQUIRIES of VENDOR

Please reply as precisely as possible to the following enquiries to obviate the need for further clarification.

....
Proposed Purchaser

....Date

Re ....15 Lone Pine Close, Hutton.........

(Seller) .. Brown..............................

To (Buyer) ... Ford............................

ENQUIRIES	REPLIES
1. Planning etc. Consents	1.
a. When did the current use of the property begin?	a. 1959
b. Has the current use been continuous since it began?	b. Yes
c. During the previous 4 years:	c.
(i) Were any buildings forming part of the property erected or have any been altered in any way?	(i) No
(ii) Have all conditions of any planning consents been complied with?	(ii) Yes
d. Please supply a copy of any planning consent giving permission for the present use of the property and for the erection and/or alteration of any buildings on the property	d. Please apply to the Local Authority for copy of Planning Consent
e. Please also supply a copy of any bye-law or building regulation consent relating to the property	e. As d above
2. Rates and other Outgoings	2.
a. What is the rateable value of the property?	a. £359
b. What were the total annual charges for rates, sewerage and water in the previous year?	b. £654.50
c. What other periodic charges affect the property or its occupier? Please specify.	c. None other than gas and similar utility charges.
3. Fixtures and Fittings	3.
a. Please specify which of the following now on the property or growing thereon or attached thereto are included in the sale price: Trees, shrubs, flowers, garden produce, sheds, greenhouses, TV aerials, fitted furniture, garden	a. All the items listed are included in the sale price except the garden shed and fitted carpets which are available for purchase by separate arrangement.

Ole SERIES PRE-CONTRACT ENQUIRIES page 2

ENQUIRIES	REPLIES
furniture and/or ornaments, electric switches, power points, ceiling and wall lights and fittings, curtain slide rails and fittings, fitted carpets as laid.	
b. Please confirm that all chattels, fixtures, fittings and separate items included in the sale price are the Vendor's property free of any bill of sale, lien, hire purchase or any other third party claim.	b. Confirmed
c. Please specify what fixtures and fittings affixed to the property are not included in the sale price.	c. None
4. Boundaries	4.
a. Is the property fenced, hedged or walled on all sides? Please state to whom these boundary fences, hedges or walls belong.	a. Yes. We understand that the Northern boundary fence belongs to No. 17 and the remainder to the Vendors.
b. Which of these has the Vendor maintained and regarded as his responsibility?	b. Please see 4a above.
c. Do the boundaries correspond with the filed plan annexed to or drawn on the Deeds?	c. Yes, so far as the Vendors are aware but the Purchasers should rely upon their own inspection.
5. Disputes	5.
a. Is the Vendor aware of any current or past disputes relating to the boundaries, easements, covenants, nuisance or any other matters affecting the property or its use?	a. No
b. Has the Vendor received any notices relating to the property or its use?	b. No
6. Rights of Way	6.
a. Please state whether any person has a right of way over land which forms part of the property being sold.	a. Not to the Vendor's knowledge but the property is sold subject to any there may be.
b. Does the Vendor have a right of way over a shared drive passage or track to gain access to a garage or other part of the property?	b. No
7. Services	7.
a. Is the water supply direct from the mains?	a. Yes, so far as the Vendor is aware.
b. Is the drainage of the property direct to a main drain?	b. The Purchasers should rely upon their own inspection.
c. Are there any drains pipes or cables which serve another property running under or over the property being sold?	c. The usual services are connected but the Purchasers should rely upon their own inspection for the route of pipes etc.

Ole SERIES PRE-CONTRACT ENQUIRIES page 3

ENQUIRIES	REPLIES
8. Guarantees	8.
a. Please state whether there is a current N.H.B.C. certificate in force in respect of the property.	a. No
b. Please supply copies of any other current guarantees relating to the property, the benefit of which will be assigned to the Purchaser.	b. Copy of Cavity Wall insulation guarantee herewith.
c. Have any claims been made under the terms of these guarantees which remain to be settled or are any pending?	c. No
9. Persons Residing in the Property	9.
a. Please give the full names (and ages if under 18 years of age) of all persons resident in the property (other than the Vendor).	a. Only the Vendors are in residence.
b. What legal or equitable rights in the property, if any, has each person named?	
10. Completion	10.
Please state when after exchange of contracts the Vendor will be able to give vacant possession of the whole of the property?	4 weeks subject to contract.

ADDITIONAL ENQUIRIES should be attached on a separate sheet

Ole SERIES PRE-CONTRACT ENQUIRIES page 4

LEASEHOLD PROPERTIES (Delete if not applicable)	REPLIES
a. Please state whether the Lease under which the property is held is a head lease or an underlease	
b. Please state the names and addresses of the Lessor, any superior Lessor and their respective receivers of the ground rent	
c. If the consent or licence of the Lessor in the Assignment of the lease is required please state what steps have been taken to obtain the same.	
d. Has the Vendor complied with all the terms of the Lease under which the property is held?	
e. Please supply details of service charges levied in respect to the preceding 3 years and vouchers for the same.	
f. Please supply full details of the insurance policy covering the property, including the name of the Insurance Company, policy number, name(s) insured, risks covered, sum covered, premium paid an removal date.	

Above are my/our replied to the enquiries

....
Proposed Vendors's Signature

.... 198

LETTER TO ACCOMPANY ENQUIRIES BEFORE CONTRACT OF THE VENDOR'S SOLICITOR

Your Name
Your Address

Today's Date

Messrs Dodson and Fogg,
Lloyds Bank Chambers,
High Street,
Hutton.

SUBJECT TO CONTRACT

Dear Sirs,

Re: 15 Lone Pine Close, Hutton

Thank you for your letter of the ...... enclosing draft contract together with carbon copy. I now enclose pre-Contract Enquiries and copy for your use, and shall be pleased to receive your replies as soon as possible.

Yours faithfully

Your Signature

CONTRACT FOR SALE (REGISTERED LAND)

C O N T R A C T   F O R   S A L E

This agreement is made the day of 198

BETWEEN	BERTRAM BROWN and BARBARA BROWN, both of, 15 Lone Pine Close, Hutton (hereinafter called "the Vendor")
and	GERALD GEORGE FORD and JOAN FORD, both of, 112 Dorset Road, Hutton (hereinafter called "the Purchaser")

Whereby it is agreed that the Vendor shall sell and the Purchaser shall Purchase subject to the conditions printed hereon the property described in the particulars below for the sum of TWENTY NINE THOUSAND SEVEN HUNDRED AND FIFTY POUNDS (£29,750.00)

PARTICULARS

ALL THAT freehold/leasehold property situate and known as Number 15 Lone Pine Close, Hutton, in the County of Wessex as the same is registered with Title Absolute at H.M.Land Registry under Title Number XZ498031 Together With and Subject to the rights contained or referred to in the Registers of the Title

Purchase price	£29,750.00
Deposit	£ 2,975.00
Balance payable	£26,775.00
Price agreed for fixtures/fittings chattels	£
Total:	£26,775.00

CONDITIONS OF SALE on REVERSE

Signed Vendor/Purchaser

Date 19

Purchaser's Solicitors

Local Authority Hutton District Council

CONDITIONS OF SALE

1. The property is sold subject to the National Conditions of Sale Twentieth Edition (hereinafter referred to as the General Conditions) so far as they are not varied or inconsistent with these conditions of sale so however General Condition 11(7) of the general conditions shall apply in any event

2. The title of the Vendor is registered in Woolville District Land Registry with Absolute Title under Title Number XZ490831

3. ~~The abstract of title shall begin with~~

4. The property is sold subject to the restrictive covenants and matters referred to by and set out in entries numbered 1, 2 and 3 of the Charges Register and referred to or set out by entry number 1 in the Property Register. A copy of said coveants, conditions and stipulations having been supplied to the Purchasers they shall be deemed to be purchasers with full knowledge thereof and shall raise no requisition or objection thereto

5. The prescribed rate referred to in the general conditions is 4 % over the base rate for the time being of Lloyds Bank PLC

6. The contractual completion date in general condition 5 of the general conditions is 198 and the latest time for completion is 2.00 ~~am~~/pm

7. Unless herein stated to the contrary general condition 3 of the general conditions shall not apply

8. The Vendor sells as Beneficial Owner

* 9. The property is sold with vacant possession of the whole upon completion

or

* 9. ~~The property is sold subject to the following leases or tenancies or licenses~~

\+ 10. The 10% deposit shall be paid as stakeholder/agent for the Vendor to Sellright Estate Agency of 10 High Street, Hutton

11. In this agreement the term 'Solicitor' shall include the term 'Licensed Conveyancer'

12. The Vendor hereby grants an Authority to the Purchaser and/or his Solicitor to examine the Register

* Delete as appropriate

\+ If you have not instructed Estate Agents, ask your Bank Manager to hold the deposit as "stakeholder." In this case, you would amend the text thus: "...........Bankers of the Vendors, Friendly Bank PLC, 21 Moorside, Hutton"

Rv.2 OLE Series

CONTRACT FOR SALE (LEASEHOLD LAND)

CONTRACT FOR SALE

This agreement is made the day of 198

BETWEEN	JOHN JONES and MARY JONES, both of 21A LIBRARY ROAD, HUTTON (hereinafter called "the Vendor")
and	FREDERICK SMITH and ANN SMITH, both of 12 HOUGH LANE, HUTTON (hereinafter called "the Purchaser")

Whereby it is agreed that the Vendor shall sell and the Purchaser shall Purchase subject to the conditions printed hereon the property described in the particulars below for the sum of TWENTY NINE THOUSAND SEVEN HUNDRED AND FIFTY POUNDS (£ 29,750.00)

PARTICULARS

ALL THAT ~~freehold~~/leasehold Flat situate and known as *

32A Library Road, Hutton, in the County of Wessex as the same is registered at H.M. Land Registry under Title Number XZ498031 for all the residue unexpired of a Lease ("the Lease") made the day of 19 between Albert Black (1) and John Brown (2) for the term of 99 years from subject as hereinafter mentioned

Purchase price	£ 29,750.00
Deposit	£ 2,975.00
Balance payable	£ 26,775.00
Price agreed for fixtures/fittings chattels	£
Total:	£ 26,775.00

CONDITIONS OF SALE on REVERSE

Signed Vendor/Purchaser

Date 19

Purchaser's Solicitors

Local Authority Hutton District Council

CONDITIONS OF SALE

1. The property is sold subject to the National Conditions of Sale Twentieth Edition (hereinafter referred to as the General Conditions) so far as they are not varied or inconsistent with these conditions of sale so however General Condition 11(7) of the general conditions shall apply in any event

2. The title of the Vendor is registered in Woolville District Land Registry with Absolute Title under Title Number XZ498031

3. ~~The abstract of title shall begin with~~

4. The property is sold subject to the payment of the rent reserved thereby and the covenants agreements and stipulations contained in the aforesaid lease a copy of which having been supplied to the Purchasers, they shall be deemed to be Purchasers with full knowledge thereof and shall raise no requisition or objection with regard thereto.

5. The prescribed rate referred to in the general conditions is 4 % over the base rate for the time being of Lloyds Bank PLC

6. The contractual completion date in general condition 5 of the general conditions is 198 and the latest time for completion is 2.00 ~~am~~/pm

7. Unless herein stated to the contrary general condition 3 of the general conditions shall not apply

8. The Vendor sells as Beneficial Owner

* 9. The property is sold with vacant possession of the whole upon completion

or

* 9. The property is sold subject to the following leases or tenancies or licences

\+ 10. The 10% deposit shall be paid as stakeholder/agent for the Vendor to Sellright Estate Agency of 10 High Street, Hutton

11. In this agreement the term 'Solicitor' shall include the term 'Licensed Conveyancer'

12. The Vendor hereby grants an Authority to the Purchaser and/or his Solicitor to examine the Register

* Delete as appropriate

\+ If you have not instructed Estate Agents, ask your Bank Manager to hold the deposit as "stakeholder." In this case, you would amend the text thus: "...........Bankers of the Vendors, Friendly Bank PLC, 21 Moorside, Hutton"

Rv.2 OLE Series

CONTRACT FOR SALE (UNREGISTERED LAND)

C O N T R A C T   F O R   S A L E

This agreement is made the day of 198

BETWEEN	BERTRAM BROWN and BARBARA BROWN, both of 15 Lone Pine Close, Hutton (hereinafter called "the Vendor")
and	GERALD GEORGE FORD and JOAN FORD, both of 112 Dorset Road, Hutton (hereinafter called "the Purchaser")

Whereby it is agreed that the Vendor shall sell and the Purchaser shall Purchase subject to the conditions printed hereon the property described in the particulars below for the sum of TWENTY NINE THOUSAND SEVEN HUNDRED AND FIFTY POUNDS (£29,750.00)

PARTICULARS

ALL THAT freehold/~~leasehold~~ piece or parcel of land TOGETHER WITH the dwellinghouse erected thereon or on some part thereof situate and known as

15 Lone Pine Close, Hutton, in the County of Wessex

as the same was conveyed by a Conveyance ("the Conveyance") dated the 18th day of May, 1979, and made between John Brown (1) and the Vendor (2) ALL WHICH said property is for the purposes of identification only delineated on the plan annexed thereto and thereon edged red

Purchase price	£29,750.00
Deposit	£ 2,975.00
Balance payable	£26,775.00
Price agreed for fixtures/fittings chattels	£
Total:	£26,775.00

CONDITIONS OF SALE on REVERSE

Signed **Vendor/Purchaser**

Date 19

Purchaser's Solicitors

Local Authority Hutton District Council

CONDITIONS OF SALE

1. The property is sold subject to the National Conditions of Sale Twentieth Edition (hereinafter referred to as the General Conditions) so far as they are not varied or inconsistent with these conditions of sale so however General Condition 11(7) of the general conditions shall apply in any event

2. The title of the Vendor is registered ~~in~~ District Land ~~Registry with~~ ~~Title under~~ Title Number

3. The abstract of title shall begin with a Conveyance on sale dated the 20th day of June, 1964, and made between Henry Smith of the one part and John Brown of the other part.

4. The property is sold subject to the restrictive and other covenants and all other matters contained, mentioned or referred to in the Conveyance. The Purchasers having been supplied with copies of the same shall be deemed to purchase with full notice thereof and no objections shall be made or requisitions raised in respect thereof. The Purchasers will in their conveyance covenant by way of indemnity to observe and perform the same.

5. The prescribed rate referred to in the general conditions is 4 % over the base rate for the time being of Bank PLC

6. The contractual completion date in general condition 5 of the general conditions is 198 and the latest time for completion is 2.00 ~~am~~/pm

7. Unless herein stated to the contrary general condition 3 of the general conditions shall not apply

8. The Vendor sells as Beneficial Owner

* 9. The property is sold with vacant possession of the whole upon completion

or

* 9. The property is sold subject ~~to the following leases or tenancies or licences~~

\+ 10. The 10% deposit shall be paid as stakeholder/agent for the Vendor to Sellright Estate Agency of 10 High Street, Hutton

11. In this agreement the term 'Solicitor' shall include the term 'Licensed Conveyancer'

12. The Vendor hereby grants an Authority to the Purchaser and/or his Solicitor to examine the Register

* **Delete as appropriate**

\+ **If you have not instructed Estate Agents, ask your Bank Manager to hold the deposit as "stakeholder." In this case, you would amend the text thus: "............Bankers of the Vendors, Friendly Bank PLC, 21 Moorside, Hutton"**

Rv.2 OLE Series (c) Jay Publications Limited

CONTRACT FOR SALE (LEASEHOLD LAND)

CONTRACT FOR SALE

This agreement is made the   day of   198

BETWEEN	JOHN JONES and MARY JONES, both of 21A LIBRARY ROAD, HUTTON (hereinafter called "the Vendor")
and	FREDERICK SMITH and ANN SMITH, both of 12 HOUGH LANE, HUTTON (hereinafter called "the Purchaser")

Whereby it is agreed that the Vendor shall sell and the Purchaser shall purchase subject to the conditions printed hereon the property described in the particulars below for the sum of TWENTY NINE THOUSAND SEVEN HUNDRED AND FIFTY POUNDS (£ 29,750.00)

PARTICULARS

ALL THAT Freehold/Leasehold property Flat situate and known as 32A Library Road, Hutton, in the County of Wessex

for all the residue unexpired of a Lease ("the Lease") made the   day of   19   between Albert Black (1) and John Brown (2) for the term of 99 years from
subject to the terms and conditions set out or referred to herein

Purchase price	£29,750.00
Deposit	£ 2,975.00
Balance payable	£26,775.00
Price agreed for fixtures/fittings chattels	£
Total:	£26,775.00

CONDITIONS OF SALE on REVERSE

Signed   VEndor/Purchaser

Date   19

Purchasers Solicitors:

Local Authority: Hutton District Council

CONDITIONS OF SALE

1. The property is sold subject to the National Conditions of Sale Twentieth Edition (hereinafter referred to as the General Conditions) so far as they are not varied or inconsistent with these conditions of sale so however General Condition 11(7) of the General Conditions shall apply in any event

2. The title of the Vendor is registered in District Land ~~Registry with Title under~~ Title Number

3. The abstract of title shall begin with the Lease and shall continue with an Assignment made between John Brown (1) and James Lee (2) dated

4. The property is sold subject to the payment of the rent reserved thereby and the covenants agreements and stipulations contained in the aforesaid lease a copy of which having been supplied to the Purchasers, they shall be deemed to be Purchasers with full knowledge thereof and shall raise no requisition or objection with regard thereto.

5. The prescribed rate referred to in the General Conditions is 4% over the base rate for the time being of Lloyds Bank PLC

6. The contractual completion date in General Condition 5 of the General Conditions is   198 and the latest time for completion is 2.00 ~~am~~/pm

7. Unless herein stated to the contrary General Condition 3 of the General Conditions shall not apply

8. The Vendor sells as Beneficial Owner

9. The property is sold with vacant possession of the whole upon completion

or

* 9. The property is sold subject ~~to the following leases or tenancies or~~ licences

\+ 10. The 10% deposit shall be paid as stakeholder/agent for the Vendor to Sellright Estate Agency of 10 High Street, Hutton

11. In this agreement the term 'solicitor' shall include the term 'Licensed Conveyancer'

12. The Vendor hereby grants an Authority to the Purchaser and/or his Solicitor to examine the Register

* Delete as appropriate

\+ If you have not instructed Estate Agents, ask your Bank Manager to hold the deposit as "stakeholder." In this case, you would amend the text thus: ".......Bankers of the Vendors, Friendly Bank PLC, 21 Moorside, Hutton."

Rv.2 OLE Series (c) 1986 Jay Publications Limited

TYPICAL LAND CERTIFICATE (SHOWING THE 3 REGISTERS)

H.M. LAND REGISTRY

Edition 1 opened 28.4.1978 TITLE NUMBER XZ498031 Map reference VIS 312K

This register consists of 4

A. PROPERTY REGISTER

containing the description of the registered land and the estate comprised in the Title

COUNTY	DISTRICT
WESSEX	HUTTON

The Freehold land shown and edged with red on the plan of the above Title filed at the Registry registered on 28 April 1978 known as 15 Lone Pine Close, Hutton.

NOTE 1:–The Conveyance dated 2 October 1958 referred to in Entry No 3 of the Charges Reg. contains the following provision :-

"The Purchasers shall not be entitled to any right of light or air which would in any manner diminish or interfere with the free and unrestricted user of any adjoining or adjacent land forming part of the Conifer Avenue Estate for either building or any other purposes."

B. PROPRIETORSHIP REGISTER

stating nature of the Title, name, address and description of the proprietor of the land and any entries affecting the right of disposing thereof

TITLE ABSOLUTE

Entry number	Proprietor, etc.	Remarks
1	JAMES CHARLES FRENCH and FREDA FRENCH his wife both of 15 Lone Pine Close Hutton, Wessex, registered on 28 April 1978	

Any entries struck through are no longer subsisting

TYPICAL CHARGES REGISTER IN LAND CERTIFICATE

2

TITLE NUMBER XZ498031

C. CHARGES REGISTER

containing charges, incumbrances etc., adversely affecting the land and registered dealings therewith

Entry No.	The date at the beginning of each entry is the date on which the entry was made on this edition of the register	Remarks
	28 April 1978—A Conveyance of the land in this title and other land dated 20 May 1896 made between (1) Mary Jane Martin and (2) Lavinia Horsey contains restrictive covenants but neither the original Conveyance nor a certified copy or examined abstract thereof was produced on first registration.	
	28 April 1978—A Conveyance of the land tinted blue on the filed plan and other land dated 4 May 1933 made between (1) Albert Truzzel Granger and William Robert Armstrong and (2) Reuben Webb contains covenants particulars of which are set out in the Schedule annexed.	
	28 April 1978—The land is subject to the following rights reserved by a Conveyance of the land in this title dated 2 October 1958 made between (1) John Frank Jones and Elizabeth Jones (Vendors) and (2) Walter William Werner and Jane Gladys Werner :— "EXCEPT AND RESERVING unto the Vendors and their successors in title a free passage and running of water and soil to and from all other property of or to which the vendors are seised or entitled with power at any time to enter upon the property hereby conveyed and to make lay and repair pipes drains and water courses for such purpose the person or persons so entering giving reasonable notice thereof and making good all damage occasioned thereby."	

Any entries struck through are no longer subsisting

TITLE NUMBER XZ498031 Page 3

C. CHARGES REGISTER – continued.

Schedule of restrictive covenants	Remarks
The following are particulars of the covenants contained in the Conveyance dated 4 May 1933 referred to in the Charges Register. THE Purchaser thereby covenanted with Vendors with intent to bind the property thereby conveyed and all future owners thereof that the Purchaser and his successors in title would observe and perform the stipulations and conditions contained in the first schedule thereto THE FIRST SCHEDULE before referred to 1. Not to make or suffer to be made on the premises thereby conveyed any excavations except for the purpose of building on or levelling such premises or make or suffer to be made or burnt thereon any bricks tiles or other wares or make or suffer to be made any mortar on the premises thereby conveyed such as is required for building thereon. 2. Not to use or permit to be used any dwellinghouse erected on the property thereby conveyed for any purpose other than as a private dwellinghouse or for the carrying on of a learned or artistic profession and not to use any motor house erected thereon or permit the same to be used for any purpose other than a private motor house for the use of the occupier of the dwellinghouse to which it belongs 3. Not to erect or permit to be erected on the property thereby conveyed any advertisement or hoarding or temporary erection or shed of any kind other than a bicycle or garden shed (except temporary sheds to be used only as incidental to and during the erection of the buildings therein-before authorised) and to use such part of the land as is not built upon as ornamental or vegetable garden or pleasure ground and not to do or permit to be done upon the said premises anything which shall or may be or become a nuisance damage annoyance or disturbance to the Vendors or the owners or occupiers of any land or dwellinghouse in the neighbourhood and not to permit clothes linen or other articles to be hung out in front of the dwellinghouse for the purpose of drying upon the premises. 4. Not to deposit on any of the roads or footpaths abutting on the property thereby conveyed any building or other materials nor disturb the surface of any such road or footpath except for the purpose of making connections to sewers drains or mains thereunder and any such disturbance shall forthwith be made good by the Purchaser of the premises thereby conveyed.	

COPY OF FILED PLAN OF REGISTERED LAND

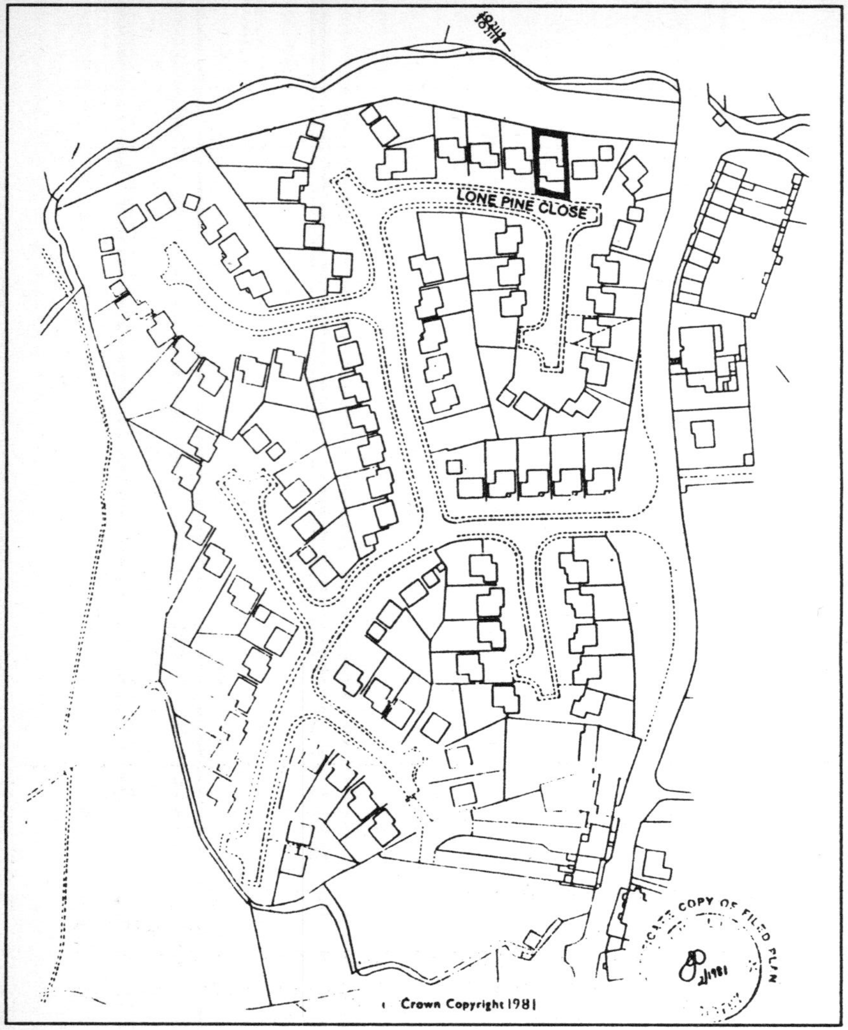

LETTER TO VENDOR'S SOLICITOR APPROVING DRAFT CONTRACT

Messrs Dodson and Fogg,
Lloyds Bank Chambers,
High Street,
Hutton.

Your Name
Your Address

Today's Date

SUBJECT TO CONTRACT

Dear Sirs,

Re: 15 Lone Pine Close, Hutton

Please refer to your letter dated . . . forwarding draft contract. As agreed on the telephone today I have added an additional clause listing the items that are included in the purchase price, and return the draft approved subject to the inclusicn of this amendment.

Yours faithfully,

Your Signature

SUGGESTED ADDITIONAL CLAUSE IN DRAFT CONTRACT LISTING ITEMS INCLUDED IN THE PURCHASE PRICE

The following items are included in the purchase price:
1. Venetian blinds as fitted to kitchen and bathroom.
2. Carpets as fitted to the lounge and dining room.
3. Garden shed

and £••• of the purchase shall be apportioned to these items.

SUGGESTED CLAUSE IN DRAFT CONTRACT TO COVER ANY GUARANTEE(S)

The following additional clause is suggested for inclusion in the contract of sale to provide for the assignment of the benefit of any guarantee(s) to the purchaser.

"On Completion the Vendors will hand over to the Purchasers the *cavity wall insulation guarantee and the *guarantee issued by Killpest Limited and will assign to the Purchasers the benefit thereof. The Vendors will also hand over the *NHBC certificate."

*Omit as appropriate

LETTER TO PURCHASER'S BUILDING SOCIETY SOLICITOR

Messrs Brown and Green
44 High West Street,
Hutton.

Your Name
Your Address
Today's date

Dear Sirs,

Re: 15 Lone Pine Close, Hutton

The Best Building Society have advised me that they have instructed you to act for them in the above matter. Will you kindly let me know what documents you will require of me before releasing the funds.

Yours faithfully

Your Signature

COVERING LETTER ON EXCHANGE OF CONTRACTS

Messrs. Dodson and Fogg.
Lloyds Bank Chambers,
High Street,
Hutton.

Your Name
Your Address

Today's Date

Dear Sirs,

Re: 15 Lone Pine Close, Hutton

I now enclose my signed part of the contract to purchase the above property, together with my cheque for £2975.00 being ten per cent of the purchase price by way of deposit. In exchange I shall be pleased to receive the part contract signed by the Vendors.

Will you also kindly send me two Authorities to Inspect the Register — one in my favour and one in favour of the solicitors acting for my Building Society, Messrs Brown and Green, 44 High West Street, Hutton.

The . . . . is agreed with the Vendors as the Completion date.

Yours faithfully,

Your Signature

LETTER TO YOUR BUILDING SOCIETY NOTIFYING EXCHANGE OF CONTRACTS

Your Name
Your Address

Today's date

The Manager,
Best Building Society,
84 High Street,
Hutton

Dear Sir,

Re: 15 Lone Pine Close, Hutton

I confirm our telephone conversation of today. I have exchanged contracts today for the purchase of the above property and as agreed, please arrange Buildings cover in the sum of £30000 with immediate effect, at the rate of £1.50 per £100.

Yours faithfully,

Your Signature

LETTER TO ACCOMPANY REQUISITIONS ON TITLE AND TRANSFER FORM

Your Name
Your Address

Today's Date

Messrs. Dodson and Fogg,
Lloyds Bank Chambers,
High Street,
Hutton.

Dear Sirs,

Re: 15 Lone Pine Close, Hutton

I now enclose Requisitions on Title with a copy for you use. Will you kindly return the form with your replies at your earliest convenience.

I also enclose two copies of Transfer Form 19(JP). If you approve, kindly treat the top copy as the engrossment and retain the second copy for your use.

Yours faithfully,

Your Signature

Ole SERIES REQUISITIONS ON TITLE (POST-CONTRACT)

REQUISITIONS ON TITLE

(POST-CONTRACT)

Re ..... 15 Lone Pine Close, Hutton ....

.... Brown ....

To ..... Ford ....

ENQUIRIES	REPLIES
1. Previous enquiries	1.
If the pre-contract enquiries replied to on behalf of the Vendor were repeated would the replies now be the same as those previously given? If not, please give full particulars of any variation.	Yes, save as may have been varied by correspondence.
2. Receipts	2.
(A) On completion the receipt for all rates and outgoings formerly payable by the Vendor must not be produced and any arrears allowed for	(A) Noted
(B) In the case of a leasehold property the receipt for ground rent due on the last rent day prior to the day of completion as well as the receipt for the last fire insurance premium must be produced on completion.	
3. Title Deeds	3.
(A) Unregistered land	
(i) Which documents of title will be handed over to the Purchaser on completion?	
(ii) Who will give the Purchaser the statutory acknowledgement and undertaking for the production and safe custody of those not handed over?	
(iii) Why will any documents not handed over be retained?	
(B) Registered land	(B)
When was the land or charge certificate last officially examined with the register?	12 August 1986
4. Mortgages	4.
(A) All subsisting mortgages must be discharged on or before completion.	(A) Agreed
(B) (i) In respect of each subsisting mortgage will the vacating receipt/discharge or registered charge be handed over on completion?	(B) (i) Please refer to (ii) below
(ii) If an undertaking to hand it over later is proposed, what are the suggested terms of the undertaking?	(ii) We will give the usual undertaking to forward a sealed Form 53

	REPLIES
5. Completion	5.
(A) Please send a completion statement.	(A) Herewith
(B) (i) Where will completion take place?	(B) (i) At this office
(ii) In whose favour and for what amounts will bankers drafts be required on completion?	(ii) We will advise as soon as possible.
6. Notices	
Please give the name and address of any Solicitor, agent, or other person to whom notice of any dealing with the property must be given.	
7. Possession	7.
(A) (i) Vacant possession of the whole of the property must be given on completion	(A) (i) Noted
(ii) What arrangements will be made to deliver the keys to the Purchaser?	(ii) We suggest that this is done through the Estate Agents.

NOTE You will appreciate that the Requisitions based on the Abstract of Title or Contract must, of course, be added to the above.

N.B. The Deeds and documents of title remain to be examined and the right is reserved to make further requisitions which may arise on each examination, the replies to the above, and enquiries before completion or otherwise.

.... Date .... Date

COMPLETED FORM 19 WITH COVENANT FOR INDEMNITY

Form 19

H.M. Land Registry

Land Registration Acts, 1925 to 1971

Stamp pursuant to section 28 of the Finance Act 1931 to be impressed here.

When the transfer attracts Inland Revenue duty, the stamps should be impressed here before lodging the transfer for registration.

(1) For a transfer by a company or corporation form 19(Co) is printed and for a transfer to joint proprietors form 19(JP) is printed

(1) **TRANSFER OF WHOLE**

(Rule 98 or 115, Land Registration Rules, 1925)

County and district (or London borough) WESSEX HUTTON

Title number(s) XZ498031

Property 15 Lone Pine Close, Hutton, Wessex

Date 19 86 In consideration of

TWENTY NINE THOUSAND SEVEN HUNDRED AND FIFTY

pounds (£29,750.00) (2) the receipt whereof is hereby acknowledged

(2) Strike out if not required

(3) In BLOCK LETTERS enter full name(s), postal address(es) and occupation(s) of the proprietor(s) of the land

I/~~We~~ (3) BERTRAM BROWN, of

15 LONE PINE CLOSE, HUTTON,

WESSEX

(4) If desired or otherwise as the case may be (See rules 76 and 77)

(4) as beneficial owner(~~s~~) hereby transfer to

(5) In BLOCK LETTERS enter full name(s), postal address(es) and occupation(s) of the transferee(s) for entry on the register

(5)

GERALD GEORGE FORD, of

112 DORSET AVENUE, HUTTON,

WESSEX

(6) Any special clause should be entered here

(7) A transfer for charitable uses should follow form 36 in the schedule to the Land Registration Rules, 1925 (see rules 121 and 122)

the land comprised in the title(s) above mentioned (6) (7) And the Transferee for himself and his successors in title hereby covenants with the Transferor by way of indemnity only to observe and perform the covenants contained or referred to in the Charges Register of the said Title so far as the same are still subsisting and capable of being enforced and relate to the property hereby transferred.

(continued overleaf)

(8) If a certificate of value for the purposes of the Stamp Act 1891 and amending Acts is not required, this paragraph should be deleted

(8) *It is hereby certified that the transaction hereby effected does not form part of a larger transaction or series of transactions in respect of which the amount or value or aggregate amount or value of the consideration exceeds £* 30,000.00

Signed, sealed and delivered by the said

BERTRAM BROWN — B. Brown

in the presence of

Name Alma Jones

Address 44 Malta Road Hutton

Occupation Clerk

Signed, sealed and delivered by the said

GERALD GEORGE FORD — G.G. Ford

in the presence of

Name John Brown

Address 9 Acre Road Hutton

Occupation Salesman

COMPLETED FORM 19 (JP) WITH COVENANT FOR INDEMNITY

Form 19(JP)
H.M. Land Registry

Land Registration Acts, 1925 to 1971

Stamp pursuant to section 28 of the Finance Act 1931, to be impressed here.

When the transfer attracts Inland Revenue duty, the stamps should be impressed here before lodging the transfer for registration

(1) For a transfer to a sole proprietor use printed form 19

NOTE This transfer must be executed by the transferees as well as the transferor(s)

(1) TRANSFER OF WHOLE TO JOINT PROPRIETORS

(Freehold or Leasehold)

(Rules 98 or 115, Land Registration Rules, 1925)

County and district (or London borough) WESSEX HUTTON

Title number(s) XZ498031

Property 15 Lone Pine Close, Hutton, Wessex

Date 19 86 In consideration of TWENTY NINE THOUSAND SEVEN HUNDRED AND FIFTY pounds (£ 29,750.000) (2) *the receipt whereof is hereby acknowledged*

(2) Strike out if not required

(3) In BLOCK LETTERS, enter full name(s), postal address(es) and occupation(s) of the proprietor(s) of the land.

~~I~~/We(3) BERTRAM BROWN and BARBARA BROWN, both of 15 LONE PINE CLOSE, HUTTON, WESSEX

(4) If desired, or otherwise as the case may be (See rules 76 and 77)

(5) In BLOCK LETTERS, enter full names, postal addresses and occupations of the transferees for entry on the register.

(4) *as beneficial owner(s)* hereby transfer to

(5) GERALD GEORGE FORD and JOAN FORD, both of 112 DORSET ROAD, HUTTON, WESSEX

the land comprised in the title above mentioned (6) (7) And the Transferees for themselves and their successors in title hereby jointly and severally covenant with the Transferors by way of indemnity only to observe and perform the covenants contained or referred to in the Charges Register of the said Title so far as the same are still subsisting and capable of being enforced and relate to the property hereby transferred.

(6) Any special clause should be entered here

(7) A transfer for charitable uses should follow form 36 (see rules 121 and 122)

(continued overleaf)

---

(8) Delete the inappropriate alternative

The transferees declare that the survivor of them(8) can / ~~cannot~~ give a valid receipt for capital money arising on a disposition of the land.

(9) If a certificate of value for the purposes of the Stamp Act, 1891, and amending Acts is not required, this paragraph should be deleted.

(9) *It is hereby certified that the transaction hereby effected does not form part of a larger transaction or series of transactions in respect of which the amount or value or aggregate amount or value of the consideration exceeds £* 30,000.00

(10) See marginal note overleaf

(10) Signed, sealed and delivered by the said BERTRAM BROWN — B. Brown
in the presence of
Name Alma Jones
Address 44 Malta Road, Hutton
Occupation Clerk

(10) Signed, sealed and delivered by the said BARBARA BROWN — Barbara Brown
in the presence of
Name Alma Jones
Address 44 Malta Road, Hutton
Occupation Clerk

(10) Signed, sealed and delivered by the said GERALD GEORGE FORD — G[illegible] Ford
in the presence of
Name John Brown
Address 7 [illegible] Road Hutton
Occupation Salesman

(10) Signed, sealed and delivered by the said JOAN FORD — Joan Ford
in the presence of
Name John Brown
Address 7 [illegible] Road Hutton
Occupation Salesman

COMPLETED FORM 201 AUTHORITY TO INSPECT THE REGISTER

HM Land Registry — Land Registration Acts 1925 to 1971

AUTHORITY TO INSPECT THE REGISTER

County and district (or London borough) WESSEX HUTTON

Title no(s) XZ 498031

Property The land and dwellinghouse known as 15 Lone Pine Close Hutton

We

Name BERTRAM BROWN AND BARBARA BROWN

Address 15 Lone Pine Close, Hutton

~~as solicitors for~~ The registered proprietors of the land in the the above-mentioned title

(insert full name(s) of registered proprietor(s))

of 15 Lone Pine Close, Hutton

~~the registered proprietor(s) of the land in the above-mentioned title(s)~~

hereby authorise Messrs Brown & Green,

of 44 High Street, Hutton,

to inspect the register of the above-mentioned title and any documents referred to in the register as being filed in the Land Registry.

Signed ....

Date .... ~~(Solicitors for the registered proprietor)~~ The registered proprietors.

Notes

1. This authority may also be used in support of an application for office copies (form A44) or for a certificate of inspection of the filed plan (form 101), or for an official search of the register (forms 94A, 94B or 94C).
2. This form, suitably adapted, can be used to give an authority to inspect the register on behalf of the proprietor of a registered charge.

LETTER TO ACCOMPANY DOCUMENTS SENT TO YOUR BUILDING SOCIETY'S SOLICITOR

Your Name
Your Address
Today's Date

Messrs Brown and Green,
44 High West Street,
Hutton,

Dear Sirs,

Re: 15 Lone Pine Close, Hutton

Thank you for your letter dated . . .*** I enclose herewith the undermentioned documents:

- Contract for sale signed by vendor
- Enquiries before Contract and replies
- Local search forms and Council's replies
- Copy of Transfer
- Authority to Inspect the Register (Form 201)
- Office copy of Land Register and plan

Yours faithfully,

Your Signature

*** Omit if inapplicable.

APPLICATION ON FORM K13

Important: Please read the notes overleaf before completing the form.

Form K13

Land Charges Act 1972
(Matrimonial Homes Act 1967)

FEE PANEL
If the fee is to be debited to your credit account put a cross (X) in this box.
If not, affix Land Registry fee stamp(s) in this space
(See Note 1 overleaf)

APPLICATION FOR CANCELLATION OF A LAND CHARGE OF CLASS F

Enter full Name(s) and Address(es) of Applicant(s)
(See notes 2 and 3 overleaf)

PARTICULARS OF APPLICANT

I. MARY MOORE

of 49 CHURCH LANE, IVANHOE, WESSEX X29 4H

hereby apply for cancellation in the register of the entry referred to below

Signature *Mary Moore* Date 12 May 1986

CERTIFICATE OF SOLICITOR(S)

We hereby certify that we are acting for the applicant and that we are satisfied that our client understands the nature of this application and the effect of the cancellation of the said entry on the register

Signature and address of Solicitors to the above applicant

Signature ...

Address ...

(See note 4 overleaf)

PARTICULARS OF ENTRY AFFECTED

Please cancel the undermentioned entry as to

Delete (a) or (b) as appropriate

(a) the whole
OR
(b) XXXXXXXXXX 90 CLIFTON CROFT ROAD, BRIGTOWN, WESSEX

CLASS	Insert number and date of the registration	Official reference no.	Date of registration
F		XZ 89211612	29. 12. 81
	Insert, if applicable, the number and date of any renewal of registration	Official reference no.	Date of registration

Only one individual or body to be entered.
(See note 5 overleaf)

PARTICULARS OF ESTATE OWNER

Forename(s) HENRY JOHN

SURNAME MOORE

Address 90 CLIFTON CROFT ROAD, BRIGTOWN, WESSEX

FOR OFFICIAL USE ONLY

1	2	3
°C		
4	5	6

KEY NUMBER

(See note 6 overleaf)

Solicitors name and address
If no Solicitor is acting enter applicant's name and address
(See note 7 overleaf)

MARY MOORE,
49 CHURCH LANE, IVANHOE, WESSEX

Solicitors' reference

COMPLETED FORM 53 DISCHARGE OF REGISTERED CHARGE

Form 53 (Co)
HM Land Registry

Land Registration Acts, 1925 to 1971

No Land Registry fee is payable

The charge certificate must accompany this application

DISCHARGE OF REGISTERED CHARGE
of which a company or corporation, including a building society, is the registered proprietor
(Rule 151, Land Registration Rules 1925)

County and district (or London borough) WESSEX HUTTON

Title number(s) XZ498031

Property 15 LONE PINE CLOSE, HUTTON, WESSEX

Date 1st October 1986 (1)

(1) In BLOCK LETTERS, enter full name and address of the registered proprietor of the charge.

BEST BUILDING SOCIETY,
BEST HOUSE, 97-99 LOMBARD ROW, RANCASTER,
WEST YORKSHIRE RG1 2XH

hereby admits that the charge dated the 5th of August 1983

(2) Strike out the words in italics if discharge is of the whole of the charge.

and registered on the 7th of August 1983 of which it is proprietor has been discharged (2)~~as to the land shown and edged with red on the accompanying plan (3), sealed by the said proprietor, being part of the land comprised in the title(s) above mentioned.~~

(3) See notes below

The common seal of
BEST BUILDING SOCIETY
was hereunto affixed (4)*by order of the board of directors*
in the presence of

(4) These words are required when the sealing is by a building society.

COMMON SEAL OF BUILDING SOCIETY

(5) Or other officers authorised by the statute, charter, articles of association, etc.

G. L. Woodward (5) *Director*

A. T. Johnson (5) *Secretary*

NOTES AS TO DISCHARGE OF PART

1. Except as stated in Note 2 below, a discharge as to part of the land comprised in a registered title must be accompanied by a plan based on the official plan of the title and, where necessary, include sufficient figured dimensions so as to define the extent of the land discharged and to fix its position by tying it to those physical features depicted by firm black lines on the official plan. This plan must be properly sealed by the chargee and securely attached to the form 53(Co).
2. A plan is not required where the part discharged is already clearly defined on the official plan by means of a colour or number reference and such particulars are entered in the form of discharge instead of those relating to an accompanying plan. A discharge which defines the part discharged by reference to the plot number(s) on an estate layout plan is not acceptable.

APPLICATION FOR SEARCH ON FORM 94A

(Numbers in brackets relate to notes overleaf)

Form 94A HM Land Registry **Land Registration (Official Searches) Rules 1981**

Application by Purchaser(1) for Official Search with priority in respect of the WHOLE of the land in a title

NEWTOWN District Land Registry(2)

67 Nelson Row,
Newtown,
Wessex

The attached duplicate must also be completed (A carbon copy will suffice).

(For an official search of part of the land in a title, use form 94B).

FOR OFFICIAL USE

County and district (or London borough)	WESSEX HUTTON
Title number(3)	XZ498031
Enter full name(s) of the registered proprietor(s)(4)	BERTRAM BROWN and BARBARA BROWN
Application is made to ascertain whether any adverse(5) entry has been made in the register since the date shown opposite being EITHER the date on which an office copy of the subsisting entries in the register was issued OR the last date on which the land or charge certificate was officially examined with the register.	1 May 1986
Enter full name(s) of the applicant(s) (*i.e. purchaser(s) lessees or chargee(s)*)	GERALD GEORGE FORD and JOAN FORD
I/We ~~solicitor(s)~~(6) the above mentioned applicant(s) certify that the applicant(s) intend(s) to:– (*Enter X in the appropriate box opposite*)	X P purchase; L take a lease of; C lend money on the security of a registered charge on — the WHOLE of the land in the above title

A WHERE A SOLICITOR IS ACTING FOR THE APPLICANT(S)
I/We certify that I/We hold the duly signed written authority of (or of the solicitor(s) for) the above mentioned registered proprietor(s) to inspect the register of the above title OR that I/We also act as solicitor(s) for the registered proprietor(s).

Indicate this by entering X in this box: [ ] A

B WHERE A SOLICITOR IS NOT ACTING FOR THE APPLICANT(S)
The duly signed written authority of (or of the solicitor(s) for) the registered proprietor(s) to inspect the register of the above title accompanies this application.

Indicate this by entering X in this box: [X] B

Key number(7)

This panel must be completed using BLOCK LETTERS and inserting the name, full address and postal code to which the official certificate or result of search is to be sent.

GERALD GEORGE FORD,
112 Dorset Road,
HUTTON,
WESSEX

Solicitor's reference(8)

Signed: G G Ford

Date: 5 June 1986

Telephone number: Hutton (0200)2999

"CLEAR" SEARCH REPORT ON FORM 94D

Form 94D H.M. Land Registry Land Registration (Official Searches) Rules 1981

This page is to be completed only by H.M. Land Registry

Official Certificate of the Result of Search

It is hereby certified that the official search applied for has been made with the following result:

Since 1–5– 19 86

Specimen

NO ADVERSE ENTRY HAS BEEN MADE THERE ON

Date of certificate 2 JUN 86 | Priority expires 11 a.m. on 14 JUL 86
THE DISTRICT LAND REGISTRY
See note below

N.B. – To obtain priority(9), the application for registration in respect of which this search is made must be delivered to the proper office at the latest by 11 am on the date when priority expires.

NOTES

(1) "Purchaser" means any person who, in good faith and for valuable consideration, acquires or intends to acquire a legal estate in land, so it includes a lessee or a chargee but not a depositee of a land or charge certificate. An official search made by such a depositee or by any person other than a "purchaser", as so defined, should be made in from 94C and a fee is payable.

(2) The application should be sent to the district land registry serving the area in which the land is situated. A list of addresses of the district land registries is set out on page 4 of this application form.

(3) A separate form must be used for each title number to be searched.

(4) The name(s) of the registered proprietor(s) should be entered as they appear on the evidence of the registered title supplied to the applicant. If there has been a change of name(s) the new name(s) should also be entered in brackets.

(5) Any entry made in the register since the date of commencement of this search but subsequently cancelled will not be revealed

(6) Where no solicitor is acting delete all or some of the words in italics as appropriate to the particular situation

(7) This should be restricted to a maximum of 10 digits including oblique strokes and punctuation.

(8) Where a key number has been allocated it should be used.

(9) The period of priority reserved for the registration of the disposition protected by the official search certificate will be shown either by a stamp impressed in the result of search above or on a separate computer printed result.

(10) Where a first registration is pending, [an official] search certificate cannot be issued unless and until the [first] registration of the title to the land affected has been completed.

(11) Fuller information about the official search procedure is contained in Practice Leaflet No. 2 entitled "Official searches of the Register", and Practice Leaflet No. 7, entitled "Development of registered building estates" which are obtainable free of charge from any district land registry

APPLICATION FOR BANKRUPTCY SEARCH ON FORM K16

Form K16

Land Charges Act 1972

APPLICATION FOR AN OFFICIAL SEARCH

(BANKRUPTCY ONLY)

Payment of fee (see Note 2 overleaf)

EITHER

Insert a cross (X) in this box if the fee is to be paid through a credit account

OR

affix stamps in this space

Application is hereby made for an official search in the index to the registers kept pursuant to the Land Charges Act 1972 in respect of the under-mentioned names for any subsisting entries of:

(i) petitions in bankruptcy in the register of pending actions
(ii) receiving orders in bankruptcy in the register of writs and orders
(iii) deeds of arrangement in the register of deeds of arrangement

For Official Use only

IMPORTANT: Please read the notes overleaf before completing the form.

NAMES TO BE SEARCHED
(Please use block letters and see note 3 overleaf)

Forename(s)	GERALD GEORGE
SURNAME	FORD
Forename(s)	JOHN
SURNAME	FORD
Forename(s)	
SURNAME	
Forename(s)	
SURNAME	
Forename(s)	
SURNAME	
Forename(s)	
SURNAME	

Particulars of Applicant (see notes, 4, 5 and 6 overleaf)

Key number	Name and address
	G.G. FORD, 11? [illegible] ROAD, HUTTON, WESSEX

Address for despatch of certificate
(Leave blank if certificate is to be returned to applicant's address)

Applicant's reference:

Date

FOR OFFICIAL USE ONLY

FORM K17 (BANKRUPTCY)

FORM K17

LAND CHARGES ACT, 1972.
CERTIFICATE OF THE RESULT OF SEARCH

CERTIFICATE No.	CERTIFICATE DATE	PROTECTION ENDS ON
10733193	17 JUL 1987	07 AUG 1987

It is hereby certified that an official search in respect of the undermentioned particulars has been made in the index to the register which are kept pursuant to the Land Charges Act, 1972. The result of the search is that there are NO SUBSISTING ENTRIES.

PARTICULARS SEARCHED

COUNTY OR COUNTIES: BANKRUPTCY ONLY. 137

NAME(S)	PERIOD	Fees £
WILLIAM HENRY * WAINWRIGHT *	---------	0.50

APPLICANT'S REFERENCE	APPLICANT'S KEY NUMBER		£
JCP/W/C	-------	AMOUNT PREPAID	0.50

Messrs Black and Brown,
49 Lower High Street,
Hutton.

Any enquiries concerning this certificate to be addressed to:-

The Superintendent,
Land Charges Department,
Burrington Way,
Plymouth, PL5 3LP.

IMPORTANT
PLEASE READ THE NOTES OVERLEAF

"CLEAR" SEARCH REPORTED ON FORM K17

FORM K17.

LAND CHARGES ACT, 1972.
CERTIFICATE OF THE RESULT OF SEARCH

CERTIFICATE No.	CERTIFICATE DATE	PROTECTION ENDS ON
X.09781546AB	05 APR 1986	26 APR 1986

It is hereby certified that an official search in respect of the undermentioned particulars has been made in the index to the register which are kept pursuant to the Land Charges Act, 1972. The result of the search is that there are NO SUBSISTING ENTRIES.

PARTICULARS SEARCHED

COUNTY OR COUNTIES: WESSEX

NAME(S)	PERIOD	Fees £
Bertram * BROWN *	1975 - 1986	.50
Barbara * BROWN *	1975 - 1986	.50

APPLICANT'S REFERENCE	GF	APPLICANT'S KEY NUMBER		£	1.00

Gerald George Ford,
112 Dorset Road,
Hutton, Wessex.

Any enquiries concerning this certificate to be addressed to:–

The Superintendent,
Land Charges Department,
Burrington Way,
Plymouth, PL5 3LP.

IMPORTANT
PLEASE READ THE NOTES OVERLEAF.

COMPLETED FORM STAMPS L(A)451

Inland Revenue
PARTICULARS OF INSTRUMENTS TRANSFERRING OR LEASING LAND

FINANCE ACT 1931
as amended by the Land Commission Act, 1967

FOR OFFICIAL USE
VO No. ....
PD No. ....
ANALYSIS CODE ....
DESC. ....
GV/NAV ....
DW. CODE ....
....
RETURN ....
O.S.No ....
OTHER ....

ATTENTION IS DRAWN TO THE NOTES OVERLEAF

1. Description of Instrument
Transfer

2. Date of Instrument
Today's date

3. Name and Address of Transferor or Lessor: *(Block Letters)*
BETRAM BROWN and BARBARA BROWN
15 LONE PINE CLOSE, HUTTON
WESSEX

4. Name and Address of Transferee or Lessee: *(Block Letters)*
GERALD GEORGE FORD and JOAN FORD,
112 DORSET ROAD, HUTTON,
WESSEX

5. Situation of the Land. Sufficient information must be given to enable the land to be identified accurately, e.g., by including any dimensions stated in the instrument and by attaching a plan to this form or by describing the boundaries in full. For premises the full postal address including the post code is required

15 Lone Pine Close, Hutton, Wessex HW92 3XX

COUNTY ....Wessex.......... RATING AUTHORITY ....HUTTON DISTRICT COUNCIL

6. Estate or Interest Transferred. Where the transaction is the assignment or grant of a lease, or the transfer of a fee simple subject to a lease, the terms of the lease, the date of commencement of the term and the rent reserved must be stated.

Fee simple

7. Consideration — State separately:

(a) any capital payment, with the date when due if otherwise than on execution of the instrument — Nil

(b) any debt released, covenanted to be paid or to which the transaction is made subject — Nil

(c) any periodical payment (including any charge) covenanted to be paid — Nil

(d) any terms surrendered — None

(e) any land exchanged — None

(f) any other thing representing money or money's worth — None

8. Any Minerals, Mineral Rights, Sporting Rights, Timber or Easements reserved: (on a separate sheet if necessary).
None

9. Any Restrictions, Covenants or Conditions affecting the value of the estate or interest transferred or granted: (on a separate sheet if necessary).
None

10. Signature of Transferee or Lessee or person on his behalf:
G.G. Ford   Date ....Today's Date

11. Name and Address of Transferor's or Lessor's Solicitor *(Block Letters)*
MESSRS DODSON & FOGG,
LLOYDS BANK CHAMBERS,
HIGH STREET,
HUTTON,
WESSEX

12. Name and Address of Signatory if other than Transferee or Lessee: *(Block Letters)*

STAMPS L(A) 451

COMPLETED FORM STAMPS 61

Inland Revenue
Stamp Duty

This form is for use when you wish to apply for impressed stamping on your documents by post
Please read the notes overleaf which tell you when and where to apply.

To: The Controller of Stamps, Inland Revenue My reference______

I request that the documents listed below be stamped with the duty (or duties) marked on them and shown below. I have put a √ by those I wish to be stamped to show that they have been produced to the Commissioners of Inland Revenue in accordance with Section 28 of Finance Act 1931. I confirm that those marked with a √ are accompanied by a completed form L(A) 451 *(available from any Stamp Office).*

Description of Document	Names of Parties to the document	√ S28	Duty to be impressed	*For official use*
Transfer	BERTRAM BROWN and BARBARA BROWN (1)			
	GERALD GEORGE FORD and JOAN FORD (2)			
		Total		

I confirm that I have
- enclosed all the documents listed above
- enclosed payment of the total duty shown
- given my reference (if applicable)
- entered my name and address below and on the return label

Signature ______

Date TODAY'S DATE

Full Name GERALD GEORGE FORD

Address 15 Lone Pine Close, HUTTON,
WESSEX

Post town HW92 3XX

Postcode ______

Telephone number 0200 98765

Return label

G.G.FORD,
15 Lone Pine Close,
Hutton,
Wessex

Stamps 61

FORM OF MORTGAGE

the Leeds PERMANENT BUILDING SOCIETY

LEGAL CHARGE
(NOT FOR BUILDING FINANCE)

LAND REGISTRY	COUNTY AND DISTRICT (OR LONDON BOROUGH)
	TITLE No

Dated the ______ day of ______ 19 ______ and made between Leeds Permanent Building Society of Permanent House The Headrow Leeds LS1 1NS ("the Society") and the Borrower and the Guarantor (if any) identified in the First Schedule.

A. The Society has paid to the Borrower (as the Borrower acknowledges) the Original Advance mentioned in the First Schedule

B. The Charge is made for securing also further advances (see Mortgage Condition 3) but the Society is not obliged to make any further advances

C. The Borrower as Beneficial Owner charges the Property identified in the First Schedule by way of legal mortgage with the payment of all moneys payable by the Borrower to the Society

D. The Borrower and the Guarantor (if any) covenant with the Society to observe be bound by and comply with the Mortgage Conditions set out in the Second Schedule

Signed sealed and delivered as follows:–

Signature	Seal	Witness
	SEAL	
	SEAL	
	SEAL	
	SEAL	

FIRST SCHEDULE

The Borrower

The Guarantor (if any)

The Property

Original Advance
£

APPLICATION ON FORM A4 (REGISTERED LAND)

Application to register **dealings with the whole of titles**

HM Land Registry — Form A4

Application number	Received stamp
	Record of fee paid
Ackd. by — Date	

Please complete the white boxes on pages 1, 4 and 2 in typescript or BLOCK CAPITALS

1 Title numbers
Enter title number(s) in this panel. If there are more than five titles please attach separate list of them and enter 'see list'.

1 Title numbers	Pending application numbers
XZ 498031	

2 Fees
Make sure you have enclosed the correct fee: refer to the current Land Registration Fee Order.
Cheques and postal orders should be crossed and made payable to HM Land Registry. Fees are payable on delivery of the application.

2 Nature of applications in priority order	Value £	Fee scale para or abatement	Fees paid £	Particulars of over/under payment
Discharge of Mortgage				
Transfer	29,750	4	65. 00	
Mortgage	10,000	Abatement		
		Total	65. 00	

3 Documents lodged
Treat each original and copy as a separate item.

3 List of all documents lodged	
Charge certificate	Mortgage
Form 53	Copy Mortgage
Transfer	Search Form 94A

4 Applicants
Name and address of person or firm lodging this application to whom any requisitions will be sent and to whom documents (including land or charge certificate) will be returned unless any special directions are given in panel 5

4 Key No. — Requisitions to be sent to and documents returned to

BROWN AND GREEN,
44 High West Street,
Hutton, Wessex.

Reference (max 10 digits): C/319 — Telephone No: Hutton 2749

5 Special directions
Specific request to the Land Registry to issue documents to a person or firm not mentioned in panel 4.

5 Description of document and addressee

Please turn to page 4 and complete panels 6 & 7

Please complete the white boxes using BLOCK CAPITALS for all names and addresses

Edition No.
Entry No. — Opened

A

6 New proprietors
For new proprietor(s) of the land enter the full name(s) and address(es) eg.
JOHN SMITH, milkman and MARY SMITH, his wife, both of 29 RYE ROAD WATFORD HERTS WD3 4TQ.
If there are no new proprietors then leave the panel blank

NB The address(es) given here will be entered on the Register as the Proprietor(s) address for service of notices etc.

6 B

I/We apply to register the following as new proprietor(s) of the land

GERALD GEORGE FORD, ENGINEER, AND JOAN FORD HIS WIFE,
15 LONE PINE CLOSE,
HUTTON, WESSEX.

(CANCEL

C — Remarks

(Date) Charge dated
registered on
to secure the moneys
the moneys including the further advances therein mentioned

7 New charges(s)
Enter the new chargee(s) full names and address(es) (Including postcode).
If there is no legal charge or mortgage to register then leave the panel blank.
If there is more than one charge enter details of the first charge in the blue area above the white box.
Please give Building Society account number if any.

NB The address(es) given here will be entered on the Register as the Proprietor(s) address for service of notices etc.

Please turn to Page 2

7 **I/We apply to register the following as new proprietor(s) of charge(s)**

Proprietor BEST BUILDING SOCIETY,
97-99 LOMBARD ROW,
RANCASIER,
WEST YORKSHIRE, RG1 2XH.

registered on
(CANCEL — and insert date)

PURCHASER'S BUILDING SOCIETY SOLICITOR'S ACCOUNT

Re: Best Building Society and
Mr. and Mrs. G.G. Ford
15 Long Pine Close, Hutton

	£	£
Mortgage Advance		15,000.00
Less Land Registry Fees	65.00	
Less our costs (including VAT)	115.75	180.75
Net amount on Completion		£14,819.25

VENDOR'S SOLICITOR'S COMPLETION STATEMENT

Dodson and Fogg
Solicitors
Lloyds Bank Chambers,
High Street, Hutton — Telephone Hutton 2555

. . . .

Mr. and Mrs. G. Ford

Re: 15 Lone Pine Close, Hutton
Completion Statement

	£	£
To Purchase money	29,750.00	
To Agreed sum for chattels	750.00	
Less Deposit paid		2,975.00
To proportion of water rates and sewerage rates 1 August-30 Sept. (61 days) @ £113.50 per year	22.27	
To balance due from you on Completion		27,547.27
	£30,522.27	£30,522.27

LETTER TO BUILDING SOCIETY SOLICITOR RE BANK DRAFTS

Messrs Brown and Green
44 High West Street,
Hutton

Your Name
Your Address
Today's Date

Dear Sirs,

Re: 15 Lone Pine close, Hutton

Thank you for your letter dated . . . . and statement showing that a net balance of £14819.25 will be available at Completion.

Will you please arrange for this sum to be split into two drafts as follows:-

1 draft in favour of Biggest Building Society	£10882.25
1 draft in favour of Dodson and Fogg (the Vendor's solicitors)	£ 3937.00
	£14819.25

Yours faithfully,

Your Signature

UNDERTAKING BY VENDOR'S BUILDING SOCIETY SOLICITOR TO SEND FORM 53

Dodson and Fogg
Solicitors
Lloyds Bank Chambers,
High Street, Hutton

Telephone Hutton 2555

. . . .

Messrs Brown and Green,
44 High West Street,
Hutton.

Today's Date

Dear Sirs,

Re: 15 Lone Pine Close, Hutton
BROWN to FORD

In consideration of your having Completed the purchase of the above property today, we hereby undertake to discharge the Mortgage dated . . . . in favour of Best Building Society and to forward *Form 53 within fourteen to twentyone days hereof.

Yours faithfully,

Dodson and Fogg

* If the land is unregistered the undertaking would read: 'and to forward the Mortgage Deed to you within fourteen to twentyone days hereof with the Receipt endorsed thereon by the Society'.

LETTER RELEASING DEPOSIT FROM STAKEHOLDER TO VENDOR'S SOLICITOR

Sellright Estate Agency, — Your Name
10 High Street, — Your Address
Hutton — Today's Date

Dear Sirs,

Re: 15 Lone Pine Close, Hutton

I have today Completed the purchase of the above property and hereby authorise you to release the sum of £100 held by you as stakeholders, to Messrs Dodson and Fogg the vendors solicitors or to their order.

Yours faithfully,

Your Signature

LETTER TO ACCOMPANY APPLICATION TO REGISTER CHANGE OF OWNERSHIP

RECORDED DELIVERY

The Superintendent, — Your Name
Newtown District Land Registry, — Your Address
67 Nelson Row,
Newtown,
Wessex — Today's Date

Dear Sir,

Re: 15 Lone Pine Close, Hutton, Wessex

I enclose herewith:

- Charge Certificate XZ 498031
- Transfer Form 19(JP)
- Search Form 94A
- Land Registry Application Form A.4.
- Photocopy of solicitor's undertaking re Form 53
- Cheque for £.... being the Land Registry fee payable.

Will you kindly acknowledge receipt of these en-closures.

Yours faithfully,

Your Signature

APPLICATION FOR OFFICE COPIES ON FORM A44

Form A44 HM Land Registry

Application for Office Copies(1)

Numbers in brackets relate to notes overleaf

NEWTOWN District Land Registry (2)

67 Nelson Row,
Newtown,
Wessex

PAYMENT OF FEES(3)

If by Land Registry fee stamp(s) affix here.

If by either of the following methods, enter X in the appropriate box.

credit account ☐

cheque or postal order ☐

FOR OFFICIAL USE ONLY

I We GERALD GEORGE FORD and JOAN FORD

(Use BLOCK LETTERS)

hereby apply for the office copies specified below

and I We declare that

(Please enter X in the appropriate box)

[X] We are the registered proprietor(s)

[ ] I We act as solicitor(s) for the registered proprietor(s)

[ ] the written authority of the registered proprietor(s) (or his solicitors) to inspect the register is enclosed.

PARTICULARS OF ACCOUNT HOLDER(4)

Key Number	Reference

Title number (4)	XZ 498031
Country and district (or London borough)	WESSEX HUTTON
Short description of property	15 LONE PINE CLOSE, HUTTON, WESSEX
Full name(s) of registered proprietor(s)	GERALD GEORGE FORD and JOAN FORD
Please state in the appropriate box(es) the NUMBER of copies required	A [X] Complete set(5) with Title plan; C [ ] Register entries; E [ ] Form 102(6); B [ ] Complete set with form 102; D [ ] Title plan; F [ ] Document(s) referred to on the register as filed(7) Specify here or state "all"

a) Where you have requested a form 102 certificate and an estate plan has been approved, enter the plot number(s) in the space opposite.
b) Where no estate plan has been approved a plan MUST be lodged in duplicate(8)

(a) Plot number(s) ☐

(b) The certificate is to be issued in respect of the land shown on the attached plan.

OFFICIAL USE FEE DEBITED	
£	p

If you are aware that an application is in the course of registration in respect of the above title and you require office copies back-dated to the day prior to the receipt of that application, enter YES in the box opposite(9) ☐

Signed G. G. Ford. Telephone No. Hutton (0200)2494 Date Today's Date

Reference

Please enter above using BLOCK LETTERS *the name, address and reference to whom the office copies are to be sent*

FOR OFFICIAL USE ONLY

ITEM	NUMBER	FEE DEBITED £	p
Complete set			
Register Entries			
Title Plan			
Form 102 certificate			
Document(s)			
TOTAL FEE DEBITED			

NOTICE TO LANDLORD'S AGENT OF CHANGE OF OWNERSHIP OF LEASEHOLD PROPERTY

Your Name
Your Address

Messrs Bloggs and Fogg,
Surveyors,
123 Higher West Street,
Hutton,
Wessex.

Today's Date

Dear Sirs,

Re: 25 Nether Lane, Hutton
NOTICE OF CHANGE OF OWNERSHIP

In the matter of a lease dated 30 April 1975 granted by John Jones to Henry Boot for a term of 99 years from the 25th day of December 1974, and in the matter of clause 6 thereof containing a covenant to give you notice of a change of ownership.

Notice is hereby given that by a *Transfer dated . . . . the property known as 25 Nether Lane Hutton was †transferred by Henry Boot to the undersigned Frederick Jones for the residue of the term of the said lease.

I enclose a cheque for £ . . . . being the fee prescribed for dealing with this matter. Please acknowledge receipt by signing and returning the enclosed duplicate copy.

Yours faithfully,

(Signed) Frederick Jones

* If unregistered land substitute 'an Assignment'
† If unregistered land substitute 'Assigned'

ABSTRACT OF TITLE

(TRACING OWNERSHIP OF UNREGISTERED PROPERTY)

Date	*Document*	*Parties*
1.3.59	Conveyance	B. Brown (1)
		J. Smith & M. Smith (2)
15.5.62	Local Search	
25.6.62	Land Charges Search 999012/62	
	Conveyance	L. Smith & M. Smith (1)
		L.J. Jones (2)
15.7.65	Local Search	
30.7.85	Land Charges Search	
5.8.65	Conveyance	L.J. Jones (1)
		D.J. Smith (2)
5.8.65	Mortgage	D.J. Smith (1)
		Best Building Society (2)
17.9.68	Mortgage dated 5.8.65 redeemed Receipt endorsed thereon All monies repaid.	
21.11.68	Conveyance	D.J. Smith (1)
		A.B. Broome (2)
12.8.71	Local Search	
5.9.71	Land Charges Search	
12.9.71	Conveyance	A.B. Broome (1)
		L.C. White (2)
12.9.71	Mortgage	L.C. White (1)
		Huge Building Society (2)
26.5.74	Mortgage dated 12.9.71 redeemed Receipt endorced thereon All monies repaid.	
6.1.83	Local Search	
28.1.83	Land Charges Search	
31.1.82	Conveyance	L.C. White (1)
		J. Wilson & L. Wilson (2)
31.8.83	Mortgage	J. Wilson & L. Wilson (1)
		Huge Building Society (2)

CONVEYANCE TO TWO PERSONS WITH JOINT TENANCY CLAUSE Page One

This Conveyance

is made the day of One thousand nine hundred and eighty

B E T W E E N BERTRAM BROWN and BARBARA BROWN both of 15 Lone Pine Close Hutton in the County of Wessex (hereinafter called "the Vendors") of the one part and GERALD GEORGE FORD and JOAN FORD both of 112 Dorset Road Hutton aforesaid (hereinafter called "the Purchasers") of the other part

W H E R E A S the Vendors are seised of the property hereinafter described for an estate in fee simple in possession subject as hereinafter mentioned but otherwise free from incumbrances and have agreed with the Purchasers for the sale to them of the said property for a like estate at the price of TWENTY NINE THOUSAND SEVEN HUNDRED AND FIFTY POUNDS and it has been agreed that the same shall be vested in the Purchasers as joint tenants in manner hereinafter appearing

N O W T H I S D E E D W I T N E S S E T H as follows:-

1. In pursuance of the said agreement and in consideration of the sum of TWENTY NINE THOUSAND SEVEN HUNDRED AND FIFTY POUNDS (£29,750.00) paid by the Purchasers to the Vendors (the receipt whereof the Vendors hereby acknowledge) the Vendors as Beneficial Owners HEREBY CONVEY unto the Purchasers ALL THAT piece or parcel of land situate in Lone Pine Close Hutton in the County of Wessex and having a frontage to the said road of Sixty feet or thereabouts and a depth therefrom of One hundred and twenty feet or thereabouts TOGETHER WITH the messuage or dwellinghouse and premises appurtenant thereto erected thereon or on some part thereof situate and known as Number 15 Lone Pine Close Hutton aforesaid ALL WHICH said piece or

CONVEYANCE TO JOINT TENANTS Page Two

parcel of land is for the purpose of identification only more particularly delineated on the plan annexed to a Conveyance (hereinafter called "the Conveyance") dated the Second day of May One thousand nine hundred and sixty four and made between John Joseph Black of the one part and the Vendors of the other part and thereon edged red TO HOLD the same unto the Purchasers in fee simple UPON TRUST for themselves as beneficial joint tenants Subject to the restrictive and other covenants contained mentioned or referred to in the Conveyance

2. The Purchasers hereby agree and declare that:-

(a) They are joint tenants in equity
(b) The trustees for sale of the property shall have powers to deal with it equal to those of a sole beneficial owner
(c) The survivor of the Purchasers shall become sole legal and beneficial owner of the property and any person dealing with the survivor may assume this unless a notice to the contrary appears on this Deed

3. With the object and intent of affording to the Vendors a full and sufficient indemnity but not further or otherwise the Purchasers hereby jointly and severally covenant with the Vendors that they the Purchasers will henceforth observe and perform the aforesaid covenants so far as the same are still subsisting and capable of being enforced and will indemnify and keep indemnified the Vendors their respective estates and effects from and against all actions claims demands and liability in respect of any future breach thereof so far as aforesaid

4. It is hereby certified that the transaction hereby effected does not form part of a larger transaction or of a series of transactions in respect of which the amount or value or the aggregate amount or value of the consideration exceeds Thirty Thousand Pounds

CONVEYANCE TO JOINT TENANTS Page Three

I N W I T N E S S whereof the parties hereto have hereunto set their hands and seals the day and year first before written

SIGNED SEALED AND DELIVERED by)
the said BERTRAM BROWN)
in the presence of:-)

SIGNED SEALED AND DELIVERED by)
the said BARBARA BROWN)
in the presence of:-)

SIGNED SEALED AND DELIVERED by)
the said GERALD GEORGE FORD)
in the presence of:-)

SIGNED SEALED AND DELIVERED by)
the said JOAN FORD)
in the presence of:-)

1. This conveyance provides for a joint tenancy, i.e. under which the property automatically passes to the survivor on the death of one of the joint Purchasers as discussed on page 12. There is a model conveyance for a sole Purchaser on page 196c.

2. At the time of writing the liability for stamp duty starts at £30001 and is 1% of the total consideration (price). If the property conveyed in this example had been sold for a figure in excess of £30,000, then clause 4 would be omitted. Similarly, if the stamp duty threshold rises in a future budget, the higher figure would be inserted in clause 4.

CONVEYANCE TO SOLE PURCHASE

This Conveyance

is made the day of One thousand nine hundred and eighty

B E T W E E N BERTRAM BROWN of 15 Lone Pine Close Hutton in the County of Wessex (hereinafter called "the Vendor") of the one part and GERALD GEORGE FORD of 112 Dorset Road Hutton aforesaid (hereinafter called "the Purchaser") of the other part

W H E R E A S the Vendor is seised of the property hereinafter described for an estate in fee simple in possession subject as hereinafter mentioned but otherwise free from incumbrances and has agreed with the Purchaser for the sale to him of the said property for a like estate at the price of TWENTY NINE THOUSAND SEVEN HUNDRED AND FIFTY POUNDS

N O W T H I S D E E D W I T N E S S E T H as follows:-

1. In pursuance of the said agreement and in consideration of the sum of TWENTY NINE THOUSAND SEVEN HUNDRED AND FIFTY POUNDS (£29,750.00) paid by the Purchaser to the Vendor (the receipt whereof the Vendor hereby acknowledges) the Vendor as Beneficial Owner HEREBY CONVEYS unto the Purchaser ALL THAT piece or parcel of land situate in Lone Pine Close Hutton in the County of Wessex and having a frontage to the said road of Sixty feet or thereabouts and a depth therefrom of One hundred and twenty feet or thereabouts TOGETHER WITH the messuage or dwellinghouse erected thereon or on some part thereof situate and known as Number 15 Lone Pine Close Hutton aforesaid ALL WHICH said piece or parcel of land is for the purpose of identification only more particularly delineated on the plan annexed to a Conveyance (hereinafter called "the Conveyance") dated the Second day of May One thousand nine hundred and sixty four and made between John Joseph Black of the one part and the Vendor of the other part and thereon edged red TO HOLD the same unto the Purchaser in fee simple Subject to the restrictive and other covenants contained mentioned or referred to in the Conveyance

2. With the object and intent of affording to the Vendor a full and sufficient indemnity but not further or otherwise the Purchaser covenants with the Vendor that he the Purchaser will henceforth observe and perform the aforesaid covenants so far as the same are still subsisting and capable of being enforced and will indemnify the Vendor from and against all actions claims demands and liability in respect of any future breach thereof so far as aforesaid

3. It is hereby certified that the transaction hereby effected does not form part of a larger transaction or of a series of transactions in respect of which the amount or value or the aggregate amount of value of the consideration exceeds Thirty Thousand Pounds

I N W I T N E S S whereof the parties hereto have hereunto set their hands and seals the day and year first before written

SIGNED SEALED AND DELIVERED by)
the said BERTRAM BROWN)
in the presence of:-)

SIGNED SEALED AND DELIVERED by)
the said GERALD GEORGE FORD)
in the presence of:-)

Ole SERIES REQUISITIONS ON TITLE (POST-CONTRACT)

REQUISITIONS ON TITLE

(POST-CONTRACT)

Re ..... 15 Lone Pine Close, Hutton ......

.... Brown ....

Jp ..... Ford ....

ENQUIRIES	REPLIES
1. Previous enquiries	1.
If the pre-contract enquiries replied to on behalf of the Vendor were repeated would the replies now be the same as those previously given? If not, please give full particulars of any variation.	Yes, save as may have been varied by correspondence.
2. Receipts	2.
(A) On completion the receipt for all rates and outgoings formerly payable by the Vendor must not be produced and any arrears allowed for	(A) Noted
(B) In the case of a leasehold property the receipt for ground rent due on the last rent day prior to the day of completion as well as the receipt for the last fire insurance premium must be produced on completion.	
3. Title Deeds	3.
(A) Unregistered land	
(i) Which documents of title will be handed over to the Purchaser on completion?	
(ii) Who will give the Purchaser the statutory acknowledgement and undertaking for the production and safe custody of those not handed over?	
(iii) Why will any documents not handed over be retained?	
(B) Registered land	(B)
When was the land or charge certificate last officially examined with the register?	12 August 1986
4. Mortgages	4.
(A) All subsisting mortgages must be discharged on or before completion.	(A) Agreed
(B) (i) In respect of each subsisting mortgage will the vacating receipt/discharge or registered charge be handed over on completion?	(B) (i) Please refer to (ii) below
(ii) If an undertaking to hand it over later is proposed, what are the suggested terms of the undertaking?	(ii) We will give the usual undertaking to forward a sealed Form 53

	REPLIES
5. Completion	5.
(A) Please send a completion statement.	(A) Herewith
(B) (i) Where will completion take place?	(B) (i) At this office
(ii) In whose favour and for what amounts will bankers drafts be required on completion?	(ii) We will advise as soon as possible.
6. Notices	
Please give the name and address of any Solicitor, agent, or other person to whom notice of any dealing with the property must be given.	
7. Possession	7..
(A) (i) Vacant possession of the whole of the property must be given on completion	(A) (i) Noted
(ii) What arrangements will be made to deliver the keys to the Purchaser?	(ii) We suggest that this is done through the Estate Agents.

NOTE You will appreciate that the Requisitions based on the Abstract of Title or Contract must, of course, be added to the above.

N.B. The Deeds and documents of title remain to be examined and the right is reserved to make further requisitions which may arise on each examination, the replies to the above, and enquiries before completion or otherwise.

.... Date .... Date

LETTER ACCOMPANYING REQUISITIONS ON TITLE AND DRAFT CONVEYANCE FOR UNREGISTERED LAND

Messrs. Dodson and Fogg, | Your Name
Lloyds Bank Chambers, | Your Address
High Street,
Hutton. | Today's Date

Dear Sirs,

Re: 15 Lone Pine Close, Hutton

I enclose herewith Requisitions on Title and a copy for your use.

I also enclose a draft Conveyance of the above property to my wife and self, with a copy which please retain for your use. I have inserted the amended purchase price as agreed and would be obliged if you will return the draft 'approved' at your early convenience.

Yours faithfully,

Your Signature

LETTER TO VENDOR'S SOLICITOR TO ACCOMPANY ENGROSSED CONVEYANCE

Messrs Dodson and Fogg | Your Name
Lloyds Bank Chambers, | Your Address
High Street,
Hutton. | Today's Date

Dear Sirs,

Re: 15 Long Pine Close, Hutton

I now have pleasure in forwarding the engrossed conveyance duly executed by my wife and self in anticipation of Completion.

Yours faithfully,

Your Signature

This Assignment

is made the day of

B E T W E E N BERTRAM BROWN and BARBARA BROWN both of 15 Lone Pine Close Hutton in the County of Wessex (hereinafter called "the Vendors") of the one part and GERALD GEORGE FORD and JOAN FORD both of 112 Dorset Road Hutton aforesaid (hereinafter called "the Purchasers") of the other part

W H E R E A S :-

1. By a Lease (hereinafter called "the Lease") dated the Second day of May One thousand nine hundred and sixty four and made between John Black of the one part and Frederick Smith of the other part ALL THAT piece or parcel of land situate in Lone Pine Close Hutton in the County of Wessex and having a frontage to the said road of Sixty feet or thereabouts and a depth therefrom of One hundred and twenty feet or thereabouts ALL WHICH said piece or parcel of land is for the purposes of identification only more particularly delineated on the plan annexed to the Lease and thereon edged red TOGETHER WITH the messuage or dwellinghouse erected thereon or on some part thereof situate and known as Number 15 Lone Pine Close Hutton aforesaid was demised by the said John Black to the said Frederick Smith for the term of Ninety nine years from the Thirtieth day of September One thousand nine hundred and sixty three Subject to the payment of the rent thereby reserved and to the covenants agreements and conditions therein contained

2. By divers mesne assurances acts in the law and events and ultimately by an Assignment dated the First day of June One thousand nine hundred and eighty three and made between Horace Hunter of the one part and the Vendors of the other part the property demised by the Lease became and is now vested in the Vendors for all the residue of the term thereby granted Subject to the rent thereby reserved and to the covenants agreements and conditions therein contained

3. The Vendors have agreed with the Purchasers for the sale to them for the sum of TWENTY NINE THOUSAND SEVEN HUNDRED AND FIFTY POUNDS of the property comprised in the Lease for the residue of the term thereby granted Subject to the rent thereby reserved and to the covenants agreements and conditions therein contained and it has been further agreed that the same shall be vested in the Purchasers as joint tenants in manner hereinafter appearing

N O W T H I S D E E D W I T N E S S E T H as follows :-

1. In pursuance of the said agreement and in consideration of the sum of TWENTY NINE THOUSAND SEVEN HUNDRED AND FIFTY POUNDS (£29,750.00) now paid to the Vendors by the Purchasers out of monies belonging to them on a joint account (the receipt whereof the Vendors hereby acknowledge) the Vendors as Beneficial Owners HEREBY ASSIGN unto the Purchasers the property comprised in and demised by the Lease TO HOLD the same unto Purchasers UPON TRUST for themselves as beneficial joint tenants for all the residue now unexpired of the said term of Ninety Nine years granted by the Lease Subject henceforth to the payment of the rent thereby reserved and to the covenants agreements and conditions therein contained and on the part of the Lessees to be observed and performed

2. The Purchasers hereby agree and declare that :-

(a) They are joint tenants in equity

(b) The trustees for sale of the property shall have powers to deal with it equal to those of a sole beneficial owner

(c) The survivor of the Purchasers shall become sole legal and beneficial owner of the property and any person dealing with the survivor may assume this unless to the contrary appears on this Deed

3. It is hereby certified that the transaction hereby effected does not form part of a larger transaction or of a series of transactions in respect of which the amount or value or the aggregate amount or value of the consideration exceeds THIRTY THOUSAND POUNDS

I N W I T N E S S whereof the parties hereto have hereunto set their hands and seals the day and year first before written

SIGNED SEALED AND DELIVERED by)
the said BERTRAM BROWN)
in the presence of :-

SIGNED SEALED AND DELIVERED by)
the said BARBARA BROWN)
in the presence of :-)

SIGNED SEALED AND DELIVERED by)
the said GERALD GEORGE FORD)
in the presence of :-)

SIGNED SEALED AND DELIVERED by)
the said JOAN FORD)
in the presence of :-)

COMPLETED APPLICATION FOR AN OFFICIAL SEARCH ON FORM K15

Form K15 — Land Charges Act 1972

Payment of fee (see note 3 overleaf)
EITHER Insert a cross (X) in this box if the fee is to be paid through a credit account
OR affix stamps in this space

APPLICATION FOR AN OFFICIAL SEARCH

NOT APPLICABLE TO REGISTERED LAND

Application is hereby made for an official search in the index to the registers kept pursuant to the Land Charges Act 1972 for any subsisting entries in respect of the under-mentioned particulars.

IMPORTANT: Please read the notes overleaf before completing this form

For Official Use only		NAMES TO BE SEARCHED (Please use block letters and see note 4 overleaf)	PERIOD OF YEARS (see note 5 overleaf) From	To
STX	Forename(s)	BERTRAM	1975	1986
	SURNAME	BROWN		
	Forename(s)	BARBARA	1975	1986
	SURNAME	BROWN		
	Forename(s)			
	SURNAME			
	Forename(s)			
	SURNAME			
	Forename(s)			
	SURNAME			
	Forename(s)			
	SURNAME			

COUNTY (see note 6 overleaf)	WESSEX
FORMER COUNTY	
DESCRIPTION OF LAND (see note 7 overleaf)	15 Lone Pine Close,Hutton, Wessex
FORMER DESCRIPTION	

Particulars of Applicant (see notes 8, 9 and 10 overleaf) — Key Number	Name and address	Address for despatch of certificate (Leave blank if certificate is to be returned to applicant's address)
	G.G.Ford 112 Dorset Road,Hutton	

Applicant's reference:	Date	FOR OFFICIAL USE ONLY

TYPICAL FORM OF GUARANTEE

Certificate of Insulation and Guarantee.

This is to Certify that the premises situated at
15 LONE PINE CLOSE HUTTON WESSEX

have been insulated with
Urea-Formaldehyde cavity wall insulation foam thus ensuring proper and adequate protection against heat loss through the walls and the savings in fuel costs occasioned thereby. The Insulation was carried out by in accordance with the standards and recommendations of the British Standards Institute 5617 & 5618. Certificate number FS064.

This insulation is guaranteed for 40 years from the date of this certificate, including inner wall dampness and any other damage consequential to the installation, provided this is a direct result of:- faulty surveying, site preparation, materials or workmanship by

Signed__________ (Director) Date__________

RESULT OF OFFICIAL SEARCH REPORTED ON FORM K16

FORM K18.

LAND CHARGES ACT, 1972.
CE..TIFICATE OF THE RESULT OF SEARCH

CERTIFICATE No.	CERTIFICATE DATE	PROTECTION ENDS ON
02758289HH	11 FEB 1986	05 MAR 1986

It is hereby certified that an official search in respect of the undermentioned particulars has been made in the index to the registers which are kept pursuant to the Land Charges Act, 1972. The result of the search is shown below.

PARTICULARS SEARCHED — B331909

COUNTY OR COUNTIES: WESSEX

NAME(S) / Particulars of Charge	PERIOD	Fees £
LEWIS CHARLES * WHITE *	1963–1975	.50
NO SUBSISTING ENTRY		
	1963–1975	
(1) P.A.(B) NO. 1372 DATED 10 FEB 1975 (5) NO 19 OF 1975 GUILDFORD COUNTY COURT (6) MALE OCCUPATION UNKNOWN (7) 16 CADWICK CLOSE FARNBOROUGH HANTS		
BERTRAM *BROWN *	1975 -1986	.50
NO SUBSISTING ENTRY		
BARBARA * BROWN *	1975 -1986	.50
NO SUBSISTING ENTRY		

APPLICANT'S REFERENCE	W7492RO/DD	APPLICANT'S KEY NUMBER		AMOUNT DEBITED £	01.50

GERALD GEORGE FORD
112 DORSET ROAD
HUTTON
WESSEX

Any enquiries concerning this certificate to be addressed to:-
The Superintendent,
Land Charges Department,
Burrington Way,
Plymouth, PL5 3LP.

IMPORTANT
PLEASE READ THE NOTES OVERLEAF.

COMPLETED FORM A13 LISTING DOCUMENTS SENT TO HM LAND REGISTRY

N.B SUBMIT IN TRIPLICATE

Form A 13
HM Land Registry

Land Registration Acts, 1925 to 1971

LIST OF DOCUMENTS SENT TO HM LAND REGISTRY

GERALD GEORGE FORD,
15 Lone Pine Close,
Hutton,
Wessex XYZ 123

Solicitor's reference

In BLOCK LETTERS, insert in panel name and address of solicitors lodging the documents and to whom acknowledgment of application is to be sent

NOTE: (1) The average time for completing the type of application to which these documents relate (assuming no requisitions have to be made) is at present .... weeks.

(2) Title number

Property 15 Lone Pine Close, Hutton, Wessex

(3) No.	Date	Nature of document	(4)	Names of parties
1	14. 7.1952	Local Search		
2	25. 7.1952	Requisitions on Title		
3	5. 8.1952	Conveyance		(1) Jones (2) Smith
4	1961	Abstract of Title		
5	21.11.1961	Conveyance		(1) Smith (2) Browne
6	20. 8.1964	Local Search		
7	30. 8.1964	Land Charges Search		
8	12. 9.1964	Conveyance		(1) Browne (2) White
9	1980	Abstract of Title		
10	1. 5.1980	Local Search		
11	21. 5.1980	Land Charges Search		
12	30. 5.1980	Conveyance		(1) White (2) Brown
13	1986	Abstract of Title		
14	15.10.1986	Local Search		
15	27.10.1986	Land Charges Search		
16	6.11.1986	Conveyance		(1) Brown (2) Ford
17	6.11.1986	Certified copy Conveyance		(1) Brown (2) Ford

(Continued overleaf)

Date 8 November 1986 — Signature of applicant ~~or his solicitor~~ G. G. Ford

(1) When returning this form as a receipt the Land Registry will insert the time likely to be taken to complete the application.
(2) On first registration, a title number will be allocated and inserted in this space by the Land Registry. In the case of a dealing with registered land, the existing title number(s) should be inserted by the applicant.
(3) The documents should be numbered and listed in sequence; copies should also be numbered and entered as separate documents.
(4) This column is for official use only. An asterisk officially placed in this column indicates that the document against which it appears will be retained in the Land Registry.

APPLICATION FOR FIRST REGISTRATION FREEHOLD LAND

Page One

Form 1A
HM Land Registry

Land Registration Acts, 1925 to 1971

APPLICATION BY OWNER(S) FOR FIRST REGISTRATION OF FREEHOLD LAND
–NO SOLICITOR ACTING

NOTE - Before completing this Form you are advised to read Explanatory Leaflet No. 2 entitled "Application for first registration made by an owner in person" which can be obtained free of charge from any office of HM Land Registry.

FOR OFFICIAL USE ONLY

Date stamp	Title number	Record of fee paid

PROPERTY

County ....WESSEX..........

District or Borough ....HUTTON..........
(Insert local authority name)

Short description ....15 LONE PINE CLOSE, HUTTON, WESSEX XYZ 123..........
(Including parish or place)

Acknowledged by
☐ A13 list
☐ Postcard
Initials ....
Date ....

Particulars of underpayment or overpayment

LAND REGISTRY FEE

Value of property £	Fee paid (Scale 1) £	p
29,750.00	35	00

Cheques should be crossed and drawn in favour of "HM Land Registry".

(1) In BLOCK LETTERS, enter full name(s), address(es) (including any postal code) and occupation(s) for entry on the register.

~~I~~/We(1) ....GERALD GEORGE FORD and JOAN FORD, both of..........
..........15 LONE PINE CLOSE, HUTTON,..........
..........WESSEX XYZ 123..........
....
....

hereby apply to be registered as proprietor(s) with absolute title of the freehold land described above (hereinafter referred to as "the land") which was conveyed by the accompanying deed(2) dated ....6th day of.......... November 1986 .... made between ....BERTRAM BROWN and BARBARA BROWN of the one part..........
....
and ....GERALD GEORGE FORD and JOAN FORD of the other part.
....

(2) The most recent transfer document.

Page Two

2

(3) Strike out the statements which do not apply.

~~I~~/We declare as follows:

1. (a) (3) ~~I am the sole owner and am entitled to the land for my own benefit.~~

OR

(b) (3) *We are joint owners and hold the land beneficially for ourselves as joint tenants so that the survivor of us will be able to give a valid receipt for capital money.*

OR

(c) (3) ~~*We are joint owners and hold the land beneficially for ourselves as tenants in common so that the survivor of us will not be able to give a valid receipt for capital money.*~~

OR

(d) (3) ~~*I am/We are entitled to the land as*~~

~~*personal representative(s).*~~
or
~~*trustees on behalf of*~~ .... *Charity.*
or
~~*trustees for sale under a trust deed dated*~~ ....
or
~~*tenant for life (or statutory owners) of settled land.*~~

(4) This schedule must be lodged together with two copies (Official form A13 may be used)

2. The deeds and documents accompanying this application and listed in the accompanying schedule(4) signed by me/us are all the deeds and documents relating to the title which I/we hold or can call for (including such documents as enquiries before contract, contracts for sale, requisitions on title, and official certificates of search).

3. Any abstracts of title deeds are marked as verified by the solicitors who examined them with the original documents and particulars of grants of probate or letters of administration, marriages and deaths set out therein as separate items are also marked as verified. Such abstracts contain a copy or full extract of all restrictive covenants, stipulations and easements to which the land is subject. All copies of documents are certified to be true copies.

(5) Strike out words inapplicable

4. (a) *None of the/*~~*Only (5) the following*~~ entries disclosed in the certificate of official search in the Land Charges Department lodged herewith or referred to in an abstract of title affect the land:
....

(b) *The instruments creating the entries are those dated* .... *which, or abstracts of which, accompany this application.*

5. *I/We hereby apply that no note be made on the register of the sub-lease dated* .... *which has been determined by merger. I/We declare that I am/we are not aware of any underlease or other incumbrance affecting the said sub-lease.*

6. (a) (3) ~~*Immediately prior to the completion of my/our purchase I was/we were in occupation of the whole of the land under an existing lease dated*~~ .... ~~*tenancy/licence*~~

OR

(b) (3) *I/We have completed the purchase of the land with vacant possession.*

OR

(c) (3) ~~*I/We have completed the purchase of the land and the tenants have been authorised to pay the rent(s) to me/us.*~~

OR

(d) (3) ~~*Since the date of the(5) assignment/transfer to me/us dated*~~ .... ~~*I/we have been in undisputed occupation of the whole of the land or in receipt of the rent(s) therefrom.*~~

7. I/We have not entered into or created, and the land is not subject to, any contract for sale, sub-lease or agreement for sub-lease, easement, mortgage, charge (including any Inland Revenue charge for unpaid capital transfer tax), lien for unpaid purchase money or otherwise, rentcharge, restrictive covenant or other right or incumbrance affecting the land or any part thereof except as stated in the (5) *assignment/transfer* dated ....15 July 1986.......... or in the schedule below.

8. I am/We are not aware of any adverse claim to the land.

APPLICATION FOR FIRST REGISTRATION FREEHOLD LAND
Page Three

THE SCHEDULE OF INCUMBRANCES

(This schedule should include any incumbrances of the kind mentioned in paragraph 7 of this declaration which are not referred to in the assignment to the applicant. In particular it should include any mortgage(s) or charge(s) created by the applicant(s). If there are no such incumbrances, enter the word "NONE" below)

NONE

TO THE BEST OF MY/OUR KNOWLEDGE AND BELIEF THE STATEMENTS CONTAINED IN THE ABOVE DECLARATION ARE CORRECT.

(FAILURE TO COMPLETE THE DECLARATION HONESTLY AND WITH PROPER CARE MAY DEPRIVE THE APPLICANT(S) OF PROTECTION UNDER THE LAND REGISTRATION ACTS IF, AS A RESULT, A MISTAKE IS MADE IN THE REGISTER).

Signature(s) of applicant(s) G G Ford

Joan Ford

Date 18 July 1986

This declaration must be signed by all the applicants. However, in the case of joint ownership, it may be signed by one of the applicants alone on behalf of the others if this form is required to be handed over to mortgagees after completion of the purchase, provided that the assignment contains a declaration showing the beneficial ownership (see paragraph 1(b) and (c) above) and is executed by the purchasers as well as by the vendor.

INSTRUCTIONS REGARDING DOCUMENTS

Note: A certified true copy of a. the assignment/transfer to the applicant and b. any subsisting mortgage that is to be entered on the register must be supplied for filing: the originals will be returned on completion of the registration in accordance with the directions given in Panels 1 and 2 below. It is essential that these panels be completed correctly so that the acknowledgment of receipt of this application is sent to the right person(s) and the documents to be issued on completion of the registration are sent to the person(s) entitled to have them.

1. Name and address of person(s) to whom the acknowledgment of the application and all requisitions made by the Land Registry, including requests for unpaid fees, are to be sent:

BLOCK LETTERS

Name GERALD GEORGE FORD,
Address 15 LONE PINE CLOSE, HUTTON,
WESSEX XYZ 123
Reference .... Telephone number Hutton (0200) 2494

IMPORTANT

The documents not retained in the Land Registry, together with the land certificate (or charge certificate(s) as the case may be), will, on the completion of the registration, be returned to the above address. If a particular document is required to be issued to some other person or firm upon completion of the registration or in connection with any requisition which may arise, please complete panel 2 below.

2. Additional instructions (if any) for the issue of any document to some person or firm other than as mentioned in panel 1 above:

BLOCK LETTERS

Description of document ....
Name ....
Address ....
....
Reference ....

CHARGE CERTIFICATE Front Page

HM LAND REGISTRY

DIEU ET MON DROIT

LAND REGISTRATION ACTS 1925 to 1971

CHARGE CERTIFICATE

This is to Certify that the charge annexed is registered at HM Land Registry against the title numbered as stated on the back page of this certificate. There are also annexed to this certificate office copies of the entries in the register of that title and of the official plan and, where so indicated in the register, of documents filed in the Land Registry.

Under section 68 of the Land Registration Act 1925 and rule 264 of the Land Registration Rules 1925, this certificate shall be admissible as evidence of the matters contained herein and, under section 64 of the said Act, must be produced to the Chief Land Registrar on every entry in the register of a disposition by the registered proprietor of the charge and on every transmission thereof.

Consequent on the registration of the said charge the land certificate has been deposited and is retained at HM Land Registry pursuant to section 65 of the said Act.

WARNING

1. No endorsement, note, notice of entry made in this certificate other than those officially made at HM Land Registry shall have any operation.

2. **All persons are cautioned against altering, adding to or otherwise tampering with this certificate or any document annexed thereto.**

APPLICATION FOR FIRST REGISTRATION LEASEHOLD LAND

Page One

Form 2A
H M Land Registry

Land Registration Acts, 1925 to 1971

APPLICATION BY OWNER(S) FOR FIRST REGISTRATION OF LEASEHOLD LAND OTHER THAN ON THE GRANT OF A NEW LEASE–NO SOLICITOR ACTING

NOTE – Before completing this Form you are advised to read Explanatory Leaflet No. 2 entitled "Application for first registration made by an owner in person" which can be obtained free of charge from any office of HM Land Registry.

FOR OFFICIAL USE ONLY		
Date stamp	Title number	Record of fee paid

PROPERTY

County ...... WESSEX ...... HUTTON ......

District or Borough ...... HUTTON ......
(Insert local authority name)

Short description ...... 15 Lone Pine Close, Hutton, Wessex ......
(Including parish or place)

Acknowledged by: ☐ A13 list ☐ Postcard
Initials
Date
Particulars of underpayment or overpayment

LAND REGISTRY FEE

Value of property £	Fee paid (Scale 1) £	p
29,750.00	35	00

Cheques should be made payable to "HM Land Registry"

(1) In BLOCK LETTERS, enter full name(s), address(es) (including any postal code) and occupation(s) for entry on the register.

~~I~~/We [(1)] GERALD GEORGE FORD and JOAN FORD, both of 15 LONE PINE CLOSE, HUTTON, WESSEX

hereby apply to be registered as proprietor(s), with **Good Leasehold** title, of the leasehold land described above

(2) Strike out or amend as appropriate.

(hereinafter referred to as "the land") held for the residue of the term of ...... 99 years ...... years[(2)] *(less* ...... *days)* from ...... 25 May 1964 ...... demised by the [(2)]*lease/underlease* dated ...... 31st December 1964 ...... made between:

(1) ...... WILLIAM JOHNSON and ......

(2) ...... BERTRAM BROWN and BARBARA BROWN ......

( ) ......

...... and comprised

in the accompanying [(2)] *assignment/~~transfer~~* to me/us dated ...... 15th July 1986 ......

(OVER)

Page Two

~~I~~/We declare as follows

(3) Strike out the statements which do not apply.

1. (a) [(3)] ~~*I am the sole owner and am entitled to the land for my own benefit.*~~

OR

(b) [(3)] *We are joint owners and hold the land beneficially for ourselves as joint tenants so that the survivor of us will be able to give a valid receipt for capital money.*

OR

(c) [(3)] ~~*We are joint owners and hold the land beneficially for ourselves as tenants in common so that the survivor of us will not be able to give a valid receipt for capital money.*~~

OR

(d) [(3)] ~~*I am/We are entitled to the land as*~~

~~*personal representative(s).*~~

or

~~*trustees on behalf of*~~ ...... *Charity*

or

~~*trustees for sale under a trust deed dated*~~ ......

or

~~*tenant for life (or statutory owners) of settled land*~~

(4) This schedule must be lodged together with two copies. (Official form A13 may be used.)

2. The deeds and documents accompanying this application and listed in the accompanying schedule[(4)] signed by me/us are all the deeds and documents relating to the title which I/we hold or can call for (including such documents as enquiries before contract, contracts for sale, requisitions on title, and official certificates of search).

3. Any abstracts of title deeds are marked as verified by the solicitors who examined them with the original documents and particulars of grants of probate or letters of administration, marriages and deaths set out therein as separate items are also marked as verified. Such abstracts contain a copy or full extract of all restrictive covenants, stipulations and easements to which the land is subject. All copies of documents are certified to be true copies.

(5) Strike out words inapplicable.

4. (a) *None of the/~~Only~~ [(5)] ~~the following~~* entries disclosed in the certificate of official search in the Land Charges Department lodged herewith or referred to in an abstract of title affect the land: ......

(b) *The instruments creating the entries are those dated* ...... *which, or abstracts of which, accompany this application.*

5. ***I/We hereby apply that no note be made on the register of the sub-lease dated*** ...... ***which has been determined by merger. I/We declare that I am/we are not aware of any underlease or other incumbrance affecting the said sub-lease.***

6. (a) [(3)] ~~***Immediately prior to the completion of my/our purchase I was/we were in occupation of the whole of the land under an existing lease dated***~~ ...... ~~***tenancy/licence***~~

OR

(b) [(3)] ***I/We** have completed the purchase of the land with vacant possession*

OR

(c) [(3)] ~~***I/We have completed the purchase of the land and the tenants have been authorised to pay the rent(s) to me/us.***~~

OR

(d) [(3)] ~~***Since the date of the[(5)] assignment/transfer to me/us dated*** ...... ***I/we have been in undisputed occupation of the whole of the land or in receipt of the rent(s) therefrom.***~~

7. **I/We have not entered into or created, and the land is not subject to, any contract for sale, sub-lease or agreement for sub-lease, easement, mortgage, charge (including any Inland Revenue charge for unpaid capital transfer tax), lien for unpaid purchase money or otherwise, rentcharge, restrictive covenant or other right or incumbrance affecting the land or any part thereof except as stated in the [(5)] *assignment/transfer* dated** ...... 15 July 1986 ...... or in the schedule below.

8. **I am/We are not aware of any adverse claim to the land.**

APPLICATION FOR FIRST REGISTRATION LEASEHOLD LAND Page Three

3

THE SCHEDULE OF INCUMBRANCES

(This schedule should include any incumbrances of the kind mentioned in paragraph 7 of this declaration which are not referred to in the assignment to the applicant. In particular it should include any mortgage(s) or charge(s) created by the applicant(s). If there are no such incumbrances, enter the word "NONE" below).

NONE

TO THE BEST OF MY/OUR KNOWLEDGE AND BELIEF THE STATEMENTS CONTAINED IN THE ABOVE DECLARATION ARE CORRECT.

(FAILURE TO COMPLETE THE DECLARATION HONESTLY AND WITH PROPER CARE MAY DEPRIVE THE APPLICANT(S) OF PROTECTION UNDER THE LAND REGISTRATION ACTS IF, AS A RESULT, A MISTAKE IS MADE IN THE REGISTER).

Signature(s) of applicant(s) G G Ford

Joan Ford

Date 18 July 1986

This declaration must be signed by all the applicants. However, in the case of joint ownership, it may be signed by one of the applicants alone on behalf of the others if this form is required to be handed over to mortgagees after completion of the purchase, provided that the assignment contains a declaration showing the beneficial ownership (see paragraph 1(b) and (c) above) and is executed by the purchasers as well as by the vendor.

INSTRUCTIONS REGARDING DOCUMENTS

Note: A certified true copy of a. the assignment/transfer to the applicant and b. any subsisting mortgage that is to be entered on the register must be supplied for filing; the originals will be returned on completion of the registration in accordance with the directions given in Panels 1 and 2 below. It is essential that these panels be completed correctly so that the acknowledgment of receipt of this application is sent to the right person(s) and the documents to be issued on completion of the registration are sent to the person(s) entitled to have them.

1. Name and address of person(s) to whom the acknowledgment of the application and all requisitions made by the Land Registry, including requests for unpaid fees, are to be sent:

BLOCK LETTERS

Name GERALD GEORGE FORD,

Address 15 LONE PINE CLOSE, HUTTON,

WESSEX XYZ 123

Reference .... Telephone number Hutton (0200) 2494

IMPORTANT

The documents not retained in the Land Registry, together with the land certificate (or charge certificate(s) as the case may be), will, on the completion of the registration, be returned to the above address. If a particular document is required to be issued to some other person or firm upon completion of the registration or in connection with any requisition which may arise, please complete panel 2 below.

2. Additional instructions (if any) for the issue of any document to some person or firm other than as mentioned in panel 1 above:

BLOCK LETTERS

Description of document ....

Name ....

Address ....

Reference ....

FORMS AND LETTERS FOR SELLING A PROPERTY

The sample forms and draft letters which follow are used when selling a property; they tie in directly with Chapter 6. The forms appear in the same order as they occur in the text.

LETTER CONFIRMING AGREEMENT TO SELL 'SUBJECT TO CONTRACT'

Your Name
Your Address
Today's Date

Mr. and Mrs. G.G. Ford,
112 Dorset Road,
Hutton.

Dear Mr. and Mrs. Ford,

Re: 15 Lone Pine Close, Hutton

I write to confirm our agreement of today that, subject to contract, I will sell to you the above mentioned freehold property for the sum of £30000 (thirty thousand pounds).

As I informed you I will be carrying out my own Conveyancing and will send your solicitor a draft contract within the next few days.

Yours truly,

Your Signature

Copy to:
Black and Brown,
Solicitors,
49 Lower High Street,
Hutton.

LETTER TO YOUR BUILDING SOCIETY RE REDEMPTION OF MORTGAGE ON SALE: REGISTERED LAND

Your Name
Your Address

Today's Date

The Manager,
Best Building Society,
Best house,
High Street,
Hutton.

Dear Sir,

Re: 15 Lone Pine Close, Hutton.
Roll Number ABC/12345

I write to advise that I am arranging to sell the above property which is mortgaged to your society.

Will you kindly appoint a firm of solicitors on your panel who are located conveniently to me to act for you in the redemption of the mortgage and advise their name and address at your early convenience.

Yours faithfully,

Your Signature

***If the land is leasehold, add:
Will you also please forward a copy of the Lease.

LETTER TO YOUR BUILDING SOCIETY RE REDEMPTION OF MORTGAGE ON SALE: UNREGISTERED LAND

Your Name
Your Address

Today's Date

The Manager,
Best Building Society,
Best House,
High Street,
Hutton.

Dear Sir,

Re: 15 Lone Pine Close, Hutton.
Roll No. ABC/12345

I write to advise that I am arranging to sell the above property which is mortgaged to your society.

Will you please arrange for the title deeds to be sent to a firm of solicitors on your panel who are located conveniently to me to whom you require the mortgage redemption monies to be paid, and kindly advise their name and address when the deeds have been forwarded.

Yours faithfully,

Your Signature

***If the land is leasehold, add:
Will you also please forward a copy of the Lease.

LETTER TO PREVIOUS SOLICITOR WHO HANDLED YOUR PURCHASE

Your Address
Your Address

Today's Date

Messrs Whyte and Snow,
Solicitors,
4 Main Street,
Anytown.

Dear Sirs,

You will recall that you acted for me in the purchase of the above property in 1984. I would be obliged if you would kindly forward to me the file of that transaction. I will be happy to reimburse the postage incurred.

Yours sincerely,

Your Signature

LETTER TO BUYER'S SOLICITOR TO ACCOMPANY DRAFT CONTRACT FOR SALE

Your Name
Your Address
Today's Date

Messrs Black and Brown,
49 Lower High Street,
Hutton.

Dear Sirs,

Re: 15 Lone Pine Close, Hutton

I understand that you are acting for Mr. and Mrs. G.G. Ford who have agreed to purchase my house as above, for the sum of £30000 subject to contract.

I enclose draft contract and a copy for your use, and also an ‡Office copy of the land register.

Yours faithfully,

Your Signature

‡If the property is unregistered land substitute the following: 'copies of restrictive covenants affecting the land'.

COMPLETED APPLICATION FORM OFFICE COPIES ON FORM A44

Form A44 HM Land Registry

Application for Office Copies(¹)

Numbers in brackets relate to notes overleaf

NEWTOWN District Land Registry (²)

67 Nelson Row,
Newtown,
Wessex

PAYMENT OF FEES(³)
If by Land Registry fee stamp(s) affix here.
If by either of the following methods, enter X in the appropriate box.

credit account ☐

cheque or postal order ☐

FOR OFFICIAL USE ONLY

I We GERALD GEORGE FORD and JOAN FORD
(in BLOCK LETTERS)

hereby apply for the office copies specified below

and I We declare that

(Please enter X in the appropriate box)

[X] ~~I am~~ We are the registered proprietor(s)

[ ] I We act as solicitor(s) for the registered proprietor(s)

[ ] the written authority of the registered proprietor(s) (or his solicitors) to inspect the register is enclosed

PARTICULARS OF ACCOUNT HOLDER(⁴)

Key Number	Reference

Title number (¹)	XZ 498031
Country and district (or London borough)	WESSEX HUTTON
Short description of property	15 LONE PINE CLOSE, HUTTON, WESSEX
Full name(s) of registered proprietor(s)	GERALD GEORGE FORD and JOAN FORD
Please state in the appropriate box(es) the NUMBER of copies required	A [X] Complete set(⁵) with Title plan; C [ ] Register entries; E [ ] Form 102(⁶); B [ ] Complete set with form 102; D [ ] Title plan; F [ ] Document(s) referred to on the register as filed(⁷) Specify here or state "all"

a) Where you have requested a form 102 certificate and an estate plan has been approved, enter the plot number(s) in the space opposite.
b) Where no estate plan has been approved a plan MUST be lodged in duplicate(⁸)

(a) Plot number(s)
(b) The certificate is to be issued in respect of the land shown on the attached plan.

OFFICIAL USE FEE DEBITED £ p

If you are aware that an application is in the course of registration in respect of the above title and you require office copies back-dated to the day prior to the receipt of that application, enter YES in the box opposite(⁹)

Signed *G. G. Ford.* Telephone No. Hutton (0200)2494 Date Today's Date

Reference

Please enter above using BLOCK LETTERS the name, address and reference to whom the office copies are to be sent

FOR OFFICIAL USE ONLY

ITEM	NUMBER	FEE DEBITED £	p
Complete set			
Register Entries			
Title Plan			
Form 102 certificate			
Document(s)			
TOTAL FEE DEBITED			

LAND CERTIFICATE

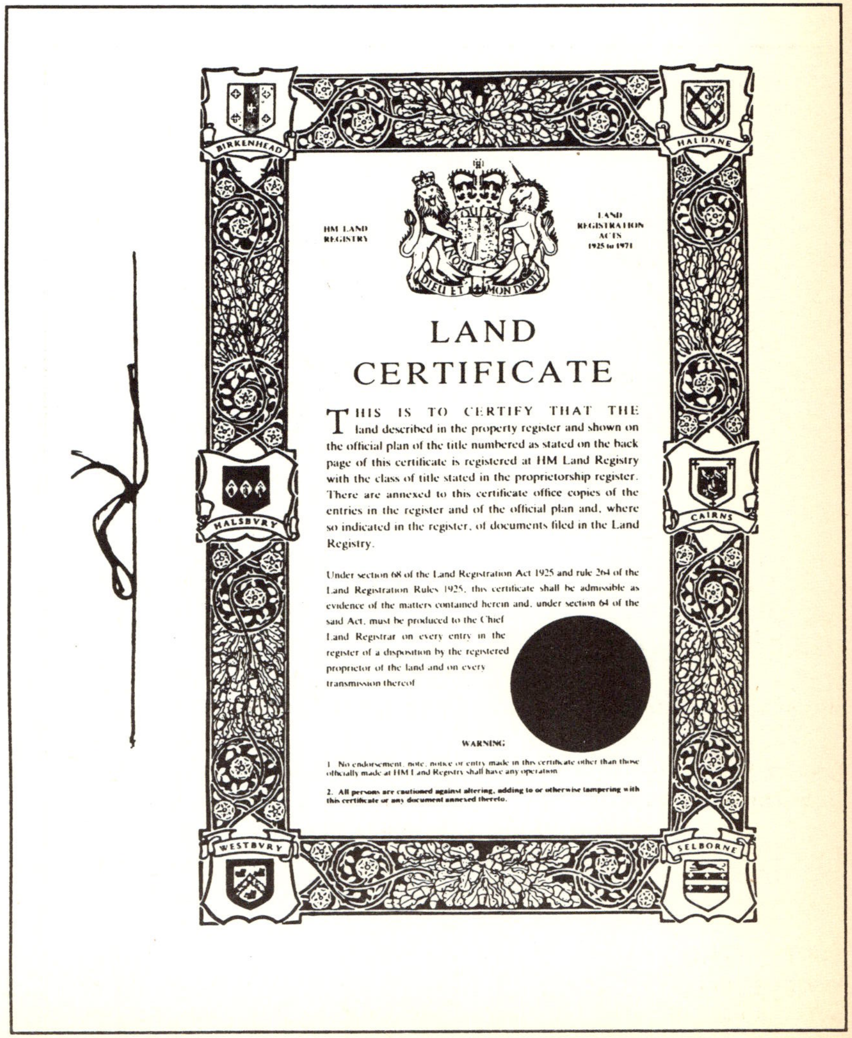

HM LAND REGISTRY

LAND REGISTRATION ACTS 1925 to 1971

LAND CERTIFICATE

THIS IS TO CERTIFY THAT THE land described in the property register and shown on the official plan of the title numbered as stated on the back page of this certificate is registered at HM Land Registry with the class of title stated in the proprietorship register. There are annexed to this certificate office copies of the entries in the register and of the official plan and, where so indicated in the register, of documents filed in the Land Registry.

Under section 68 of the Land Registration Act 1925 and rule 264 of the Land Registration Rules 1925, this certificate shall be admissible as evidence of the matters contained herein and, under section 64 of the said Act, must be produced to the Chief Land Registrar on every entry in the register of a disposition by the registered proprietor of the land and on every transmission thereof.

WARNING

1. No endorsement, note, notice or entry made in this certificate other than those officially made at HM Land Registry shall have any operation.

2. All persons are cautioned against altering, adding to or otherwise tampering with this certificate or any document annexed thereto.

A TYPICAL LAND CERTIFICATE SHOWING THE 3 REGISTERS

Page Two

H.M. LAND REGISTRY

Edition 1 opened 28.4.1978 TITLE NUMBER XZ498031. Map reference VXS 312K

This register consists of 4

A. PROPERTY REGISTER

containing the description of the registered land and the estate comprised in the Title

COUNTY	DISTRICT
WESSEX	HUTTON

The Freehold land shown and edged with red on the plan of the above Title filed at the Registry registered on 28 April 1978 known as 15 Lone Pine Close,Hutton.

NOTE 1:-The Conveyance dated 2 October 1958 referred to in Entry No 3 of the Charges Reg. contains the following provision :-

"The Purchasers shall not be entitled to any right of light or air which would in any manner diminish or interfere with the free and unrestricted user of any adjoining or adjacent land forming part of the Conifer Avenue Estate for either building or any othe purposes."

B. PROPRIETORSHIP REGISTER

stating nature of the Title, name, address and description of the proprietor of the land and any entries affecting the right of disposing thereof

TITLE ABSOLUTE

Entry number	Proprietor, etc.	Remarks
1	JAMES CHARLES FRENCH and FREDA FRENCH his wife both of 15 Lone Pine Close Hutton,Wessex, registered on 28 April 1978	

Any entries struck through are no longer subsisting

2 TITLE NUMBER XZ498031

C. CHARGES REGISTER

containing charges, incumbrances etc., adversely affecting the land and registered dealings therewith

Entry number	The date at the beginning of each entry is the date on which the entry was made on this edition of the register	Remarks
	28 April 1978-A Conveyance of the land in this title and other land dated 20 May 1896 made between (1) Mary Jane Martin and (2) Lavinia Horsey contains restrictive covenants but neither the original Conveyance nor a certified copy or examined abstract thereof was produced on first registration.	
	28 April 1978-A Conveyance of the land tinted blue. on the filed plan and other land dated 4 May 1933 made between (1) Albert Truzzel Granger and William Robert Armstrong and (2) Reuben Webb contains covenants particulars of which are set out in the Schedule annexed.	
	28 April 1978-The land is subject to the following rights reserved by a Conveyance of the land in this title dated 2 October 1958 made between (1) John Frank Jones and Elizabeth Jones (Vendors) and (2) Walter William Werner and Jane Gladys Werner :- "EXCEPT AND RESERVING unto the Vendors and their successors in title a free passage and running of water and soil to and from all other property of or to which the vendors are seised or entitled with power at any time to enter upon the property hereby conveyed and to make lay and repair pipes drains and water courses for such purpose the person or persons so entering giving reasonable notice thereof and making good all damage occasioned thereby."	

LAND CERTIFICATE SHOWING THE 3 REGISTERS Page Three

TITLE NUMBER XZ498031 — Page 3

C. CHARGES REGISTER – continued.

Schedule of restrictive covenants	Remarks
The following are particulars of the covenants contained in the Conveyance dated 4 May 1933 referred to in the Charges Register. THE Purchaser thereby covenanted with Vendors with intent to bind the property thereby conveyed and all future owners thereof that the Purchaser and his successors in title would observe and perform the stipulations and conditions contained in the first schedule thereto THE FIRST SCHEDULE before referred to 1. Not to make or suffer to be made on the premises thereby conveyed any excavations except for the purpose of building on or levelling such premises or make or suffer to be made or burnt thereon any bricks tiles or other wares or make or suffer to be made any mortar on the premises thereby conveyed such as is required for building thereon. 2. Not to use or permit to be used any dwellinghouse erected on the property thereby conveyed for any purpose other than as a private dwellinghouse or for the carrying on of a learned or artistic profession and not to use any motor house erected thereon or permit the same to be used for any purpose other than a private motor house for the use of the occupier of the dwellinghouse to which it belongs 3. Not to erect or permit to be erected on the propertythereby conveyed any advertisement or hoarding or temporary erection or shed of any kind other than a bicycle or garden shed (except temporary sheds to be used only as incidental to and during the erection of the buildings thereinbefore authorised) and to use such part of the land as is not built upon as ornamental or vegetable garden or pleasure ground and not to do or permit to be done upon the said premises anything which shall or may be or become a nuisance damage annoyance or disturbance to the Vendors or the owners or occupiers of any land or dwellinghouse in the neighbourhood and not to permit clothes linen or other articles to be hung out in front of the dwellinghouse for the purpose of drying upon the premises. 4. Not to deposit on any of the roads or footpaths abutting on the propertythereby conveyed any building or other materials nor disturb the surface of any such road or footpath except for the purpose of making connections to sewers drains or mains thereunder and any such disturbance shall forthwith be made good by the Purchaser of the premises thereby conveyed.	

COPY OF FILED PLAN

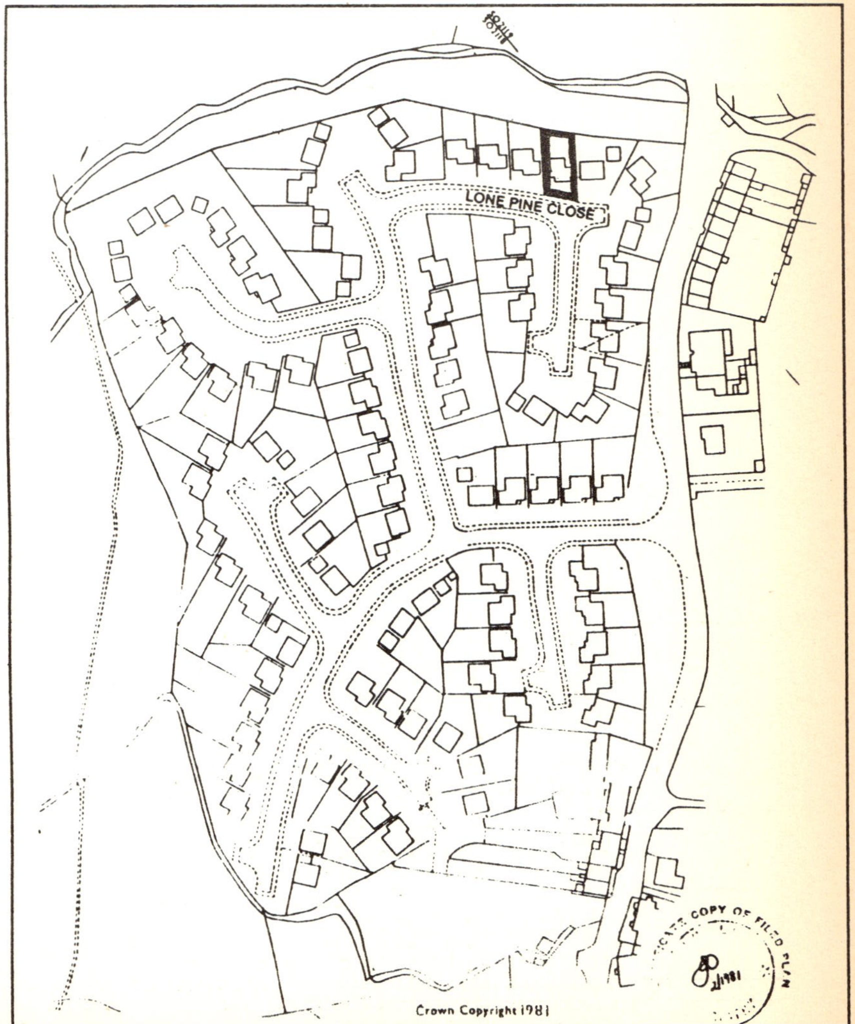

CONTRACT FOR SALE OF REGISTERED LAND

CONTRACT FOR SALE

This agreement is made the day of 198

BETWEEN BERTRAM BROWN and BARBARA BROWN, both of, 15 Lone Pine Close, Hutton (hereinafter called "the Vendor")

and GERALD GEORGE FORD and JOAN FORD, both of, 112 Dorset Road, Hutton (hereinafter called "the Purchaser")

Whereby it is agreed that the Vendor shall sell and the Purchaser shall Purchase subject to the conditions printed hereon the property described in the particulars below for the sum of TWENTY NINE THOUSAND SEVEN HUNDRED AND FIFTY POUNDS (£29,750.00)

PARTICULARS

ALL THAT freehold/leasehold property situate and known as Number 15 Lone Pine Close, Hutton, in the County of Wessex as the same is registered with Title Absolute at H.M.Land Registry under Title Number XZ498031 Together With and Subject to the rights contained or referred to in the Registers of the Title

Purchase price	£29,750.00
Deposit	£ 2,975.00
Balance payable	£26,775.00
Price agreed for fixtures/fittings chattels	£
Total:	£26,775.00

CONDITIONS OF SALE on REVERSE

Signed **Vendor/Purchaser**

Date 19

Purchaser's Solicitors

Local Authority Hutton District Council

CONDITIONS OF SALE

1. The property is sold subject to the National Conditions of Sale Twentieth Edition (hereinafter referred to as the General Conditions) so far as they are not varied or inconsistent with these conditions of sale so however General Condition 11(7) of the general conditions shall apply in any event

2. The title of the Vendor is registered in Woolville District Land Registry with Absolute Title under Title Number XZ490831

~~3. The abstract of title shall begin with~~

4. The property is sold subject to the restrictive covenants and matters referred to by and set out in entries numbered 1, 2 and 3 of the Charges Register and referred to or set out by entry number 1 in the Property Register. A copy of said covenants, conditions and stipulations having been supplied to the Purchasers they shall be deemed to be purchasers with full knowledge thereof and shall raise no requisition or objection thereto

5. The prescribed rate referred to in the general conditions is 4 % over the base rate for the time being of Lloyds Bank PLC

6. The contractual completion date in general condition 5 of the general conditions is 198 and the latest time for completion is 2.00 ~~am~~/pm

7. Unless herein stated to the contrary general condition 3 of the general conditions shall not apply

8. The Vendor sells as Beneficial Owner

* 9. The property is sold with vacant possession of the whole upon completion

or

* 9. ~~The property is sold subject to the following leases or tenancies or licences~~

\+ 10. The 10% deposit shall be paid as stakeholder/agent for the Vendor to Sellright Estate Agency of 10 High Street, Hutton

11. In this agreement the term 'Solicitor' shall include the term 'Licensed Conveyancer'

12. The Vendor hereby grants an Authority to the Purchaser and/or his Solicitor to examine the Register

* **Delete as appropriate**

\+ If you have not instructed Estate Agents, ask your Bank Manager to hold the deposit as "stakeholder." In this case, you would amend the text thus: "............Bankers of the Vendors, Friendly Bank PLC, 21 Moorside, Hutton"

Rv.2 OLE Series

CONTRACT FOR SALE OF UNREGISTERED LAND

CONTRACT FOR SALE

This agreement is made the day of 198

BETWEEN	BERTRAM BROWN and BARBARA BROWN, both of 15 Lone Pine Close, Hutton (hereinafter called "the Vendor")
and	GERALD GEORGE FORD and JOAN FORD, both of 112 Dorset Road, Hutton (hereinafter called "the Purchaser")

Whereby it is agreed that the Vendor shall sell and the Purchaser shall Purchase subject to the conditions printed hereon the property described in the particulars below for the sum of TWENTY NINE THOUSAND SEVEN HUNDRED AND FIFTY POUNDS (£29,750.00)

PARTICULARS

ALL THAT freehold/~~leasehold~~ piece or parcel of land TOGETHER WITH the dwellinghouse erected thereon or on some part thereof situate and known as 15 Lone Pine Close, Hutton, in the County of Wessex

as the same was conveyed by a Conveyance ("the Conveyance") dated the 18th day of May, 1979, and made between John Brown (1) and the Vendor (2) ALL WHICH said property is for the purposes of identification only delineated on the plan annexed thereto and thereon edged red

Purchase price	£29,750.00
Deposit	£ 2,975.00
Balance payable	£26,775.00
Price agreed for fixtures/fittings chattels	£
Total:	£26,775.00

CONDITIONS OF SALE on REVERSE

Signed Vendor/Purchaser

Date 19

Purchaser's Solicitors

Local Authority Hutton District Council

CONDITIONS OF SALE

1. The property is sold subject to the National Conditions of Sale Twentieth Edition (hereinafter referred to as the General Conditions) so far as they are not varied or inconsistent with these conditions of sale so however General Condition 11(7) of the general conditions shall apply in any event

2. The title of the Vendor is registered ~~in~~ District Land Registry ~~with Title under~~ Title Number

3. The abstract of title shall begin with a Conveyance on sale dated the 20th day of June, 1964, and made between Henry Smith of the one part and John Brown of the other part.

4. The property is sold subject to the restrictive and other covenants and all other matters contained, mentioned or referred to in the Conveyance. The Purchasers having been supplied with copies of the same shall be deemed to purchase with full notice thereof and no objections shall be made or requisitions raised in respect thereof. The Purchasers will in their conveyance covenant by way of indemnity to observe and perform the same.

5. The prescribed rate referred to in the general conditions is 4 % over the base rate for the time being of Bank PLC

6. The contractual completion date in general condition 5 of the general conditions is 198 and the latest time for completion is 2.00 ~~am~~/pm

7. Unless herein stated to the contrary general condition 3 of the general conditions shall not apply

8. The Vendor sells as Beneficial Owner

* 9. The property is sold with vacant possession of the whole upon completion

or

* 9. The property is sold subject ~~to the following leases or tenancies or licences~~

\+ 10. The 10% deposit shall be paid as stakeholder/agent for the Vendor to Sellright Estate Agency of 10 High Street, Hutton

11. In this agreement the term 'Solicitor' shall include the term 'Licensed Conveyancer'

12. The Vendor hereby grants an Authority to the Purchaser and/or his Solicitor to examine the Register

* Delete as appropriate

\+ If you have not instructed Estate Agents, ask your Bank Manager to hold the deposit as "stakeholder." In this case, you would amend the text thus: "...........Bankers of the Vendors, Friendly Bank PLC, 21 Moorside, Hutton"

Rv.2 OLE Series

CONTRACT FOR SALE OF REGISTERED LEASEHOLD LAND

CONTRACT FOR SALE

This agreement is made the day of 198

BETWEEN	JOHN JONES and MARY JONES, both of 21A LIBRARY ROAD, HUTTON (hereinafter called "the Vendor")
and	FREDERICK SMITH and ANN SMITH, both of 12 HOUGH LANE, HUTTON (hereinafter called "the Purchaser")

Whereby it is agreed that the Vendor shall sell and the Purchaser shall Purchase subject to the conditions printed hereon the property described in the particulars below for the sum of TWENTY NINE THOUSAND SEVEN HUNDRED AND FIFTY POUNDS (£ 29,750.00)

PARTICULARS

ALL THAT ~~freehold~~/leasehold Flat situate and known as

32A Library Road, Hutton, in the County of Wessex as the same is registered at H.M. Land Registry under Title Number XZ498031 for all the residue unexpired of a Lease ("the Lease") made the day of 19 between Albert Black (1) and John Brown (2) for the term of 99 years from subject as hereinafter mentioned

Purchase price	£ 29,750.00
Deposit	£ 2,975.00
Balance payable	£ 26,775.00
Price agreed for fixtures/fittings chattels	£
Total:	£ 26,775.00

CONDITIONS OF SALE on REVERSE

Signed Vendor/Purchaser

Date 19

Purchaser's Solicitors

Local Authority Hutton District Council

CONDITIONS OF SALE

1. The property is sold subject to the National Conditions of Sale Twentieth Edition (hereinafter referred to as the General Conditions) so far as they are not varied or inconsistent with these conditions of sale so however General Condition 11(7) of the general conditions shall apply in any event

2. The title of the Vendor is registered in Woolville District Land Registry with Absolute Title under Title Number XZ498031

3. ~~The abstract of title shall begin with~~

4. The property is sold subject to the payment of the rent reserved thereby and the covenants agreements and stipulations contained in the aforesaid lease a copy of which having been supplied to the Purchasers, they shall be deemed to be Purchasers with full knowledge thereof and shall raise no requisition or objection with regard thereto.

5. The prescribed rate referred to in the general conditions is 4 % over the base rate for the time being of Lloyds Bank PLC

6. The contractual completion date in general condition 5 of the general conditions is 198 and the latest time for completion is 2.00 ~~am~~/pm

7. Unless herein stated to the contrary general condition 3 of the general conditions shall not apply

8. The Vendor sells as Beneficial Owner

* 9. The property is sold with vacant possession of the whole upon completion

or

* 9. The property is sold subject to the following leases or tenancies or licences

\+ 10. The 10% deposit shall be paid as stakeholder/agent for the Vendor to Sellright Estate Agency of 10 High STreet, Hutton

11. In this agreement the term 'Solicitor' shall include the term 'Licensed Conveyancer'

12. The Vendor hereby grants an Authority to the Purchaser and/or his Solicitor to examine the Register

* Delete as appropriate

\+ If you have not instructed Estate Agents, ask your Bank Manager to hold the deposit as "stakeholder." In this case, you would amend the text thus: "...........Bankers of the Vendors, Friendly Bank PLC, 21 Moorside, Hutton"

Rv.2 OLE Series

CONTRACT FOR SALE OF UNREGISTERED LEASEHOLD LAND

C O N T R A C T   F O R   S A L E

This agreement is made the   day of   198

BETWEEN	JOHN JONES and MARY JONES, both of 21A LIBRARY ROAD, HUTTON (hereinafter called "the Vendor")
and	FREDERICK SMITH and ANN SMITH, both of 12 HOUGH LANE, HUTTON (hereinafter called "the Purchaser")

Whereby it is agreed that the Vendor shall sell and the Purchaser shall purchase subject to the conditions printed hereon the property described in the particulars below for the sum of TWENTY NINE THOUSAND SEVEN HUNDRED AND FIFTY POUNDS (£ 29,750.00)

PARTICULARS

ALL THAT Freehold/Leasehold property Flat situate and known as

32A Library Road, Hutton, in the County of Wessex

for all the residue unexpired of a Lease ("the Lease")
made the   day of   19
between Albert Black (1) and John Brown (2) for the term of 99 years
from
subject to the terms and conditions set out or referred to herein

Purchase price	£29,750.00
Deposit	£ 2,975.00
Balance payable	£26,775.00
Price agreed for fixtures/fittings chattels	£
Total:	£26,775.00

CONDITIONS OF SALE on REVERSE

Signed   VEndor/Purchaser

Date   19

Purchasers Solicitors: -

Local Authority: Hutton District Council

CONDITIONS OF SALE

1. The property is sold subject to the National Conditions of Sale Twentieth Edition (hereinafter referred to as the General Conditions) so far as they are not varied or inconsistent with these conditions of sale so however General Condition 11(7) of the General Conditions shall apply in any event

2. The title of the Vendor is registered in District Land ~~Registry with Title under~~ Title Number

3. The abstract of title shall begin with the Lease and shall continue with an Assignment made between John Brown (1) and James Lee (2) dated

4. The property is sold subject to the payment of the rent reserved thereby and the covenants agreements and stipulations contained in the aforesaid lease a copy of which having been supplied to the Purchasers, they shall be deemed to be Purchasers with full knowledge thereof and shall raise no requisition or objection with regard thereto.

5. The prescribed rate referred to in the General Conditions is 4% over the base rate for the time being of Lloyds Bank PLC

6. The contractual completion date in General Condition 5 of the General Conditions is   198 and the latest time for completion is 2.00 am/pm

7. Unless herein stated to the contrary General Condition 3 of the General Conditions shall not apply

8. The Vendor sells as Beneficial Owner

* 9. The property is sold with vacant possession of the whole upon completion

or

* 9. The property is sold subject ~~to the following leases or tenancies or licences~~

\+ 10. The 10% deposit shall be paid as stakeholder/agent for the Vendor to Sellright Estate Agency of 10 High Street, Hutton

11. In this agreement the term 'solicitor' shall include the term 'Licensed Conveyancer'

12. The Vendor hereby grants an Authority to the Purchaser and/or his Solicitor to examine the Register

* Delete as appropriate

\+ If you have not instructed Estate Agents, ask your Bank Manager to hold the deposit as "stakeholder." In this case, you would amend the text thus: ".......Bankers of the Vendors, Friendly Bank PLC, 21 Moorside, Hutton."

Ole SERIES PRE-CONTRACT ENQUIRIES OF VENDOR

PRE-CONTRACT ENQUIRIES of VENDOR

Please reply as precisely as possible to the following enquiries to obviate the need for further clarification.

....
Proposed Purchaser

.... Date

Re .... 15 Lone Pine Close, Hutton ....

(Seller) ... Brown ....

To (Buyer) ... Ford ....

ENQUIRIES	REPLIES
1. Planning etc. Consents	1.
a. When did the current use of the property begin?	a. 1959
b. Has the current use been continuous since it began?	b. Yes
c. During the previous 4 years:	c.
(i) Were any buildings forming part of the property erected or have any been altered in any way?	(i) No
(ii) Have all conditions of any planning consents been complied with?	(ii) Yes
d. Please supply a copy of any planning consent giving permission for the present use of the property and for the erection and/or alteration of any buildings on the property	d. Please apply to the Local Authority for copy of Planning Consent
e. Please also supply a copy of any bye-law or building regulation consent relating to the property	e. As d above
2. Rates and other Outgoings	2.
a. What is the rateable value of the property?	a. £359
b. What were the total annual charges for rates, sewerage and water in the previous year?	b. £654.50
c. What other periodic charges affect the property or its occupier? Please specify.	c. None other than gas and similar utility charges.
3. Fixtures and Fittings	3.
a. Please specify which of the following now on the property or growing thereon or attached thereto are included in the sale price: Trees, shrubs, flowers, garden produce, sheds, greenhouses, TV aerials, fitted furniture, garden	a. All the items listed are included in the sale price except the garden shed and fitted carpets which are available for purchase by separate arrangement.

Page Two

ENQUIRIES	REPLIES
furniture and/or ornaments, electric switches, power points, ceiling and wall lights and fittings, curtain slide rails and fittings, fitted carpets as laid.	
b. Please confirm that all chattels, fixtures, fittings and separate items included in the sale price are the Vendor's property free of any bill of sale, lien, hire purchase or any other third party claim.	b. Confirmed
c. Please specify what fixtures and fittings affixed to the property are not included in the sale price.	c. None
4. Boundaries	4.
a. Is the property fenced, hedged or walled on all sides? Please state to whom these boundary fences, hedges or walls belong.	a. Yes. We understand that the Northern boundary fence belongs to No. 17 and the remainder to the Vendors.
b. Which of these has the Vendor maintained and regarded as his responsibility?	b. Please see 4a above.
c. Do the boundaries correspond with the filed plan annexed to or drawn on the Deeds?	c. Yes, so far as the Vendors are aware but the Purchasers should rely upon their own inspection.
5. Disputes	5.
a. Is the Vendor aware of any current or past disputes relating to the boundaries, easements, covenants, nuisance or any other matters affecting the property or its use?	a. No
b. Has the Vendor received any notices relating to the property or its use?	b. No
6. Rights of Way	6.
a. Please state whether any person has a right of way over land which forms part of the property being sold.	a. Not to the Vendor's knowledge but the property is sold subject to any there may be.
b. Does the Vendor have a right of way over a shared drive passage or track to gain access to a garage or other part of the property?	b. No
7. Services	7.
a. Is the water supply direct from the mains?	a. Yes, so far as the Vendor is aware.
b. Is the drainage of the property direct to a main drain?	b. The Purchasers should rely upon their own inspection.
c. Are there any drains pipes or cables which serve another property running under or over the property being sold?	c. The usual services are connected but the Purchasers should rely upon their own inspection for the route of pipes etc.

Ole SERIES PRE-CONTRACT ENQUIRIES OF VENDOR Page Three

ENQUIRIES	REPLIES
8. Guarantees	8.
a. Please state whether there is a current N.H.B.C. certificate in force in respect of the property.	a. No
b. Please supply copies of any other current guarantees relating to the property, the benefit of which will be assigned to the Purchaser.	b. Copy of Cavity Wall insulation guarantee herewith.
c. Have any claims been made under the terms of these guarantees which remain to be settled or are any pending?	c. No
9. Persons Residing in the Property	9.
a. Please give the full names (and ages if under 18 years of age) of all persons resident in the property (other than the Vendor).	a. Only the Vendors are in residence.
b. What legal or equitable rights in the property, if any, has each person named?	
10. Completion	10.
Please state when after exchange of contracts the Vendor will be able to give vacant possession of the whole of the property?	4 weeks subject to contract.

ADDITIONAL ENQUIRIES should be attached on a separate sheet

Page Four

LEASEHOLD PROPERTIES (Delete if not applicable)	REPLIES
a. Please state whether the Lease under which the property is held is a head lease or an underlease	
b. Please state the names and addresses of the Lessor, any superior Lessor and their respective receivers of the ground rent	
c. If the consent or licence of the Lessor in the Assignment of the lease is required please state what steps have been taken to obtain the same.	
d. Has the Vendor complied with all the terms of the Lease under which the property is held?	
e. Please supply details of service charges levied in respect to the preceding 3 years and vouchers for the same.	
f. Please supply full details of the insurance policy covering the property, including the name of the Insurance Company, policy number, name(s) insured, risks covered, sum covered, premium paid an removal date.	

Above are my/our replied to the enquiries

....

Proposed Vendors's Signature

....198

LETTER TO ACCOMPANY PRE-CONTRACT ENQUIRIES

Messrs Black and Brown,
49 Lower High Street,
Hutton

Your Name
Your Address
Today's Date

Dear Sirs,

Re: 15 Lone Pine Close, Hutton
SUBJECT TO CONTRACT

I am pleased to return herewith to your pre-contract enquiries in respect of the above property with my replies thereto.

Yours faithfully,

Your signature

LETTER TO PURCHASER'S SOLICITOR ON EXCHANGE OF CONTRACTS

Messrs Black and Brown,
49 Lower High Street,
Hutton.

Your Name
Your Address
Today's Date

Dear Sirs,

Re: 15 Lone Pine Close, Hutton

Thank you for your letter enclosing part of contract to purchase the above property signed by your clients, together with cheque for £3000 being ten per cent deposit which will be held by my estate agents as stakeholders as per contract.

I now enclose my signed part of contract, and have inserted the date agreed for Completion, namely . . . . on both parts of the contract. ‡I also enclose Form 201 Authority to Inspect the Register.

Yours faithfully,

Your Signature

‡If the land is unregistered omit this sentence and substitute:
I also enclose Abstract of Title.

COMPLETED AUTHORITY TO INSPECT THE REGISTER

HM Land Registry — Land Registration Acts 1925 to 1971

AUTHORITY TO INSPECT THE REGISTER

County and district (or London borough) WESSEX HUTTON

Title no(s) XZ 498031

Property The land and dwellinghouse known as 15 Lone Pine Close Hutton

We

Name BERTRAM BROWN AND BARBARA BROWN

Address 15 Lone Pine Close, Hutton

as ~~solicitors for~~ The registered proprietors of the land in the the above-mentioned title
(insert full name(s) of registered proprietor(s))

of 15 Lone Pine Close, Hutton

~~the registered proprietor(s) of the land in the above-mentioned title(s)~~

hereby authorise Messrs Brown & Green,

of 44 High Street, Hutton,

to inspect the register of the above-mentioned title and any documents referred to in the register as being filed in the Land Registry.

Signed ....

~~(Solicitors for the registered proprietor)~~ The registered proprietors.

Date ....

Notes

1. This authority may also be used in support of an application for office copies (form A44) or for a certificate of inspection of the filed plan (form 101), or for an official search of the register (forms 94A, 94B or 94C).
2. This form, suitably adapted, can be used to give an authority to inspect the register on behalf of the proprietor of a registered charge.

ABSTRACT OF TITLE

Epitome of Title

Relating to Freehold property known as

21 BOWHILL ROAD, ANYTOWN

Epitome of Title F/cap Fronts

DATE	NATURE OF DOCUMENT OR EVENT 1	PARTIES 2	WHETHER ABSTRACT OR PHOTOGRAPHIC COPY 4	DOCUMENT NUMBER 5	WHETHER ORIGINAL DOCUMENT TO BE HANDED OVER ON COMPLETION
12. 5.59	Conveyance	Eli Saul Smith (1) John Smith & Maud Smith (2)	P.C	1	Yes
14.12.68	Conveyance	J.Smith & M.Smith (1) Lionel George Jones (2)	"	2	"
14.12.68	Mortgage	L.G.Jones (1) Best Building Society (2)	"	3	"
21. 7.74	Mortgage dated 14.12.68 redeemed. Receipt endorsed thereon.		"	4	"
14. 9.76	Conveyance	L.G.Jones (1) Ernest Wade & Jane Wade (2)	"	5	"
14. 9.76	Mortgage	E.Wade & J.Wade (1) Huge Building Society (2)	"	6	"
8. 8.80	Mortgage dated 14.9.86 redeemed. Receipt endorsed thereon.		"	7	"
12. 9.83	Death of J.Wade Death Certificate of this date		"	8	No
3. 4.84	Conveyance	E.Wade (1) Edwin Fuller & Leah Fuller (2)	"	9	Yes
3. 4.84	Mortgage	E.Fuller & L.Fuller (1) Largest Building Society (2)	"	10	"
28. 5.86	Mortgage dated 3.4.84 redeemed. Receipt endorsed thereon.		"	11	"

NOTES

1. An abstract may be in the form of an Epitome accompanied by photographic copies of documents or abstracts in traditional form (examined or not as appropriate) or photographic copies of such abstracts.
2. Indicate on the copy any parts of a document not relevant to the transaction.
3. Where the document is a search certificate state the person against whom search was made.
4. Photographic copies must be (i) permanent, i.e., must be capable of remaining legible for the thirty years or so for which an abstract is usually required even if frequent reference is made to it, (ii) capable of being marked, (iii) printed black on white paper, (iv) clear and definite so as to permit further photographic reproduction. Photographic copies of plans must also be satisfactorily coloured and show all the details of the originals.
5. Documents accompanying the Epitome should be identified by number and that number stated in this column, numbers should continue in sequence when further documents are added (e.g. if the Epitome is used when the property is resold).

SUGGESTED LETTER TO ASCERTAIN SUM REQUIRED TO REDEEM MORTGAGE

Messrs. Hue and Cryer,
Solicitors,
219 New High Road,
Hutton.

Your Name
Your Address

Today's Date

Dear Sirs,

Re: Best Building Society
Roll No. ABC/12345

I am pleased to advise that contracts have now been exchanged with Mr. and Mrs. G.G. Ford for the purchase of this property which is mortgaged to Handy Building Society.

Completion has been fixed for (date) and I would be obliged if you will please ascertain the sum required to redeem the mortgage on that date. Will you please also advise the daily rate in the event that Completion is delayed.

Yours faithfully,

Your Signature

LETTER TO LANDLORD'S AGENTS NOTIFYING YOUR INTENTION TO ASSIGN BENEFIT OF RESIDUE OF LEASE

Messrs Able and Jones,
Surveyors,
112 High Street,
Hutton.

Your Name
Your Address

Today's Date

Dear Sirs,

Re: 16 Long Meadow Lane, Hutton

Reference clause 6 of the lease dated 25 May 1964 made between JOHN BROWN (1) and JAMES JONES (2), NOTICE is hereby given in accordance therewith that the undersigned has exchanged contracts for the sale of the leasehold interest in the property described above, being the residue of the said lease, with ALBERT BUYER.

Completion of the purchase of the said leasehold interest has been fixed for (date).

I enclose a cheque for £ . . . . being the fee prescribed for dealing with this matter. Please acknowledge receipt by signing and returning the duplicate copy of this notice.

Yours faithfully,

Your Signature

Ole SERIES REQUISITIONS ON TITLE (POST-CONTRACT)

REQUISITIONS ON TITLE

(POST-CONTRACT)

Re ...15 Lone Pine Close, Hutton........

......Brown..................................

To .....Ford.................................

ENQUIRIES	REPLIES
1. Previous enquiries	1.
If the pre-contract enquiries replied to on behalf of the Vendor were repeated would the replies now be the same as those previously given? If not, please give full particulars of any variation.	Yes, save as may have been varied by correspondence.
2. Receipts	2.
(A) On completion the receipt for all rates and outgoings formerly payable by the Vendor must not be produced and any arrears allowed for	(A) Noted
(B) In the case of a leasehold property the receipt for ground rent due on the last rent day prior to the day of completion as well as the receipt for the last fire insurance premium must be produced on completion.	
3. Title Deeds	3.
(A) Unregistered land	
(i) Which documents of title will be handed over to the Purchaser on completion?	
(ii) Who will give the Purchaser the statutory acknowledgement and undertaking for the production and safe custody of those not handed over?	
(iii) Why will any documents not handed over be retained?	
(B) Registered land	(B)
When was the land or charge certificate last officially examined with the register?	12 August 1986
4. Mortgages	4.
(A) All subsisting mortgages must be discharged on or before completion.	(A) Agreed
(B) (i) In respect of each subsisting mortgage will the vacating receipt/discharge or registered charge be handed over on completion?	(B) (i) Please refer to (ii) below
(ii) If an undertaking to hand it over later is proposed, what are the suggested terms of the undertaking?	(ii) We will give the usual undertaking to forward a sealed Form 53
5. Completion	5.
(A) Please send a completion statement.	(A) Herewith
(B) (i) Where will completion take place?	(B) (i) At this office
(ii) In whose favour and for what amounts will bankers drafts be required on completion?	(ii) We will advise as soon as possible.
6. Notices	
Please give the name and address of any Solicitor, agent, or other person to whom notice of any dealing with the property must be given.	
7. Possession	7.
(A) (i) Vacant possession of the whole of the property must be given on completion	(A) (i) Noted
(ii) What arrangements will be made to deliver the keys to the Purchaser?	(ii) We suggest that this is done through the Estate Agents.

NOTE You will appreciate that the Requisitions based on the Abstract of Title or Contract must, of course, be added to the above.

N.B. The Deeds and documents of title remain to be examined and the right is reserved to make further requisitions which may arise on each examination, the replies to the above, and enquiries before completion or otherwise.

.... Date .... Date

Form 19

H.M. Land Registry

Land Registration Acts, 1925 to 1971

(1) TRANSFER OF WHOLE

(Rule 98 or 115, Land Registration Rules, 1925)

County and district (or London borough) WESSEX HUTTON

Title number(s) XZ498031

Property 15 Lone Pine Close, Hutton, Wessex

Date .... 19 86 In consideration of

TWENTY NINE THOUSAND SEVEN HUNDRED AND FIFTY

pounds (£29,750.00) (2) the receipt whereof is hereby acknowledged

I/~~We~~ (3) BERTRAM BROWN, of 15 LONE PINE CLOSE, HUTTON, WESSEX

(4) as beneficial owner~~(s)~~ hereby transfer to

(5) GERALD GEORGE FORD, of 112 DORSET AVENUE, HUTTON, WESSEX

the land comprised in the title(s) above mentioned (6) (7) And the Transferee for himself and his successors in title hereby covenants with the Transferor by way of indemnity only to observe and perform the covenants contained or referred to in the Charges Register of the said Title so far as the same are still subsisting and capable of being enforced and relate to the property hereby transferred.

(continued overleaf)

(8) *It is hereby certified that the transaction hereby effected does not form part of a larger transaction or series of transactions in respect of which the amount or value or aggregate amount or value of the consideration exceeds £* 30,000.00

Signed, sealed and delivered by the said BERTRAM BROWN — B. Brown

in the presence of

Name Alan Jones

Address 44 Malta Road Hutton

Occupation Clerk

Signed, sealed and delivered by the said GERALD GEORGE FORD — G.G. Ford

in the presence of

Name John Brown

Address 91 Acre Road Hutton

Occupation Salesman

COMPLETED FORM 19(JP) TO JOINT TENANTS WITH COVENANT FOR INDEMNITY CLAUSE

Form 19(JP)
H.M. Land Registry

Land Registration Acts, 1925 to 1971

Stamp pursuant to section 28 of the Finance Act 1931, to be impressed here.

When the transfer attracts Inland Revenue duty, the stamps should be impressed here before lodging the transfer for registration.

(1) For a transfer to a sole proprietor use printed form 19.

(1) **TRANSFER OF WHOLE TO JOINT PROPRIETORS**

(Freehold or Leasehold)

(Rules 98 or 115, Land Registration Rules, 1925)

NOTE: This transfer must be executed by the transferees as well as the transferor(s).

County and district (or London borough): WESSEX HUTTON

Title number(s): XZ498031

Property: 15 Lone Pine Close, Hutton, Wessex

Date: 19 86. In consideration of TWENTY NINE THOUSAND SEVEN HUNDRED AND FIFTY pounds (£ 29,750.000) (2) *the receipt whereof is hereby acknowledged*

(2) Strike out if not required.

(3) In BLOCK LETTERS, enter full name(s), postal address(es) and occupation(s) of the proprietor(s) of the land.

I/We(3) BERTRAM BROWN and BARBARA BROWN, both of 15 LONE PINE CLOSE, HUTTON, WESSEX

(4) If desired or otherwise as the case may be (See rules 76 and 77)

(4) *as beneficial owner(s)* hereby transfer to:

(5) In BLOCK LETTERS, enter full names, postal addresses and occupations of the transferees for entry on the register.

(5) GERALD GEORGE FORD and JOAN FORD, both of 112 DORSET ROAD, HUTTON, WESSEX

the land comprised in the title above mentioned (6) (7) And the Transferees for themselves and their successors in title hereby jointly and severally covenant with the Transferors by way of indemnity only to observe and perform the covenants contained or referred to in the Charges Register of the said Title so far as the same are still subsisting and capable of being enforced and relate to the property hereby transferred.

(6) Any special clause should be entered here

(7) A transfer for charitable uses should follow form 36 (see rules 121 and 122)

(continued overleaf)

(8) Delete the inappropriate alternative.

The transferees declare that the survivor of them(8) can ~~cannot~~ give a valid receipt for capital money arising on a disposition of the land.

(9) If a certificate of value for the purposes of the Stamp Act, 1891, and amending Acts is not required, this paragraph should be deleted.

(9) *It is hereby certified that the transaction hereby effected does not form part of a larger transaction or series of transactions in respect of which the amount or value or aggregate amount or value of the consideration exceeds £* 30,000.00

(10) See marginal note overleaf.

(10) Signed, sealed and delivered by the said BERTRAM BROWN — B. Brown
in the presence of
Name: Alma Jones
Address: 44 Malta Road, Hutton
Occupation: Clerk

(10) Signed, sealed and delivered by the said BARBARA BROWN — Barbara Brown
in the presence of
Name: Alma Jones
Address: 44 Malta Road, Hutton
Occupation: Clerk

(10) Signed, sealed and delivered by the said GERALD GEORGE FORD — G.G. Ford
in the presence of
Name: John Brown
Address: 7 ... Road Hutton
Occupation: Salesman

(10) Signed, sealed and delivered by the said JOAN FORD — Joan Ford
in the presence of
Name: John Brown
Address: 7 ... Road Hutton
Occupation: Salesman

LETTER TO PURCHASER'S SOLICITOR APPROVING DRAFT PURCHASE DEED: REGISTERED LAND

Messrs Black and Brown
49 Lower High Street
Hutton

Your Name
Your Address
Today's Date

Dear Sirs,

Re: 15 Lone Pine Close, Hutton

I thank you for your lette dated . . . enclosing Transfer of Whole Form 19(JP). I am pleased to formally approve the form as drawn and return the same for execution by the Purchasers.

I am grateful for the carbon copy for my file.

Yours faithfully,

Your Signature

LETTER TO PURCHASER'S SOLICITOR APPROVING DRAFT PURCHASE DEED: UNREGISTERED LAND

Messrs Black and Brown,
49 Lower High Street,
Hutton.

Your Name
Your Address
Today's Date

Dear Sirs,

Re: 15 Lone Pine Close, Hutton

Thank you for your letter dated . . . enclosing draft conveyance in respect of the purchase of the above property by your clients. I return the top copy of the draft marked 'approved', and am obliged for the carbon copy for my use.

Yours faithfully,

Your Signature

CONVEYANCE OF UNREGISTERED LAND TO SOLE PURCHASER WITH COVENANT FOR INDEMNITY

This Conveyance

is made the day of One thousand nine hundred and eighty

B E T W E E N BERTRAM BROWN of 15 Lone Pine Close Hutton in the County of Wessex (hereinafter called "the Vendor") of the one part and GERALD GEORGE FORD of 112 Dorset Road Hutton aforesaid (hereinafter called "the Purchaser") of the other part

W H E R E A S the Vendor is seised of the property hereinafter described for an estate in fee simple in possession subject as hereinafter mentioned but otherwise free from incumbrances and has agreed with the Purchaser for the sale to him of the said property for a like estate at the price of TWENTY NINE THOUSAND SEVEN HUNDRED AND FIFTY POUNDS

N O W T H I S D E E D W I T N E S S E T H as follows:-

1. In pursuance of the said agreement and in consideration of the sum of TWENTY NINE THOUSAND SEVEN HUNDRED AND FIFTY POUNDS (£29,750.00) paid by the Purchaser to the Vendor (the receipt whereof the Vendor hereby acknowledges) the Vendor as Beneficial Owner HEREBY CONVEYS unto the Purchaser ALL THAT piece or parcel of land situate in Lone Pine Close Hutton in the County of Wessex and having a frontage to the said road of Sixty feet or thereabouts and a depth therefrom of One hundred and twenty feet or thereabouts TOGETHER WITH the messuage or dwellinghouse erected thereon or on some part thereof situate and known as Number 15 Lone Pine Close Hutton aforesaid ALL WHICH said piece or parcel of land is for the purpose of identification only more particularly delineated on the plan annexed to a Conveyance (hereinafter called "the Conveyance") dated the Second day of May One thousand nine hundred and sixty four and made between John Joseph Black of the one part and the Vendor of the other part and thereon edged red TO HOLD the same unto the Purchaser in fee simple Subject to the restrictive and other covenants contained mentioned or referred to in the Conveyance

2. With the object and intent of affording to the Vendor a full and sufficient indemnity but not further or otherwise the Purchaser covenants with the Vendor that he the Purchaser will henceforth observe and perform the aforesaid covenants so far as the same are still subsisting and capable of being enforced and will indemnify the Vendor from and against all actions claims demands and liability in respect of any future breach thereof so far as aforesaid

3. It is hereby certified that the transaction hereby effected does not form part of a larger transaction or of a series of transactions in respect of which the amount or value or the aggregate amount of value of the consideration exceeds Thirty Thousand Pounds

I N W I T N E S S whereof the parties hereto have hereunto set their hands and seals the day and year first before written

SIGNED SEALED AND DELIVERED by)
the said BERTRAM BROWN)
in the presence of:-)

SIGNED SEALED AND DELIVERED by)
the said GERALD GEORGE FORD)
in the presence of:-)

CONVEYANCE OF UNREGISTERED LAND TO JOINT TENANTS WITH COVENANT FOR INDEMNITY

This Conveyance

is made the day of One thousand nine hundred and eighty

B E T W E E N BERTRAM BROWN and BARBARA BROWN both of 15 Lone Pine Close Hutton in the County of Wessex (hereinafter called "the Vendors") of the one part and GERALD GEORGE FORD and JOAN FORD both of 112 Dorset Road Hutton aforesaid (hereinafter called "the Purchasers") of the other part

W H E R E A S the Vendors are seised of the property hereinafter described for an estate in fee simple in possession subject as hereinafter mentioned but otherwise free from incumbrances and have agreed with the Purchasers for the sale to them of the said property for a like estate at the price of TWENTY NINE THOUSAND SEVEN HUNDRED AND FIFTY POUNDS and it has been agreed that the same shall be vested in the Purchasers as joint tenants in manner hereinafter appearing

N O W T H I S D E E D W I T N E S S E T H as follows:-

1. In pursuance of the said agreement and in consideration of the sum of TWENTY NINE THOUSAND SEVEN HUNDRED AND FIFTY POUNDS (£29,750.00) paid by the Purchasers to the Vendors (the receipt whereof the Vendors hereby acknowledge) the Vendors as Beneficial Owners HEREBY CONVEY unto the Purchasers ALL THAT piece or parcel of land situate in Lone Pine Close Hutton in the County of Wessex and having a frontage to the said road of Sixty feet or thereabouts and a depth therefrom of One hundred and twenty feet or thereabouts TOGETHER WITH the messuage or dwellinghouse and premises appurtenant thereto erected thereon or on some part thereof situate and known as Number 15 Lone Pine Close Hutton aforesaid ALL WHICH said piece or parcel of land is for the purpose of identification only more particularly delineated on the plan annexed to a Conveyance (hereinafter called "the Conveyance") dated the Second day of May One thousand nine hundred and sixty four and made between John Joseph Black of the one part and the Vendors of the other part and thereon edged red TO HOLD the same unto the Purchasers in fee simple UPON TRUST for themselves as beneficial joint tenants Subject to the restrictive and other covenants contained mentioned or referred to in the Conveyance

2. The Purchasers hereby agree and declare that:-

(a) They are joint tenants in equity

(b) The trustees for sale of the property shall have powers to deal with it equal to those of a sole beneficial owner

(c) The survivor of the Purchasers shall become sole legal and beneficial owner of the property and any person dealing with the survivor may assume this unless a notice to the contrary appears on this Deed

3. With the object and intent of affording to the Vendors a full and sufficient indemnity but not further or otherwise the Purchasers hereby jointly and severally covenant with the Vendors that they the Purchasers will henceforth observe and perform the aforesaid covenants so far as the same are still subsisting and capable of being enforced and will indemnify and keep indemnified the Vendors their respective estates and effects from and against all actions claims demands and liability in respect of any future breach thereof so far as aforesaid

4. It is hereby certified that the transaction hereby effected does not form part of a larger transaction or of a series of transactions in respect of which the amount or value or the aggregate amount or value of the consideration exceeds Thirty Thousand Pounds

CONVEYANCE OF UNREGISTERED LAND TO JOINT TENANTS WITH COVENANT FOR INDEMNITY Page Three

I N W I T N E S S whereof the parties hereto have hereunto set their hands and seals the day and year first before written

SIGNED SEALED AND DELIVERED by)
the said BERTRAM BROWN)
in the presence of:-)

SIGNED SEALED AND DELIVERED by)
the said BARBARA BROWN)
in the presence of:-)

SIGNED SEALED AND DELIVERED by)
the said GERALD GEORGE FORD)
in the presence of:-)

SIGNED SEALED AND DELIVERED by)
the said JOAN FORD)
in the presence of:-)

1. This conveyance provides for a joint tenancy, i.e. under which the property automatically passes to the survivor on the death of one of the joint Purchasers as discussed on page 12. There is a model conveyance for a sole Purchaser on page 196c.

2. At the time of writing the liability for stamp duty starts at £30001 and is 1% of the total consideration (price). If the property conveyed in this example had been sold for a figure in excess of £30,000, then clause 4 would be omitted. Similarly, if the stamp duty threshold rises in a future budget, the higher figure would be inserted in clause 4.

CONVEYANCE OF UNREGISTERED LAND TO TENANTS IN COMMON WITH COVENANT FOR INDEMNITY

This Conveyance

is made the day of One thousand nine hundred and eighty

B E T W E E N BERTRAM BROWN and BARBARA BROWN both of 15 Lone Pine Close Hutton in the County of Wessex (hereinafter called "the Vendors) of the one part and JOHN METRO and VALERIE AUSTIN both of 112 Dorset Road Hutton aforesaid (hereinafter called "the Purchasers" of the other part

W H E R E A S the Vendors are seised of the property hereinafter described for an estate in fee simple in possession subject as hereinafter mentioned but otherwise free from incumbrances and have agreed with the Purchasers for the sale to them of the said property for a like estate at the price of TWENTY NINE THOUSAND SEVEN HUNDRED AND FIFTY POUNDS

N O W THIS DEED WITNESSETH as follows :-

1. In pursuance of the said agreement and in consideration of the sum of TWENTY NINE THOUSAND SEVEN HUNDRED AND FIFTY POUNDS (£29750.00) paid by the Purchasers to the Vendors (the receipt whereof the Vendors hereby acknowledge the Vendors as Beneficial Owners HEREBY CONVEY unto the Purchasers ALL THAT piece or parcel of land situate in Lone Pine Close Hutton in the County of Wessex and having a frontage to the said road of Sixty feet or thereabouts and a depth therefrom of One hundred and twenty feet or thereabouts TOGETHER WITH the messuage or dwellinghouse and premises appurtenant thereto erected thereon or on some part thereof situate and known as Number 15 Lone Pine Close Hutton aforesaid ALL WHICH piece or parcel of land is for the purpose of identification only more particularly delineated on the plan annexed to a Conveyance (hereinafter called "the Conveyance") dated the Second day of May One thousand nine hundred and sixty four and made between John Joseph Black of the one part and the Vendors of the other part and thereon edged red TO HOLD the same unto the Purchasers as beneficial tenants in common in equal shares SUBJECT to the restrictive and other covenants contained mentioned or referred to in the Conveyance

2. With the object and intent of affording to the Vendors a full and sufficient indemnity but not further or otherwise the Purchasers hereby jointly and severally covenant with the Vendors that they will henceforth observe and perform the aforesaid covenants so far as the same are still subsisting and capable of being enforced and will indemnify and keep indemnified the Vendors their respective estates and effects from and against all actions claims demands and liability in respect of any future breach thereof so far as aforesaid

3. It is hereby certified that the transaction hereby effected does not form part of a larger transaction or of a series of transactions in respect of which the amount or value or the aggregate amount or value of the consideration exceeds Thirty Thousand Pounds

I N W I N E S S whereof the parties hereto have hereunto set their hands and seals the day and year first before written

CONVEYANCE OF UNREGISTERED LAND TO TENANTS IN COMMON WITH COVENANT FOR INDEMNITY Page Three

SIGNED SEALED AND DELIVERED by)
the said BERTRAM BROWN)
in the presence of :-)

SIGNED SEALED AND DELIVERED by)
the said BARBARA BROWN)
in the presence of :-)

SIGNED SEALED AND DELIVERED by)
the said JOHN METRO)
in the presence of :-)

SIGNED SEALED AND DELIVERED by)
the said VALERIE AUSTIN)
in the presence of :-)

TYPICAL COMPLETION STATEMENT FOR YOUR SALE

COMPLETION STATEMENT as at 30 April 1986

Re: 15 Lone Pine Close, Hutton

JONES to BROWN

Purchase price		£ 30,000.00
Less Deposit paid		£ 3,000.00
		£27,000
Add Chattels purchased from Vendor	275.00	
Add proportion of water rates @ £52 per year 30 April-30 Sept. (153 days)	21.42	
Add proportion of sewerage charges @ £100 per year 30 April-30 Sept. (153 days)	41.31	337.73
		£27,337.73

1 Draft for £8,961.50 in favour of Best Building Society and
1 Draft for £18,356.23 in our favour, please.

LETTER TO PURCHASER'S SOLICITOR ACCOMPANYING COMPLETION STATEMENT

Your Name
Your Address
Today's Date

Messrs Black and Brown,
49 Lower High Street,
Hutton.

Dear Sirs,

Re: 15 Lone Pine Close, Hutton
Jones to Brown

I now enclose herewith completion statement in respect of the purchase of the above property by Mr. and Mrs. Brown.

I take the opportunity to confirm that the venue for the Completion will be at the offices of my building society's solicitors, Messrs Hue and Cryer, as mentioned to you on the telephone yesterday. The agreed time for Completion is 10.30 a.m.

Yours faithfully,

Your Signature

Glossary

Obscure legal jargon and delightfully flowery phrasing is part and parcel of the legal scene, for with lawyers a spade will always be 'an aforesaid digging implement'. Nowhere is this jungle of language quite as lush as with the buying and selling of property. This modest glossary is designed to help you fathom some of the more common words and phrases you will encounter in the various letters and forms of your conveyancing.

You may encounter many of the following words and phrases in this book or when dealing with the various letters and forms of your conveyance. The bulk is legal jargon which it is, unfortunately, not possible to avoid.

Abstract of title A summary of the deeds constituting the title to land which are furnished by the vendor to an intending purchaser. These used to be typed summaries of the title deed but nowadays, with the widespread use of photocopiers, the Abstract usually consists of photocopies of the actual deeds.

Administrators Persons authorised to administer the estate of one who died 'intestate' (without leaving a valid will).

Apportionments The division between the buyer and seller of a property of sums paid or to be paid for water and sewerage charges and other outgoings.

Assent (Think of it as consent.) A document used to pass the legal estate in land to a beneficiary. It must be in writing and must be signed by all the personal representatives and must name the person in whose favour it is given. It need not be sealed and is an exception to the general rule that a legal estate can only be transferred by means of a deed. Where there is a sole personal representative and he has been left property in a will he must sign an assent in his own favour, from himself as personal representative. See also Personal Representatives.

Assign The term used to make over a right or interest to another. In the context of this book to transfer a lease from one person to another.

Assignee One to whom leasehold property is assigned.

Assignment The name used for the document which transfers unregistered leasehold property from one person to another.

Assignor One who assigns (transfers) leasehold property to another.

Assurance Now outdated but used to be the term used for a conveyance, i.e. the legal evidence of the transfer of property.

Attestation The signing by a witness of his name to a deed executed by another.

Attestation clause	The clause to a deed or other document by which a witness certifies to be genuine.
Attorney — power of	One who has been appointed by another to do something in his stead, e.g. to sign and seal deeds.
Auction	A public sale of goods or land to the highest bidder at the fall of the hammer.
Auctioneer	An agent licensed to conduct sales or auctions. He is deemed to be the agent of both seller and buyer and, in the case of land, can bind both parties by his signature to a memorandum of sale under section 40 Law of Property Act 1925.
Authority to inspect the register	The document which when signed by the registered proprietor(s) of land authorises another person to make an official search of the register. Now usually effected by completing Form 201 or by an Authority incorporated in the contract of sale.
Backside	An old term used to denote a yard at the rear of a house and forming part of it. Rarely used today.
Banker's draft	A cheque drawn by a bank and signed on its behalf by an authorised bank employee. Regarded as the equivalent of cash.
Beneficial occupation	Occupation of land to the benefit, ie. the advantage, of the occupier.
Beneficial owner	One who has title to land for his own benefit ('enjoyment') as opposed to someone who holds title as a trustee.
Beneficiary	One entitled to benefit under a trust or will, who then has the beneficial interest.
Bridging loan	A loan for the purpose of bridging the period between the time when a house buyer must pay the purchase price and the time when the proceeds of sale of another house are received.
Building society	A society established to raise funds by the subscriptions of its members and to accept deposits on which interest is paid. The funds thus accumulated are available to member borrowers to assist them purchase dwellings for their own occupation, such advances being secured by a mortgage on the property purchased. The first society was formed in Birmingham in 1775.
Caution	An entry on the land register which prevents the registered proprietor of the land from dealing in it without first giving notice to the cautioner.
Charge	A mortgage (or other right or interest) subject to which land may be held.
Charge certificate	In registered conveyancing, this is the certificate issued by the Land Registry to the mortgage lender showing the entry of a charge on the land register.
Chargee	One who can enforce a charge, e.g. a mortgagee.
Chattels	Moveable personal property, clothes, motor cars, carpets, furniture.
Completion	The final step leading up to transfer of ownership of a property when the vendor hands over the

	documents of title in exchange for the purchase price.
Completion moneys	The sum payable by a buyer to complete a purchase.
Completion statement	The statement completed and sent to the buyer showing the exact amount payable on completion of the transaction.
Compulsory registration	The requirement that in areas of England and Wales, which have been designated areas of compulsory registration, transfer of land must be registered with the District Land Registry upon transfer. If the land is unregistered, e.g. because when last sold the area had not been designated an area of compulsory registration, an application must be made for first registration of title.
Contract	A document in two identical parts, one signed by the seller and one by the purchaser which, when exchanged, binds the parties to complete the sale of a house. This is completed by transferring ownership in exchange for the purchase price.
Conveyance	The document which transfers freehold unregistered land from seller to buyer.
Conveyancing	The term used to describe the procedures involved in transferring property from one person to another.
Covenant	A promise or undertaking in a deed whereby one party promises to do or not to do any act or to give something to another.
Daily interest rate	The rate at which interest accrues on a loan. It is this sum times the number of days that is added to the completion figure if completion is delayed. See page 106 and clause 5 of the contracts on pages 135 and 137, 177 and 179.
Deed	A written instrument signed sealed and delivered. In practice the term is used to describe deeds, conveyances, mortgages etc. according to the nature of the document.
Delivery	Delivery of a deed is held to take place at the moment the party executing the deed places his finger on the seal and says 'I deliver this my act and deed'.
Demise	The grant of a lease.
Deposit	The agreed part of the purchase price, usually ten per cent, which is paid by the purchaser upon or before exchange of contracts. This normally is held by the vendor's solicitor as stakeholder. The vendor may not use the deposit money without the purchaser's agreement.
Discharge of a registered charge	The document on which a building society or other lender acknowledges that all monies secured by the mortgage on a registered property have been repaid.
Draft	May be a shortened form of 'banker's draft', or the first copy of a legal document before it has been engrossed.

Easement — A right enjoyed by the owner of a property over the land of his neighbour, such as a right of way, of light, of support, etc.

Endowment mortgage — An endowment type policy specially developed for home-owners which provides for interest only payments on the mortgage loan, the principal sum being paid off at the end of the term from the proceeds of the policy. Many variations are marketed and are discussed in Chapter 7.

Engrossment — The fair copy of a deed or other legal document which is to be executed in contrast to a draft of it.

Enquiries before contract — A series of questions concerning a property which a purchaser asks of a vendor. Also known as preliminary enquiries. Most solicitors use a standard printed form Conveyancing 29 (Long) for the questions.

Enquiries of local councils — A series of questions concerning a property which a purchaser asks of a local authority. The questions are on a printed form Con 29 A (England and Wales) or Con 29 D (London).

Estate — An interest in land. The term is also used to denote an area of land and also the total value of a deceased person's assets.

Exceptions and reservations — These are rights in favour of adjoining and neighbouring properties. They include rights of way and the right to carry water, gas and drainage pipes across a property.

Exchange of contracts — The point in the procedures leading up to the transfer of land at which the vendor signs an engrossment of the contract of sale and sends it to the purchaser. Exchange takes places at the moment of posting by the vendor at which point both parties are legally bound to go through with the transaction.

Execute — To sign, seal and deliver a deed.

Executors — Persons appointed by the will of a deceased person. They may 'prove' the will in the High Court by applying for grant of probate and their duty is the administration and distribution of the estate of the deceased person.

Fee simple — The most absolute title which a subject may possess in land. Freehold.

Filed plan — The plan prepared for use with a particular registered property in the land register.

Fittings — Chattels which do not form part of the land, such as freestanding bookcase, washing machine, dish washer, etc. See fixtures.

Fixtures — Items which become part of the structure of a property, e.g. a central heating system, bath, double glazing, by being attached by pipes or screws or ducting, etc. Such items are deemed to form part of the property and included in a sale. Fixtures and fittings are a frequent source of subsequent dispute between vendor and purchaser and the parties should agree any doubtful points at a very early stage.

Form 53	The form on which a building society, bank or other lender acknowledges that a mortgage on a property with *registered title* has been redeemed (paid off). Also called 'discharge of a registered charge'.
Freehold	Absolute title to land in contrast to leasehold. See fee simple.
Good leasehold title	This is effectively the same as an absolute leasehold title with the difference that the right of the lessor to grant a lease has not been investigated by the District Land Registry, and the right of the lessor to grant the lease is not guaranteed.
Ground rent	The annual rent paid by the holder of the property under a lease (a leaseholder) to the landlord or his agent.
Inhibition	An entry on the Land Register prohibiting partly or wholly the exercise of a proprietor's power to deal in the land. With the exception of bankruptcy inhibitions, inhibitions are rarely encountered.
Intestate	Without making a will.
Joint and several covenant	When joint purchasers give a covenant it is usual for it to be expressed as 'jointly and severally'. The effect is that the covenant can be enforced not only against both covenantors (those who gave the covenant) but against either of them at the option of the person in whose favour the covenant was given. There is an example of such a covenant at the bottom of the Form 19(JP) on page 187.
Joint tenants	Land held by two or more persons jointly in such manner that upon the death of one all the property passes to the survivor. Typically joint tenants are two persons and frequently husband and wife. Contrast joint tenants with tenants in common.
Land certificate	The certificate issued by the Land Registry to the proprietor of registered land.
Land charges registry	The government department located in Plymouth which maintains a register of various charges on *unregistered* land. It should not be confused with the Land Registry which is concerned only with *registered* land.
Landlord	The person entitled to receive the rent from a property which he has leased. Also known as a lessor.
Land registry	A government department headed by the Chief Land Registrar. The head office is in London and there are several District Land Registries in the provinces. These maintain the register of land with registered title.
Leasehold	Land held for a fixed number of years granted by a lease. Such a lease may be sold, i.e. assigned.
Leaseholder	The person who holds land under a lease, also known as a lessee.
Lessor	One who grants a lease.
Letters of administration	The document issued by the High Court to administrators authorising them to act for one who

died intestate.

Licence In land law a licence is the authority to do an act which otherwise would be a trespass.

Licensee One who is granted a licence.

Local authority Responsible for education, social services, housing, planning and many other services that are paid for partly from the rates levied on property and partly from central government grants.

Local search An application made to the district council on printed form LLC1.

LVA form Officially known as Stamps L(A)451 and unofficially as a PD (particulars delivered). This is the form on which a purchaser provides the Inland Revenue with details of his purchase and it is then stamped 'Presented'. Obtainable from Inland Revenue stamp offices.

Merge The submerging or drowning of a lesser estate in a greater estate because they coincide in one and the same person. Thus a leaseholder may buy the freehold (fee simple) of the property he occupies under the lease (the freehold reversion) and so hold both the freehold and the leasehold interests. The leasehold interest may be merged in the fee simple and exist no more. The formal verbiage use in a conveyance or transfer to give effect to a merger of interests runs 'TO THE INTENT that the term granted by the Lease shall forthwith merge and be extinguished in the fee simple thereof'.

Messuage A house, bungalow etc., comprising also outbuildings and garden. An example of the use of the term is in clause 1 of the conveyance on page 190.

Mortgage The deed whereby land is pledged as security for a loan. Often called a legal charge.

Mortgagee The lender who loans money that is secured by a pledge of land (i.e. building society and banks).

Mortgagor The borrower who pledges land as security for a loan.

Office copy An officially authorised copy of a document of which the relevant organisation holds the original.

Personal representatives Those who are appointed by the High Court to act for one who has died. Persons appointed under the will of the deceased are called 'Executors' and they may apply to the court for Grant of Probate to distribute the estate of the deceased. If the deceased died intestate (without leaving a will), application may be made to the court for Letters of Administration empowering the distribution of the estate to those by law entitled to it.

Planning permission Permission granted by a local authority to 'develop', e.g. build on, land under the Town and Country Planning Acts. Certain work is declared by the Act not to be development, and by a General Development Order 1977 the Secretary of State granted 23 separate categories of development for which

	permission is not required. Individual applications for planning permission are not required if the development falls within one of these categories, but an application must still be made to the local planning authority for Building Regulations consent.
Preliminary enquiries	See Enquiries before Contract.
Premium	The periodic payments made to obtain insurance cover.
Probate — grant of	The document issued by the High Court which signifies that the executors have authority under a will to deal with the property of the deceased.
Property register	One of the three parts of a register of land with registered title. The property register contains a description of the land and any easements, rights or privileges that go with the land.
Proprietorship register	One of the three parts of the land register. The proprietorship register states the type of title owned by the proprietor, e.g. 'title absolute', and gives the name and address of the registered proprietor and the date on which the proprietorship was registered.
Realty	Real estate, i.e. freehold land.
Registered land	Land, the title to which is registered at a District Land Registry.
Registered proprietor	A person who owns land with a registered title and is shown as such in the proprietorship register held at the Land Registry.
Requisitions on title	Written enquiries made of the vendor concerning queries or apparent defects in the title. Strictly, requisitions should be confined to such queries but in practice other matters are also raised such as last receipts for outgoings to be produced on Completion and other details concerning Completion arrangements.
Restrictive covenant	A covenant binding the owner of land from doing certain things on the land, e.g. carry on a trade.
Rights and exceptions	See Exceptions and Reservations
Root of title	The title deed, being at least fifteen years old, with which a vendor of unregistered land commences his abstract of title.
Seal	A red wafer affixed to a document alongside the signature. Originally the seal was of wax and was impressed with a device as a mark of authenticity.
Search	An application for information recorded in the official records of a local authority, a District Land Registry or the Land Charges Registry.
Search certificate	The official certificate of the result of a search.
Solicitor's undertaking	A personal undertaking given by a solicitor, in the form of a letter, that he will forward the sealed vacating receipt or Form 53, having first paid off his client's mortgage. A personal undertaking by a solicitor is enforceable, and the solicitor may have

	disciplinary action taken against him by the Law Society if he fails to honour it.
Stakeholder	One who holds money pending the outcome of an event and not as agent of one of the parties.
Stamp duty	In the context of this book a tax levied on the transfer, conveyance or assignment of land at a price in excess of £30,000.
Subject to contract	A provisional contract not meant to be legally binding.
Tenants in common	Two or more persons who hold distinct separate shares in a single property. The share of one who dies forms part of his estate. Tenants in common may hold unequal interests, e.g. if there are two, one may hold an interest in one-third and the other an interest in two-thirds of the property. See also Joint Tenants.
Tenement	A general term meaning a freehold or leasehold property. Was once much used in conveyances but is rarely encountered today.
Tenure	The manner whereby property is held, e.g. freehold or leasehold.
Term of years	The phrase used to denote an interest in leasehold land to be enjoyed for a fixed period.
Title	Ownership of a property.
Title absolute	The highest form of freehold title under the system of land registration. Absolute leasehold is the highest form of leasehold title granted.
Title — covenants for	When property is sold the purchaser is entitled to covenants for title. These are implied by the use of such terms as beneficial owner, trustee for sale, personal representative etc.
Title deeds	The deeds and other documents which prove title to unregistered freehold or leasehold land. Sometimes also applied to the land certificate issued for registered land.
Transfer	A deed which transfers title to freehold or leasehold registered land. A standard printed form is normally used.
Trust	Spouses frequently vest their joint purchase of their home in a trust for the benefit of themselves. See page 159 clause 2 for a declaration of a trust and page 146 (8) which has a similar effect.
Trustees for sale	Trustees, often husband and wife, who have the duty of selling the assets of a trust and then distributing them. In practice these asets consist of the home, and 'Trustees for sale' is a capacity in which the vendors of a property express themselves to convey or transfer it on sale to another. See page 159 clause 2 for a declaration of trust and page 146 (8) which has similar effect.
Vacating receipt	An acknowledgement endorsed on a mortgage, by duly authorised officers of a building society, bank, or other lender, that the loan moneys secured thereby have been repaid to the lender.
Vendor	The person selling a property.

Index

Do-It-Yourself Conveyancing Backup Service

Details of the Backup Service

Provided that you follow the step by step procedures simply laid out in *Do-It-Yourself Conveyancing* you should complete your conveyancing transaction without any problems.

However, there are two further areas where assistance will be useful to you if you are about to embark on the conveyancing road. This service is offered by Clearcrest Limited — a specialist company offering help and assistance to anyone doing their own conveyancing.

Set of Conveyancing Forms

Throughout the book mention has been made of the many different forms which have to be filled in. Under normal circumstances these are obtained from a variety of sources. One or two are free but most cost money and to obtain them all requires effort and cost.

To make your life easier at a time when you have so much to think about, Clearcrest Limited supply you with a forms pack. This pack contains all the forms needed for you to carry out your own conveyancing at a cost of £7.95 postage paid.

Conveyancing Assurance Service

What happens if you do get stuck halfway through a transaction and have nobody to turn to for help? Legal fees might be prohibitive if you hand it all over. You might delay things badly if you sort out the problem yourself and you may lose your sale or purchase.

Clearcrest Limited offers peace of mind through an assurance service which should be seen as a backup to your efforts. If you get a problem this backup service should get things quickly back on course by putting you in touch with experienced and knowledgeable conveyancers. This service costs £14.95 payable on registration.

The Two Services Together

These two services are available separately or together as a package. As has been stated the cost of the forms pack is £7.95 postage paid and of the assurance service £14.95. As a package the forms and assurance service cost a total of £19.95 — a saving of £2.95 on the individual price.

Clearcrest Limited
P.O. Box 18
Bridport
Dorset DT6 3XG

How does the Backup Service Work?

Once you have registered with the assurance service you are supplied with two copies of the *Request for Service* form. Having completed them send one copy to Clearcrest Limited whose experts process the form immediately and send you their suggestions regarding the problem. The other copy you retain for your own records. The form is simple to complete; it asks you for basic details about your transaction and then requests specific information about your problem.

The service must be in writing and not over the telephone. Most problems can be solved quickly and easily by an exchange of correspondence and it is essential that records are kept. There is no reason for any real delay.

The registration fee covers the provision of advice in respect of one problem only. Additional *Request for Service* forms are available by reregistering at a cost of £14.95. You should apply for reregistration as soon as you have used up your problem because you will not be covered by the backup service should you experience a further problem. Registration forms are printed on pages 209 and 211.

Clearcrest Limited cannot undertake to take over your transaction within the terms of the assurance service but may be prepared to provide you with a quotation for so doing. Please send your request for such services to

Clearcrest Limited
P.O. Box 18
Bridport
Dorset DT6 3XG

DO IT YOURSELF CONVEYANCING BACKUP SERVICE: REGISTRATION CARD

Office use: Registration No.....................
Date ....

☐ I apply to register for the CONVEYANCING ASSURANCE SERVICE and require one complete set of CONVEYANCING FORMS. I enclose cheque for £19.95.

☐ I apply to register for the CONVEYANCING ASSURANCE SERVICE and enclose cheque for £14.95.

☐ Please forward ....complete set(s) of CONVEYANCING FORMS. I enclose cheque for....@ £7.95 per set.

In applying to enrol in the DO IT YOURSELF CONVEYANCING ASSURANCE SERVICE I accept the terms and conditions applying thereto which are printed overleaf.

Name ....

Address ....

....

Post code ....Tel. ....

Signed ....Date ....

Clearcrest Limited, P.O. Box 18, Bridport, Dorset DT6 3XG

DO IT YOURSELF CONVEYANCING BACKUP SERVICE: REGISTRATION CARD

Office use: Registration No.....................
Date ....

☐ I apply to register for the CONVEYANCING ASSURANCE SERVICE and require one complete set of CONVEYANCING FORMS. I enclose cheque for £19.95.

☐ I apply to register for the CONVEYANCING ASSURANCE SERVICE and enclose cheque for £14.95.

☐ Please forward ....complete set(s) of CONVEYANCING FORMS. I enclose cheque for....@ £7.95 per set.

In applying to enrol in the DO IT YOURSELF CONVEYANCING ASSURANCE SERVICE I accept the terms and conditions applying thereto which are printed overleaf.

Name ....

Address ....

....

Post code ....Tel. ....

Signed ....Date ....

Clearcrest Limited, P.O. Box 18, Bridport, Dorset DT6 3XG

DO IT YOURSELF CONVEYANCING BACKUP SERVICE: REGISTRATION CARD

Office use: Registration No.....................
Date ....

☐ I apply to register for the CONVEYANCING ASSURANCE SERVICE and require one complete set of CONVEYANCING FORMS. I enclose cheque for £19.95.

☐ I apply to register for the CONVEYANCING ASSURANCE SERVICE and enclose cheque for £14.95.

☐ Please forward ....complete set(s) of CONVEYANCING FORMS. I enclose cheque for....@ £7.95 per set.

In applying to enrol in the DO IT YOURSELF CONVEYANCING ASSURANCE SERVICE I accept the terms and conditions applying thereto which are printed overleaf.

Name ....

Address ....

....

Post code ....Tel. ....

Signed ....Date ....

Clearcrest Limited, P.O. Box 18, Bridport, Dorset DT6 3XG

Terms and Conditions

1. Provided that you have followed the procedures set out in *D-I-Y-Conveyancing* every effort will be made to provide a resolution of your problem.

2. However, if you have failed to follow the procedures set out in this book and/or the resolution of your problem would involve an unreasonable amount of time it must be clearly understood that it may not be posible to completely resolve your problem. Clearcrest Limited shall be the sole judge of what is an unreasonable amount of time for the purpose of this condition.

3. Whilst every care will be taken to provide advice and/or guidance appropriate to the resolution of the problem you pose, Clearcrest Limited accept no liability whatsoever for the same.

4. Neither Prism Press nor the Author are Agents of Clearcrest Limited and accept no liability for any advice and/or guidance provided by Clearcrest Limited.

5. No employee or servant of Clearcrest Limited is empowered to vary the terms and conditions herein set out, on which basis alone the assurance service is provided.

6. Your enrolment fee covers the provision of advice and/or guidance in respect of one problem. Additional *Request for Service* forms are available, priced £14.95 each, cheque with order.

7. Documents sent for scrutiny when submitting a *Request for Service* form should be sent by Recorded Delivery. A stout self-addressed envelope bearing appropriate postage stamps should be enclosed to cover their return by first class post. If you wish return to be by Recorded Delivery service please include for this service when affixing the postage stamps.

8. Clearcrest Limited accept no responsibility for the safety of any documents placed in their custody.

Terms and Conditions

1. Provided that you have followed the procedures set out in *D-I-Y-Conveyancing* every effort will be made to provide a resolution of your problem.

2. However, if you have failed to follow the procedures set out in this book and/or the resolution of your problem would involve an unreasonable amount of time it must be clearly understood that it may not be posible to completely resolve your problem. Clearcrest Limited shall be the sole judge of what is an unreasonable amount of time for the purpose of this condition.

3. Whilst every care will be taken to provide advice and/or guidance appropriate to the resolution of the problem you pose, Clearcrest Limited accept no liability whatsoever for the same.

4. Neither Prism Press nor the Author are Agents of Clearcrest Limited and accept no liability for any advice and/or guidance provided by Clearcrest Limited.

5. No employee or servant of Clearcrest Limited is empowered to vary the terms and conditions herein set out, on which basis alone the assurance service is provided.

6. Your enrolment fee covers the provision of advice and/or guidance in respect of one problem. Additional *Request for Service* forms are available, priced £14.95 each, cheque with order.

7. Documents sent for scrutiny when submitting a *Request for Service* form should be sent by Recorded Delivery. A stout self-addressed envelope bearing appropriate postage stamps should be enclosed to cover their return by first class post. If you wish return to be by Recorded Delivery service please include for this service when affixing the postage stamps.

8. Clearcrest Limited accept no responsibility for the safety of any documents placed in their custody.

Terms and Conditions

1. Provided that you have followed the procedures set out in *D-I-Y-Conveyancing* every effort will be made to provide a resolution of your problem.

2. However, if you have failed to follow the procedures set out in this book and/or the resolution of your problem would involve an unreasonable amount of time it must be clearly understood that it may not be posible to completely resolve your problem. Clearcrest Limited shall be the sole judge of what is an unreasonable amount of time for the purpose of this condition.

3. Whilst every care will be taken to provide advice and/or guidance appropriate to the resolution of the problem you pose, Clearcrest Limited accept no liability whatsoever for the same.

4. Neither Prism Press nor the Author are Agents of Clearcrest Limited and accept no liability for any advice and/or guidance provided by Clearcrest Limited.

5. No employee or servant of Clearcrest Limited is empowered to vary the terms and conditions herein set out, on which basis alone the assurance service is provided.

6. Your enrolment fee covers the provision of advice and/or guidance in respect of one problem. Additional *Request for Service* forms are available, priced £14.95 each, cheque with order.

7. Documents sent for scrutiny when submitting a *Request for Service* form should be sent by Recorded Delivery. A stout self-addressed envelope bearing appropriate postage stamps should be enclosed to cover their return by first class post. If you wish return to be by Recorded Delivery service please include for this service when affixing the postage stamps.

8. Clearcrest Limited accept no responsibility for the safety of any documents placed in their custody.

DO IT YOURSELF CONVEYANCING BACKUP SERVICE: REGISTRATION CARD

Office use: Registration No. ....
Date ....

☐ I apply to register for the CONVEYANCING ASSURANCE SERVICE and require one complete set of CONVEYANCING FORMS. I enclose cheque for £19.95.

☐ I apply to register for the CONVEYANCING ASSURANCE SERVICE and enclose cheque for £14.95.

☐ Please forward .... complete set(s) of CONVEYANCING FORMS. I enclose cheque for .... @ £7.95 per set.

In applying to enrol in the DO IT YOURSELF CONVEYANCING ASSURANCE SERVICE I accept the terms and conditions applying thereto which are printed overleaf.

Name ....

Address ....

....

Post code .... Tel. ....

Signed .... Date ....

Clearcrest Limited, P.O. Box 18, Bridport, Dorset DT6 3XG

DO IT YOURSELF CONVEYANCING BACKUP SERVICE: REGISTRATION CARD

Office use: Registration No. ....
Date ....

☐ I apply to register for the CONVEYANCING ASSURANCE SERVICE and require one complete set of CONVEYANCING FORMS. I enclose cheque for £19.95.

☐ I apply to register for the CONVEYANCING ASSURANCE SERVICE and enclose cheque for £14.95.

☐ Please forward .... complete set(s) of CONVEYANCING FORMS. I enclose cheque for .... @ £7.95 per set.

In applying to enrol in the DO IT YOURSELF CONVEYANCING ASSURANCE SERVICE I accept the terms and conditions applying thereto which are printed overleaf.

Name ....

Address ....

....

Post code .... Tel. ....

Signed .... Date ....

Clearcrest Limited, P.O. Box 18, Bridport, Dorset DT6 3XG

DO IT YOURSELF CONVEYANCING BACKUP SERVICE: REGISTRATION CARD

Office use: Registration No. ....
Date ....

☐ I apply to register for the CONVEYANCING ASSURANCE SERVICE and require one complete set of CONVEYANCING FORMS. I enclose cheque for £19.95.

☐ I apply to register for the CONVEYANCING ASSURANCE SERVICE and enclose cheque for £14.95.

☐ Please forward .... complete set(s) of CONVEYANCING FORMS. I enclose cheque for .... @ £7.95 per set.

In applying to enrol in the DO IT YOURSELF CONVEYANCING ASSURANCE SERVICE I accept the terms and conditions applying thereto which are printed overleaf.

Name ....

Address ....

....

Post code .... Tel. ....

Signed .... Date ....

Clearcrest Limited, P.O. Box 18, Bridport, Dorset DT6 3XG

Terms and Conditions

1. Provided that you have followed the procedures set out in *D-I-Y-Conveyancing* every effort will be made to provide a resolution of your problem.

2. However, if you have failed to follow the procedures set out in this book and/or the resolution of your problem would involve an unreasonable amount of time it must be clearly understood that it may not be posible to completely resolve your problem. Clearcrest Limited shall be the sole judge of what is an unreasonable amount of time for the purpose of this condition.

3. Whilst every care will be taken to provide advice and/or guidance appropriate to the resolution of the problem you pose, Clearcrest Limited accept no liability whatsoever for the same.

4. Neither Prism Press nor the Author are Agents of Clearcrest Limited and accept no liability for any advice and/or guidance provided by Clearcrest Limited.

5. No employee or servant of Clearcrest Limited is empowered to vary the terms and conditions herein set out, on which basis alone the assurance service is provided.

6. Your enrolment fee covers the provision of advice and/or guidance in respect of one problem. Additional *Request for Service* forms are available, priced £14.95 each, cheque with order.

7. Documents sent for scrutiny when submitting a *Request for Service* form should be sent by Recorded Delivery. A stout self-addressed envelope bearing appropriate postage stamps should be enclosed to cover their return by first class post. If you wish return to be by Recorded Delivery service please include for this service when affixing the postage stamps.

8. Clearcrest Limited accept no responsibility for the safety of any documents placed in their custody.

Terms and Conditions

1. Provided that you have followed the procedures set out in *D-I-Y-Conveyancing* every effort will be made to provide a resolution of your problem.

2. However, if you have failed to follow the procedures set out in this book and/or the resolution of your problem would involve an unreasonable amount of time it must be clearly understood that it may not be posible to completely resolve your problem. Clearcrest Limited shall be the sole judge of what is an unreasonable amount of time for the purpose of this condition.

3. Whilst every care will be taken to provide advice and/or guidance appropriate to the resolution of the problem you pose, Clearcrest Limited accept no liability whatsoever for the same.

4. Neither Prism Press nor the Author are Agents of Clearcrest Limited and accept no liability for any advice and/or guidance provided by Clearcrest Limited.

5. No employee or servant of Clearcrest Limited is empowered to vary the terms and conditions herein set out, on which basis alone the assurance service is provided.

6. Your enrolment fee covers the provision of advice and/or guidance in respect of one problem. Additional *Request for Service* forms are available, priced £14.95 each, cheque with order.

7. Documents sent for scrutiny when submitting a *Request for Service* form should be sent by Recorded Delivery. A stout self-addressed envelope bearing appropriate postage stamps should be enclosed to cover their return by first class post. If you wish return to be by Recorded Delivery service please include for this service when affixing the postage stamps.

8. Clearcrest Limited accept no responsibility for the safety of any documents placed in their custody.

Terms and Conditions

1. Provided that you have followed the procedures set out in *D-I-Y-Conveyancing* every effort will be made to provide a resolution of your problem.

2. However, if you have failed to follow the procedures set out in this book and/or the resolution of your problem would involve an unreasonable amount of time it must be clearly understood that it may not be posible to completely resolve your problem. Clearcrest Limited shall be the sole judge of what is an unreasonable amount of time for the purpose of this condition.

3. Whilst every care will be taken to provide advice and/or guidance appropriate to the resolution of the problem you pose, Clearcrest Limited accept no liability whatsoever for the same.

4. Neither Prism Press nor the Author are Agents of Clearcrest Limited and accept no liability for any advice and/or guidance provided by Clearcrest Limited.

5. No employee or servant of Clearcrest Limited is empowered to vary the terms and conditions herein set out, on which basis alone the assurance service is provided.

6. Your enrolment fee covers the provision of advice and/or guidance in respect of one problem. Additional *Request for Service* forms are available, priced £14.95 each, cheque with order.

7. Documents sent for scrutiny when submitting a *Request for Service* form should be sent by Recorded Delivery. A stout self-addressed envelope bearing appropriate postage stamps should be enclosed to cover their return by first class post. If you wish return to be by Recorded Delivery service please include for this service when affixing the postage stamps.

8. Clearcrest Limited accept no responsibility for the safety of any documents placed in their custody.

Other Books of Interest

Plans for Dream Homes
Plans for Dream Homes by Murray Armor is a collection of plans for real dream homes: 400 houses and bungalows of all sizes designed in recent years by five leading design practices. Selected and introduced by Murray Armor, the plans reflect the traditional and regional styles that are now returning to the housing scene, and the book is an exhaustible source of advice, information and design ideas for those choosing the plans for a new home.

A4, 480pp, £10.45 postage inclusive

Building Your Own Home
By Murray Armor, now in its ninth edition. More than 10,000 people build their own homes each year and this book has become the standard textbook on the subject. Completely revised and updated every year, this book contains the latest costings and planning regulations, together with some recent case histories.

What they said about the earlier editions:

'A must for self builders' *Do-It-Yourself Magazine*

'Photographs galore and packed with factual data' *House and Garden*

'Excellent publication for anyone contemplating building a house' *Country Landowner*

'Building Your Own Home is a must' *Farmers Weekly*

'An all-embracing handbook' *Daily Telegraph*

192 pp, £7.45 postage inclusive.

Home Plans for the Eighties
This widely acclaimed consumer guide by Murray Armor, first published in 1983, is now in its third edition and has been completed updated and contains 230 home and bungalow plans and text features.

What they said about earlier editions:

'A mouth watering book with an authoritative text' *Ideal Home*

'Crammed with advice about costing, materials, windows, roofs, kitchens and bathrooms' *Daily Mail*

'A useful reference book' *Building Trades Journal*

'Of absorbing interest' *House and Garden*

'The book claims to be the most comprehensive yet published and this reviewer could not deny this' *Popular DIY*

A4, 340 pp, £9.45 postage inclusive